Participation and empowerment in child protection

Edited by
Christopher Cloke
Murray Davies

PITMAN PUBLISHING
128 Long Acre, London WC2E 9AN

A Division of Pearson Professional Limited

First published in Great Britain 1995

© Pearson Professional Limited 1995

British Library Cataloguing in Publication Data
A CIP catalogue record for this book can be obtained from the British
Library

ISBN 0–273–61621–8

10 9 8 7 6 5 4 3 2 1

Phototypeset by Northern Phototypesetting Co Ltd, Bolton

Printed at Redwood Books, Trowbridge, Wiltshire.

To Jane, Thomas and Rosalind whose capacity to participate was curtailed
by Chris' work on this book.
and
To Corin and Sorcha for sharing their lives with Murray and Val.

Contents

*The opinions expressed in this book are those of the individual authors
and do not necessarily represent the policies or practice of the NSPCC.*

Contributors

Peter Appleton is a clinical psychologist who has worked for twenty years with children with multiple health problems. He trained in clinical psychology at Glasgow University and at Strathclyde University and he is currently completing a doctorate in epidemiology at Liverpool University. He is Head of Clinical Psychology in Clwyd and is an honorary lecturer in psychology at University of Wales, Bangor. His interests also include psychosocial aspects of pregnancy and population-oriented mental health services for children and young people.

Nancy Asdigian received her Ph.D. in social psychology at the University of New Hampshire and now works as a research associate with the university's Family Research Laboratory. She has worked on research projects related to missing children and victimisation prevention among children. She has been involved in investigations of alcohol abuse and marital violence.

Ann Buchanan is lecturer in Applied Social Studies at the University of Oxford with a responsibility for child welfare research and teaching on the professional MSc for social workers. Previously she taught at the University of Southampton. Ann Buchanan has also taught residential workers and for ten years she was a practising social worker. She has published widely on child-related topics.

Ian Butler has been a lecturer in the School of Social and Administrative Studies, University of Wales, Cardiff since October 1990. Prior to that he worked as a local authority social worker and in intermediate treatment before being appointed Assistant Director of the Rayner Foundation in 1982. In 1987 he worked as a manager of services for adolescents with Barnardos and for a West Midlands local authority. He has written on child care for academic journals, particularly in relation to the legal regulation of child-care practice. **Christopher Cloke** is Head of the Secretariat to the National Commission of Inquiry into the Prevention of Child Abuse. Prior to that he was Head of Policy Development with the NSPCC, where he has worked for six years. He has been particularly involved in the Society's campaigning activities, which have sought to change public and professional attitudes to children. Prior to joining the NSPCC he worked with a number of voluntary agencies including Age Concern England where he covered health and social services issues.

Murray Davies qualified in social work, social administration, and applied social studies at Dundee University and gained a masters degree in business administration at Bradford University. His social work practice has been in child and family settings in health, local authority and voluntary organisations. He moved to the NSPCC in 1980 and is currently the Regional Director with responsibility for the Society's work in Wales and the Midlands. He has worked with the Central Council for Education and Training in Social Work and with the Department of Health on training initiatives and was an external practice assessor to the Lancaster University post-qualifying course in child protection. He is a co-author of *Dangerous Families* and a co-editor of *Child Protection Policy and Practice in Europe*.

John Dotchin graduated as an engineer and worked in that field and in manufacturing before moving into the service sector where he became interested in the provision of quality service. At Bradford University he has carried out research into service users' expectations and perceptions, and their effect on satisfaction with services. He has recently worked with the NSPCC on a project helping to understand children's and young people's perceptions of the services they receive. John Dotchin is currently senior lecturer in Total Quality Management at Sheffield Hallam University and is a research and development associate with the NSPCC.

Jennifer Dziuba-Leatherman is a doctoral candidate and dissertation fellow at the Department of Sociology, University of North Hampshire, and has served as a graduate project assistant at the Family Research Laboratory. She has co-authored several articles on child victimisation, victimisation prevention education, and the legal representation of children.

David Finkelhor is the co-director of the Family Research Laboratory and the Family Violence Research Program at the University of New Hampshire. His many publications on child abuse and child protection include: *Sourcebook on Child Sexual Abuse* (1986), a widely used compilation of research; *Nursery Crimes* (1988), a study of sexual abuse in day care. He has been studying the problem of family violence since 1977 and had published widely on the subject. David Finkelhor has received grants from the National Institute of Mental Health and the National Center on Child Abuse and Neglect.

Yvonne Joseph has been a Policy Development Officer at the NSPCC since 1990. Prior to this she worked as a Community Work Team Leader at a Community Relations Council and as a Community Development Officer on a large estate in Brent. Yvonne has particular responsibilities for developing work around child protection and children's rights issues. Yvonne is particularly concerned about issues affecting black and minority communities and is currently a management committee member of a black women's group and is Chair of SIA, a national organisation promoting the interests of the Black Voluntary Sector.

Ilan Katz received his degree in Social Work at the University of the Witwatersrand, Johannesburg in 1978. After qualifying he came to the UK and has worked as a social worker and social work manager in local authorities and voluntary organisations. His current post is National Evaluation Officer for the NSPCC. He has a part-time secondment to the Brunel University Centre for the Evaluation of Public Policy and Practice. Current research interests include comprehensive risk assessment, user empowerment, and area child protection committees. In 1994 he received his doctorate on 'The Construction of Racial Identity in Children of Mixed Parentage' from Brunel University.

Caroline Marks is employed by the NSPCC as a project manager for the Nottingham Black Families Project. In addition to providing a service from a black perspective for black children and families, she is also a trainer for the Nottinghamshire Area Child Protection Committee.

Panna Modi has been working for the NSPCC since July 1994 as a project manager with responsibility for developing and delivering services for black children and their families. She qualified as a social worker in 1982 and has worked for local authorities for over five years. In 1987 she took up a post as a family therapist with Leicester Family Services Unit and in 1991 she was appointed co-ordinator to the Department of Health project working with adolescent sex offenders. Since 1992 she had lectured on the Diploma/MA course in child protection studies at Leicester University. As a practitioner she has been working on child protection issues with offender families, looking at issues of rehabilitation and risk assessment across gender and cultures.

Rhonda Wattley is a community social worker with the Black Families Project in Nottingham. She has a background in equal opportunities training, group work, and youth work. Rhonda Wattley is also an associate director of the Centre for Social Action.

Helen Westcott is Research Officer with the NSPCC, based in London. Her research interests include children's views on interviewing and communicating about personal issues, children as witnesses, and the abuse of disabled children. She has written widely on these topics, and has addressed a number of national and international conferences. Helen is currently studying for her doctorate at Leicester University.

Chris Wilson graduated in business administration in 1972 before pursuing a career in personnel management, industrial relations and consultancy in both England and Australia where he was involved in various social research projects. On returning to Scotland in 1980 he became a local authority social worker in inner city Dundee. He went on to work for the NSPCC. Chris Wilson is now the Children's Rights Officer for Warwickshire. He is married with two young children.

Howard Williamson is currently a part-time senior research associate, NSPCC research fellow, and Assistant Director in the Social Research Unit, University of Wales, Cardiff. He is also a practising youth worker in Birmingham. In 1989 the Minister of State at the Welsh Office appointed him Chair of Wales Youth Work Partnership and in 1992 he was appointed Vice Chair of the newly formed Wales Youth Agency (Cyngor Leuenctid Cymru). He has published widely on youth issues and his research work includes juvenile delinquency, enterprise development, special needs housing in Wales, youth service curriculum, and ascertaining children's and young people's views about appropriate forms of professional interventions and support. With Ian Butler, he is the author of *Children Speak – children, trauma, and social work* published by Longman, 1994.

Foreword

With the ratification of the UN Convention on the Rights of the Child and the implementation of the Children Act, a framework has been set for encouraging children and young people to participate in decisions which affect their lives. These changes are to be welcomed. The commitment to participation is a long-standing priority of the NSPCC. In 1989 the NSPCC ran its first *Listen to Children Week* which sought to encourage parents, carers, and professionals to listen to children. We felt – and still feel – that this is important if children are to be effectively protected. The child who is listened to is more likely to turn to a parent or adult when she or he needs help. An adult who listens to children is more likely to understand their needs. Our latest campaign – *A Cry for Children* – takes forward and builds on these important messages.

It was the *Listen to Children* initiatives which led to the publication by Longman in 1990 of *Listening to Children: The Professional Response to Hearing the Abused Child*. Since then it was hoped that considerable progress would have been made in empowering children and young people to have greater control over their destinies.

Unfortunately, it is not possible to draw that conclusion as *Participation and Empowerment* clearly demonstrates. Ironically, for example, following on from the Children Act, it is parents who seem to have benefited from the encouragement to attend child protection case conference and not children. The effect of the *Memorandum of Good Practice on Interviewing Children* may have been to make it *more* difficult for children to give evidence in court.

That it should be difficult for professionals to enable and empower children and young people to take part in children's services should really come as little surprise. Relating to children in this way is highly challenging to professionals, many of whom have been taught that they have the 'expertise' and 'knowledge' to make sound judgements which will be for the benefit of 'their clients'. It takes time and resources to empower users of our services – and so much more so if they are of a young age. It also requires a fundamental change in our attitudes and in the culture of our institutions. Such changes are slow to occur.

The NSPCC seeks to encourage its staff to listen to, and empower, the children and young people with whom they work. We do this in a variety of ways. Partly it is achieved by ensuring that decisions about the planning and development of services are taken as closely as possible to the recipients of the services. In addition, we have a set of *Principles, Standards and Indicators* for our children's services to which our staff are held accountable and against which our services are inspected by our Independent Inspection Unit. Also, we are committed to consulting with children and young people on their expectations of the services which they receive.

Participation and Empowerment is very timely. It indicates that there is a commitment from professionals to empowering children and young people and which they are struggling to achieve. There is a gap between the principles and practice. *Participation and Empowerment* will help bridge that gap through enhancing understanding and by giving practical information and guidance.

This book is also important in reaffirming the need for a clear commitment to children's rights at a time when some people are questioning whether the pendulum has swung too far in favour of the interests of children.

Professionals are in a privileged, albeit at times difficult, position in that they work closely with children, young people and their families. This affords them great insight into children's needs. It is important that this understanding and experience is used to promote the needs of the users of our services. As we approach the likely revisions of the Children Act and the government's *Working Together* guidance on child protection, it is important that all of us working with children recognise that the promotion of children's rights will lead to their greater protection. *Participation and Empowerment* will help secure that much needed goal.

Chistopher Brown, Director and Chief Executive
NSPCC London, March, 1995

Introduction

Christopher Cloke and Murray Davies

In recent years, client participation in decision-making has gained increasing importance. As recently as the late 1980s such participation was not seen as a priority by practitioners, and clients' views were not seen as accurate or valid indicators of the effectiveness of social work intervention or performance. Indeed, there has been an historical resistance to client participation associated with some of the theoretical underpinnings of practice, such as psycho-dynamic theory, and systems theory. Social welfare systems, such as the inter-agency co-ordinated approach to child protection, have, until more recently, also discouraged client participation, for example, in child protection care conferences and reviews.

This recent concern about the level of participation parallels a move towards more openness and accountability of public agencies to their customers or consumers. Service providers are exhorted by government to respect the 'wishes' and needs of the citizen. This is the key principle behind the Citizen's Charter and accompanying documents which, as a way of providing quality services, encourage citizen participation.

Over the last 25 years, a few research studies have examined clients' views of social work, but there has been little research in respect of children's involvement. While experience and some research now points increasingly to parents and carers participating in deci-

sions about their children, this is not the case with children themselves.

The UN Convention on the Rights of the Child 1989, and the
Children Act 1989, provide a fresh impetus for children to participate more actively in decisions affecting their lives, and challenge
established adult and professional views, practices and prejudices.
This book explores the development of our understanding about
children's rights, and the implications in respect of greater participation; it examines some of the difficulties for practitioners in listening to, and taking account of, children's views, and in reconciling
the conflict between children's rights, wishes, and needs, and the
views of adults. It offers suggestions and models of participation
which allow children's wishes and expectations to be expressed and
respected; and, finally, the book addresses the social policy implications for child protection services, including the limitation that children are not viewed by Government as citizens.

The child's right to participate

It is over 200 years since a newly independent United States of
America adopted the Declaration of the Rights of Man. England, at
this time, was experiencing the beginning of the industrial revolu-
tion, with young children working long hours in mills and factories,
often being beaten to keep them awake, prompting William Cobbett
to comment in the House of Commons;

> all our greatness and prosperity, and superiority over other
> nations is owing to 300,000 little girls in Lancashire. We have
> made the discovery that, if these little girls worked two hours less
> in a day, it would occasion the ruin of this country.

Progress in achieving equal rights for all from this time was very
slow indeed as the history of slavery, or the battle to establish rights
and votes for women, demonstrates. As this book shows, establishing a recognition of children's rights has taken much longer, and the
1989 United Nations' Convention on the Rights of the Child is the
first legally binding international human rights treaty to confer a
wide range of rights specifically on children.

In America, in 1874, there were laws against the ill-treatment of
animals, but no laws to protect children, and when a little girl called
Mary Ellen was found neglected, beaten and cut in a New York ten-
ement, it was argued and established in court that as a member of the
animal kingdom she was entitled to protection.

The late nineteenth century saw the beginnings of adult activity

to protect children from abuse and ill-treatment, with the establishment in New York and in England of Societies for the Prevention of
Cruelty to Children. The first legislation for the Prevention of Cruelty was introduced in in 1889. This protectionist movement has
been active during the twentieth century, promoting legislation and
establishing institutions specifically for the protection of children
and the promotion of their welfare.

Measures to protect children were of vital importance at the
beginning of the twentieth century but, in the second half of this
century, the balance between the right to protection, and children's
rights to autonomy and independence has come under increasing
debate and scrutiny. Protecting children can, and does, restrict
autonomy, and reflects an adult view about the inherent incompetence of children, and the need for adults to protect and safeguard
children's best interests. Inherent in this approach is the view that
children are not afforded the same rights as are adults.

Children are amongst the most vulnerable members of our
society, but are denied basic civil rights, perhaps most fundamentally the right to participate in decisions affecting them. While there
has been considerable progress in respect of the right to provision,
for example, through education, health and standards of living, and
the right to protection, the right to participation, which involves
freedom of expression, and rights to be consulted, heard and taken
seriously, have been largely ignored. Children remain recipients of
adult actions, rather than participants in decision-making.

Changes have been taking place. A century ago, children were
seen mainly as their father's property, and people under 21 years had
to depend on adults to decide and speak on their behalf. The fairly
recent Gillick ruling has emphasised that parents have rights over
their children only in so far as these enable parents to fulfil their responsibility to care for their child. While this points to children
having the right to be consulted about decisions which personally
affect them, the Children Act requires only that children's views
should be taken into account, not that they should be observed.

The UN Convention on the Rights of the Child has signalled the
requirement for greater opportunities for participation, affirming in
Article 12 that children are human beings who must be taken seriously and respected as participants in their own lives. The Convention advocates measures to preserve children's physical integrity,
and to respect their personhood.

However, the debate about the balance between parental and
children's rights, and children's entitlements to participate in decision-making continues. The issues raised here are expanded and
considered in much greater detail in the early chapters of this book.
The way in which it is the predominance of a protective model in the

construction of our relationships with children, which has inhibited the development of appropriate recognition of children's real capacity for participation, is examined closely. Questions about rights versus responsibilities are explored, looking at the proposition that much of the hostility to the concept of children's rights is rooted in the belief that children cannot have rights until they are competent to accept responsibilities. The idea that children have rights is seen as profoundly threatening to many adults, rousing fears of disruption to family life. The way in which these concerns derive from a failure to distinguish between self-determination and participation in considering a child's best interests is examined.

The debate about children's rights raises the requirement that, if the child's right to be heard is to be taken seriously, then our preconceptions and understanding about the best interests of the child must be questioned and reviewed. If we are truly to respect the child's integrity, and fully to take account of the child's wishes and feelings, we have to recognise that less protection may be afforded, but greater control and autonomy for the child over outcomes will be created. The early chapters offer the reader the opportunity to read the arguments in respect of this dilemma, and to consider their own viewpoint, before moving on to hear opinions and views from children and young people.

Promoting participation – listening to children

Listening to children, and hearing what they have to say, are at the root of developing effective human rights for children. Rethinking childhood in terms of rights opens the way for children to be consulted more fully in defining their interests. Decision-making involves the right to consent, to agree, to decide on one's own best interests and preferences, to make an informed choice without coercion. Beliefs about the best way to care for children, and to balance their conflicting rights, vary radically over time, and between individuals, so seeking children's consent provides a way of involving them in deciding the best balance. The result, the child's choice, may be different from an adult decision.

Listening to children values the views of children, but is not achieved easily, or accepted universally. It challenges the protectionist view that it is not fair to involve children in difficult decision-making, particularly because children may become involved in considering painful or upsetting outcomes for themselves. The protectionist view would avoid the exposure of children to such further 'unnecessary' pain.

Listening to children requires a commitment from practitioners who may already be trying to juggle with competing demands on their time, and children, coming from a powerless group, are easier to set aside. This attitude feeds into professional arrogance, particularly for those professionals defined as experts in certain areas of practice, whose opinions are considered to reflect children's requirements. To acknowledge a need to seek views and opinions directly from children is threatening and, defensively, it is argued that children's opinions are not to be trusted because children are not really capable of forming opinions, and their views are so easily influenced by others.

The validity of listening to children is also challenged on methodological grounds, with the argument put forward that it is not possible to get accurate and reliable information. Interestingly, this view is challenged by research and experience in the private sector, particularly in marketing and advertising, where children's power in the market place is recognised and responded to with approaches and communication particularly sensitive to the needs of children.

Several authors draw attention to the crucial issue of 'access' between children and adults. This covers many different aspects, but language and presentation are crucial. It is not easy to get children and young people to express their views. they are not used to such requests. Their experience has often been that their opinions are only of value to themselves, an experience regularly confirmed by the adults in their lives. With vulnerable young people, those who most need to be heard are often those hardest to reach, so ways of hearing the voices of children and young people who lack confidence, who are not used to sharing their thoughts, and who may not have the words to express their feelings, are essential.

Examples of different approaches are provided in the book. There is a need for flexibility, trying different approaches to the same topic, for tolerance and patience, for sensitivity, for humour and self-effacement and, above all, for 'tuning in' to each person. Children are very fashion-conscious, and this applies to language and to dress. This awareness and sensitivity is vital if communication is to be established. The additional requirements of disabled children need to be considered, for example, signing with deaf children, if they are not to be further *dis*-abled and isolated. For all children, there is a need to be responsive to their own first language or preferred language for communication, if additional communication barriers are not to be introduced.

Access to children can also be frustrated by 'gatekeepers': those adults responsible for their care. Several authors draw attention to these frustrations, which may reflect adult fears about what may be said, and demonstrate that there is not universal acceptance of the value of children's views, and their right to express them. These issues, and how they have been handled in different settings, are commented on by several authors.

Consultation: listening to the views of children in different settings reveals important new information and perspectives. It demonstrates that children's perceptions, as users and recipients of services, are influenced by different considerations to those of the professionals who provide them, reinforcing the danger of relying only on adult and professional views. Numerous examples of children's views not being taken into account, which result in surprising omissions, are quoted in the book. Child abuse prevention programmes have been established without hearing from children about their worries and fears. There is evidence that children demonstrate that they do have views about the dangers they face, what they consider to be harmful, and the sort of help they want. They also confirm that adults do not listen to them. They doubt adult commitment and ability to understand, with the result that there are probably large numbers of children 'at risk' about whom adults never get to hear.

Black children

For some children, especially for black children, and for disabled children, there are additional requirements which must be heard and responded to, and two authors address these requirements.

For black children, participation is affected by the racist attitudes and behaviours which pervade social life in Britain, in addition to other adversities. Issues of empowerment and participation are addressed in the context of a white-dominated oppressive system, and in the context of the different perspectives which have attempted to make sense of the needs of minority ethnic and black children and families. To these, a black perspective is provided, shaped by experience of racism and powerlessness, both past and present, which should assist white people in working from an anti-racist perspective. It also highlights the difficulty facing black professionals who equally feel trapped and powerless, with little influence in designing and delivering services to black children and families. Any consideration of oppression requires an acknowledgement of racism, and a shift in focus from 'helping disadvantaged blacks' to 'tackling oppressors' and focusing on 'black people being oppressed'. Recognising and facing up to personal racism and tackling it, can be discomforting and distressing. It also highlights the additional barriers and attitudes black children and young people face. A commitment to anti-oppressive practice is a prerequisite to empowering both children and adults, and particularly black children and adults. This is not easy to achieve because of the practices and behaviours, such as denial, or negation of black people's specific experiences as black people, which work against the establishment of anti-racist practice.

All practioners involved with black children and young people have a positive contribution to make in enhancing and nurturing a positive racial identity – built on an inner core of pride and positive feelings. Children as young as three are very aware of their identity, and are sensitive to racial issues and, in a society where white is the norm, for some children their sense of blackness is repressed. Participation requires empowerment, and for black children a holistic approach is advocated which takes account of the 'total child' – race, culture, religion, language amongst other aspects which make up the child – can only serve to empower. Assessing need in relation to black children and young people and their families must take account of racism and oppression, and practical guidelines are offered in this respect.

Disabled children

For disabled children, the perception that they are less capable, and less able, has a very disempowering effect. To be labelled 'in need' automatically on a diagnosis of physical or sensory impairment portrays disabled children as weak and incapable of independence, rather than presenting their particular abilities and competences. Disabled children have the right to be regarded as of equal value to non-disabled children, and not to be labelled and regarded as 'special'. Disabled children do not have special needs, this is victimising and blaming, but rather society has needs if disabled children are to be accommodated so that society can benefit from their presence. This book illustrates the ways in which children and young people are able to present their views and opinions, and the ways in which this is inhibited. Disabled children are no different, and their thoughts and feelings about their social world are also expressed. They need to be listened to, and they are anxious about the ability of adults to understand, and about the isolating effects of labelling which limit opportunities.

Accommodated children

Not all children are able to live with their natural parents; some are looked after by local authorities and experience substitute relationships. This can be a very disempowering experience, and it does not follow automatically that, because children are accommodated by local authorities, this care is better. It has to be worked at. The UK

Government's First Report to the UN Committee on the Rights of the Child, presented by the Government, points out that guidance on the conduct of children's homes emphasises the need to take into account the wishes of the children in the home in the day-to-day running of the home, but does not offer any evaluation of achievement in this area, or any presentation of children's perceptions. Young people, as this book reveals, want more opportunities to make choices in their lives, for example, choices about the day-to-day running of their establishment. Young people know about complaints procedures, and could challenge and complain, but are reluctant to do so. Merely providing policies or procedures for involvement or complaint are insufficient in themselves. Young people need to experience empowerment.

As contributors to this book point out, young people who are being looked after become expert at saying what they are expected to say, and are highly selective with whom they share their innermost feelings. This is a common theme in respect of childen's perceptions of adults. What is also reported from residential and other settings is that young people have very positive and relevant things to say about how their lives could be improved. What they need is to be heard, and to receive full, and not partial or pre-selected, information in order to make the decisions that affect their lives.

Isolation is also a feature which can affect accommodated children, and opportunities to link young people together, to provide mutual support, and to obtain collective views of provision and service, are not generally developed. Some contributors describe the benefits of groups, and provide evidence of the way in which, in relaxed group settings, young people are prepared to share information about very sensitive issues. Young people describe how they were empowered by such groups and demonstrate that they value the opportunities to share common experiences with other young people in care.

Of particular concern is that young people in residential accommodation highlight their distress from their experiences of being bullied, and the apparent inability of carers to contain this, and ensure that young people do not experience further harm away from home. In so many different settings, with concern about bullying, it emerges that there is clearly a need for much concerted action to promote anti-bullying strategies wherever children are together.

Participation in practice – overcoming barriers

Recent studies reported in this book, while confirming that the move to client participation still has some way to go, and demonstrating that there are important lessons to be learnt, also show some areas and examples of progress.

In particular, the confusion about the difference between empowerment and participation and the implications of this, are discussed. The requirements of child protection procedures, and practice during the initial investigation and assessment of a suspected case of child abuse, can leave adults and children feeling powerless, and feeling that they have not participated in the decision-making. This sense of powerlessness is perpetuated in the process of establishing written agreements to describe the work in which practitioners, adults and children will be engaged, where the important decisions, and even some less important decisions, were made by the practitioner. It is noted that, occasionally, participants had a say in the content of the agreement, but this was not universal. This highlights the complex relationship between empowerment and participation, and the self-defeating process of going through the motions of participation without empowering people to participate effectively.

Participation requires more than arrangements to take part in existing organisational structures and processes; it requires more flexibility to listen to the wishes and feelings of children and their carers, and to agree arrangements which respect these.

The process of empowerment is also influenced by the amount of information made available, and in particular sharing information about rights, including the right to access to information. This process would be enhanced by the availability of written information for children and young people, which makes clear their rights, and entitlements.

The need for children, adults, and practitioners to agree from the outset explicit aims, objectives and focus for work is confirmed in a study of practice which reveals differences in the way in which participants view casework. There is evidence of children and adults focussing on the process and of practitioners focussing on content, and on what they are seeking to achieve. But it is suggested that practitioners do not express clearly their expectations and the issues they deem to be important, and so it is not surprising that children and adults are confused about the role and purpose of social work visits. If practitioners remain unaware of the importance of the process to adults and children, unaware of expectations in respect of humour, empathy, friendliness, and caring, then differences in view will remain.

These differences challenge the ability of practitioners to promote effective partnership, affect motivation, and in many cases undermine the success of casework. This illustrates the importance of establishing agreements between practitioners and children and adults about the aims, objectives and focus for the work.

Children, in particular, need to be empowered to contribute, otherwise their views, wishes and feelings will be lost. This point is demonstrated in the example of an advocacy service in Devon where real changes in participation were brought about when an advocate was provided. Although there is a policy commitment to the participation of children and young people in child protection case conferences, and reviews of plans for looked after children, as shown in the UK's response to the UN Committee on the Rights of the Child, there is no guidance or proposals about how children may be empowered to participate effectively. The concern reported by the Devon project was in relation to the small numbers of children participating, and in the very limited extent to which children's views were being expressed at child protection case conferences. It was felt that children needed information, that they needed independent support to participate, and that they should also have a choice in the manner in which they participated. The way in which this particular service was established, the issues that were dealt with; in particular, the young person's right to confidentiality, and an evalation by young people of the provision and its benefits to them, are described in detail in this book.

The challenge remains for policy-makers and professionals to make participation a reality for all children and young people so that they are empowered to make contributions to the decisions that affect them. This requires more than a tokenistic approach of involving children in a decision-making process as a one-off without any follow-up. Commitment to an on-going process is required.

Involving children and young people in decision-making is not only about recognising their rights; it is about developing co-operation and working relationships, and about providing skills and experiences which can be taken into future relationships. Such involvement extends beyond individual decisions, and can lead to local authorities, for example, consulting regularly with a permanent council of children and young people, an organisation having a separate committee of children and young people, or a permanently established school council. Empowerment as an ultimate goal requires more commitment in time and resources from an organisation. Control, it is suggested in one chapter, is the overall goal, where children and young people run the organisation, or project, with the role of adults being one of 'support'. It will be interesting to watch the development of the emerging Article 12 organization which seeks to be run by children and young people, for children and young people. This approach does require a change in adult attitudes, with adults having to give up power in the decision-making process. Sometimes, unwittingly, adults create barriers which prevent children being involved successfully, for example, preventing access by arranging meetings during school hours, or setting venues which are comfortable for adults rather than for young people. A further disadvantage for young people is the information which adults possess, which tilts the power balance in their favour; children and young people very rarely have access to their own information networks and, without information will remain isolated and powerless.

When children and young people are involved, are brought together and invited to contribute to the development and provision of services, it is possible to establish valid and reliable statements which adults can work to and be monitored against. One example, 'Viewpoint' outlined in this book, demonstrates a particular method of work with children and young people. This approach identifies and quantifies some of the key requirements from a child's perspective of community-based services. This approach draws on the experiences of researchers in the 1980s, investigating with adults the concept of service quality, which found that consumers used basically similar criteria to evaluate the quality of a service in different organisations. Meeting the requirements of customers becomes a crucial gauge of quality, and in 'Viewpoint' the approach has been adapted to focus on children's expectations of the help being provided for them in response to their needs.

Children have not been accorded the same attention as adults but, as this example demonstrates, it is possible to use developments in the field of service quality to promote the participation of children and young people in the design of the services provided for them, so that their needs and expectations are reflected in service provision. Here is further evidence that children's perceptions as users and recipients of services are influenced by different considerations to the adults who provide them. There is a need to find different ways to empower children, to bring out their views, their wishes and feelings, and to respect and act on them.

Social policy implications

There is growing evidence from children and young people about the issues that concern them, and about the nature of the help they require, but the oppressive nature of our children and young people's services permits only tokenistic participation. Historically, adults have maintained a protectionist stance in relation to 'young citizens', and it is not easy to shift adult and professional attitudes and behaviours to those which permit more participation and empowerment.

A key requirement of any organisation seeking to create oppor-

tunities for children and young people to participate in an effective
and meaningful way is to develop and formalise a policy Such a
policy requires a commitment and ownership from all levels of the
organisation, and will need to address the resistance adults
inevitably will experience, and the barriers which will have to be
overcome. Children do not lack the knowledge and ability to participate, but are adults prepared to permit their empowerment?

These policy issues are addressed in the final chapter in a context
where Government policy is encouraging service providers to respect the 'wishes' and needs of the citizen. Whether this policy
extends to the young citizen in any meaningful way is questionable.
The implications of these policy issues for child protection services
are addressed, and readers of this book will see that there are opportunities for action on behalf of children and young people if they
choose to take them.

Only an individual young citizen can tell why he or she ran away
or played truant from school. Only a group of young citizens can say
what provision would meet their needs in a particular area. The lack
of knowledge and experience lies with adults, and with adult professionals, who fail to listen, to draw out and act on the knowledge,
skills and experience of our young citizens.

1 Child protection rights:
can an international declaration be an effective instrument for protecting children
Yvonne Joseph

In recent years, interest in the children's rights debate has been given an added impetus as a result of the United Kingdom ratification of the United Nations Convention on the Rights of the Child and the passing of the 1989 Children Act. Both these measures seek to safeguard children's welfare and place special emphasis on their right to a safe and secure environment. In particular, they both highlight the child's right to protection from abuse and exploitation.

This chapter focusses on the issue of a child's right to protection from physical harm, and on the relevance of the broad principles outlined in the Convention and in the Chidren Act. It seeks to define what is meant by children's rights and addresses key questions:

- can international declarations and conventions really protect children?

- how are such measures implemented on a national level?

- how can broad principles be translated into practice?

It is divided into two parts, the first of which reviews the current debate on children's rights, beginning with a general discussion of the broader theoretical issues before focussing on key protective and welfare rights aspects of the debate.

The second part of the study will seek to examine how the principles outlined in both these measures relate to child protection and how they might be translated into practice in the actual work of protecting chidren.

Children and 'childhood'

The concepts of 'child' and 'childhood' are relatively recent Eurocentric inventions before which children, whatever their age, were considered as small adults belonging to society in general. Plumb has pointed out

> The very idea of childhood is a European invention of the last 400 years, before then as soon as the child could live without the constant solicitude of his mother, his nanny, or his cradle rocker, he belonged to an adult society. (Plumb, 1972)

There can therefore be no one simple definition of a 'child' since childhood is itself not a single universal experience of fixed duration that is common to all people. It is rather a cultural, social, and historical construct reflecting the diversity and relativity of the concept. But, despite this lack of specificity, the terms are commonly taken to mark an arbitrary separation between a young person and an adult both in terms of chronology and taken status.

Children can also be regarded as a homogenous group *vis à vis*, their relationship to adults, where, as well as the division into distinct age-linked stages, there is also an assumption of their 'inherent incompetence'. Veerman identifies several key features associated with that period of time when children are not yet considered to be adults. These include

• being disenfranchised with no political rights or power

• having economic disadvantage and a lack of independent financial power

• having essentially 'passive' legal status and being considered to be the property of their parents.

• being the subject of adult discipline, especially from parents.

During this time, children are denied basic human rights because of their age. Their freedom and autonomy is limited in areas which are as diverse as a choice of which film to watch, what clothes to wear, and what time to go to bed. They are denied the vote and in short are 'a large, long-suffering and oppressed grouping – a silent and unrepresented minority who are undeserving of civil rights'. They live in what Martin Luther King Junior described as a state of 'nobody-ness' (quoted in Freeman, 1983).

In addition, some children may experience additional hardships and restrictions due, for example, to poverty, physical and/or mental disability, and different forms of abuse and exploitation, but, despite any differences, all children are likely to suffer political, economic, legal, educational and domestic restrictions simply because they are children.

In the final analysis, childhood and adolescence are processes of learning, and since all children experience the most mental and physical development in their first years of life, adequate resources must be made available to protect and assist their development.

Children's rights – theoretical perspectives

Contemporary views of childhood and children are commonly based on at least two myths which, to a large extent, serve to distort and suppress an accurate reflection of the reality facing most children. The first is that the treatment of children is based on respect and a wish to protect and safeguard their best interests. In the second, childhood is seen as a golden age and a special time in which children should be protected from the harshness of adult life, should have no responsibilities and anxieties, and have the freedom to play, learn and participate in recreational activities.

The facts, however, belie this arcadian view. For example, large numbers of children are abused and neglected each year, and many children in the United Kingdom live in poverty, bad housing, or are in institutional care. According to a study by the Birmingham Low Pay Unit, children also feature highly in employment figures with one in three children in the UK working part-time, 80% of them illegally and in poor health and safety conditions (Birmingham Low Pay Unit, 1992). Until fairly recently, this blend of fantasy and unreality has served to obscure the fact that children have special rights of their own.

Soon after gaining its independence, the Government of the United States adopted the *Declaration on Rights of Man* in 1776. Some people feared the spread of this new radicalism to England, and that the next step on the rights agenda would be to put forward ridiculous ideas about the rights of youngsters, children and babies. (Franklin, 1986) For some time therefore, rights of children, like rights and votes for women and slaves, continued to be degraded and ignored.

However, to show how things have changed, a little less than two centuries after the end of the American civil war, 1979 was designated as the International Year of the Child by the United Nations, and a Children's Legal Centre was established in England with the sole aim of advocating and promoting children's rights. Since then, children's rights have become a serious social issue which can no longer be ignored being based upon the fundamental principle that children's rights should be essentially no different from the human rights to which every human person is entitled. This is most clearly expressed in the United Nations Declaration on Human Rights.

Historically, the development of general theories of rights and justice was based on the philosophies of law and education in which the specific rights of children received little attention. This is because children have always been considered to be incompetent and therefore unable to bear responsibility. The fact that they have little or no power, and are politically disenfranchised led Franklin to observe that they lacked basic human rights to such an extent that they are frequently subjected to treatment which, if inflicted upon any other grouping in society, would be considered a moral outrage and would undoubtedly become the source of substantial political activity (Franklin, 1989).

While the 1960s civil rights movement heightened the 'rights' debate generally, as far as children were concerned, there has never really been a general consensus about whether they do indeed have rights, and if so, how these could be implemented.

Consistent attempts have been made to ridicule the concept of children's rights by conjuring up ridiculous caricatures; for example, images of 2 year-olds with the vote, and toddlers negotiating with cowed parents. Franklin argues that a major reason for the neglect of children's rights is the difficulty of getting people to take the matter seriously. Some of this reluctance is almost certainly due to the complex nature of the issues involved and to the difficulty of applying the concept to the broad age range of children to which it must apply. However, many children's rights advocates would argue that age should not be a significant factor in achieving children's rights, which should be an intrinsic part of the human rights objectives that every society should strive to achieve for both children and adults.

Different aspects of the 'children's rights' debate are prioritised according to the different perspective and interests of its proponents, for example, more legal and financial responsibilities, more basic food, clothing, and medical care, more general rights including human dignity, autonomy, privacy, and respect. Essentially, this varied 'bag' of rights falls into two main categories.

- Legal rights describe existing practices which are recognised and endorsed in law and which can be enforced through legal means.

- Moral rights relate to commonly agreed principles of behaviour and what is commonly perceived as justifiable entitlements even where these are not backed up by legal force.

These support and inform each other and are interdependent to the extent that improvements in one area will inevitably impact on the other.

In terms of their safety in general and child protection in particular, these broad categories can be narrowed down even further to include: the right to protection and the rights to freedom from abuse and neglect, both of which feature fairly high on the rights agenda. Here the two dominant ideologies are

- liberationist – the right to more independence

- protectionist – the right to welfare and protection.

In summary, liberationists stress the importance of rights which would give children autonomous control over their environment and various other aspects of their lives. They argue that children should have the same rights as adults to vote, work, drive a car, and so on. They should not be forced to undergo compulsory education, and their rights should not be based solely on arbitrary age divisions but should take account of uneven patterns of human development and acknowledge different capacities and competencies at different stages. Also, children should have greater independence from parents and adults including more autonomy to make decisions on a range of 'family' issues.

Protectionists adopt a more pragmatic approach and, while still highlighting many of the same issues, they place slightly more emphasis on meeting needs than fulfilling rights. Freeman suggests three possible approaches in this area:

- the need to accept as inevitable some age restrictions while at the same time attempting to reduce existing injustices

- the abolition of all age-related restrictions

- the need to carry out a case by case judgement; however, he acknowledged that this approach would be difficult and could lead to increased discrimination.

Inherent in this approach is the belief that protection rights should be integral and not only a matter of protection – children should also be given rights to independence and autonomy. The protectionist stresses the responsibility of society to provide a range of beneficial objects, environments, services, experiences, etc for all people including children.

Rogers and Wrightsman also carry out an assessment, the protectionist versus the liberationist view of children's rights. They conclude that the protectionist or 'child-saving' movement promotes legislation and the creation of insititutions specifically for protecting children and promoting their welfare, while liberationists believe that children have the same rights as adults and that consideration of their rights should be integral to any legislative or other action taken by society.

Despite such slight differences in analysis, all are united in advocating the view that, while children do indeed have needs that merit special attention and protection, they should on the whole, have rights which are no greater or lesser than those of adults. These rights should be regarded as necessary and relevant and should not be conditional or mutually exclusive – indeed adults can and do have the broad range and, even though they do sometimes conflict, one does not generally supplant the other.

Possibly because of the complex nature of the issues involved, the concept of children's rights has proved to be a particularly elusive one. This is probably partly why Jeremy Bentham (1987) has described it as a 'slogan in search of a definition'. But, even without agreeing absolutely with that view, it is obvious that children's rights raise complex philosophical, moral, legal, and social issues which will necessarily require a great deal of work and energy before a resolution is achieved.

International children's rights:

The UN Convention on the rights of the child

International declarations are binding treaties between states expressing statements of principles which provide a framework for guiding policy and practice. Ratifying states agree to abide by these principles and to carry out any specific obligations they contain.

The concept of children's rights was first defined 30 years ago in the UN Declaration on the Rights of the Child. The Declaration was the brain-child of Eglantyne Jebb, a British woman who was a pioneer in the struggle for international children's rights and a founder member of the Save the Children Fund. She believed that all the world's children, wherever they were, needed better protection, and she drew on her wide experience to draft a 'Code For Children' which was adopted in 1922 by the Save the Children Fund Union, and by the General Assembly of the League of Nations in 1924, and again by the General Assembly of the United Nations in 1959.

The Code sets out ten key principles which give children rights and was the first international measure aimed at protecting them. Although it was not legally binding, and essentially only a 'statement of intent' ratifying states undertook to look after the interests of children within their boundaries. Despite any shortcomings, this statement played a key role in establishing for the first time the principle of universality which emphasised that all children have rights which were linked to the obligations of adults to protect them at parental, national and international levels.

In 1959, as a result of pressures from the International Union of Children's Welfare to amend the Code, the UN Social Committee drew up a children's charter which was unanimously adopted in 1959 as the UN Declaration on the Rights of the Child.

One of the most important principles contained in the 1959 Declaration was that children needed special protection by reason of their physical and mental immaturity. Responsibility was placed on adults and adult society to fulfil those obligations. In terms of children's rights, this Declaration went further than the earlier Code in that it also specifically addressed the needs of children to protection. Thirty years after this first Declaration, the UN adopted a re-drafted and strengthened Convention on the Rights of the Child in 1989. These various initiatives certainly placed children's rights firmly on the international agenda.

The 1989 Convention is regarded as the first 'true' piece of international children's legislation aiming to harmonise all the rights of children under a single umbrella. It is the first legally binding international human rights treaty to confer a wide range of rights specifically on children. In this respect, it is radically different from other international measures like the UN Declarations of Human Rights, the European Convention on Human Rights, and other Convention and Covenants, which do not specifically refer to children.

The Convention, which has been described as the most comprehensive international statement of children's rights, provides a yardstick to measure development on both the international and national levels. Its 54 articles cover the economic, social, civil, and cultural rights of children including the right to protection from abuse, neglect, and exploitation. It was adopted by the UN in 1989 and became law on the 2 September, 1990 after being ratified by 20 nations. Ratifying countries are legally bound to observe the children's rights principles outlined in the Convention and pledge to adopt laws, develop practice, and introduce any neccessary regulations to achieve these objectives. In the UK, after intensive lobbying and campaigning, the Convention was ratified in December 1991, one year after its adoption by the United Nations.

The Convention defines a child as 'every human being below 18'. It recognises the 'particular vunerability of children', and brings together a comprehensive code for their protection from all forms of neglect and abuse. In addition, it tries to allow for different cultural, political, and material realities by allowing scope for interpretation and adaptation of the various articles and provisions. The Convention offers a conceptual framework for action, and sets standards and targets for facilitating and planning practical action based on the following fundamental principles:

- parents have primary responsibility for the care of children
- children must not be separated from parents unnecessarily
- children must be protected from economic exploitation and harmful work
- children must be protected from drug abuse
- children have a right to receive recovery and rehabilitation services for maltreatment and neglect
- children should receive special safeguards beyond those accorded to adults
- the best environment for children is with their families
- adults and governments should act in children's interests.

These principles reinforce the central tenet that the primary responsibility of caring for children remains with the family. Emphasis is also placed on the need for international co-operation, and the responsibility of governments for taking legal, and other protective measures to protect children and promote their rights.

In terms of protection from abuse and its effects, the aim is to preserve children's physical integrity and to respect their personhood. The key articles in this area are:

- Article 3 – which allows children the right to develop to their fullest potential
- Article 39 – which guarantees the right to treatment and recovery services
- Article 19 – which guarantees protection from all forms of physical and mental abuse.

The Convention explicitly acknowledges that *all* children do indeed have rights, even though differences of opinion may still revolve around the identification of the most appropriate policies for their promotion and implementation.

Following adoption of the Convention, the UN convened the first World Summit on Children in September 1990 at the UN headquarters in New York. The Summit was attended by 91 heads of State and representatives from 159 nations including the United Kingdom's Prime Minister, Margaret Thatcher. It was the largest ever gathering of its kind, and it ended with a commitment by over 120 countries to begin addressing a range of problems facing children.

Through an agreed list of Summit goals, States also undertook to draw up detailed national plans for implementing identified objectives by the end of 1991. Some programmes were to be implemented immediately, while others especially in less developed countries might experience some delay because of their dependence on increased aid. For example, UNICEF UK estimates that about 20 million dollars per annum will be needed to achieve the summit goals by the year 2000.

The net outcome of the Summit was a detailed plan for a new world order for the world's children, including an agreed programme for, among other things, ending mass malnutrition, preventable disease and widespread illiteracy before the end of the decade. These goals are clearly an indication of the degree of the political will and commitment to tackle children's problems, including the mobilisation of appropriate resources to achieve the objectives that have been identified. Implementing the summit goals will undoubtedly encourage countries to be more aware of the likely effects on children of existing policies as well as helping them to identify formerly neglected areas and formulate specific measures to meet their needs.

Children's rights in the UK

In the decade since International Year of the Child in 1979, there have been a variety of initiatives aimed at promoting the rights of children. This includes:

- the creation of a Children's Legal Centre to protect and promote the legal rights of children

- the setting up of an autonomous organisation, the Children's Rights Development Unit (CRDU) to monitor the implementation of the UN Convention on the Rights of the Child

- a proposal that the Government should appoint a Minister for

Children who would assume responsibility for children's issues at Government level

- calls for a Children's Rights Commissioner or Ombudsman to monitor the progress of Children's rights on a national level, to receive and deal with individual complaints, comment and report on issues affecting children
- calls for a Youth Council or Youth Congress where young people can draw up their own agendas, and debate and discuss issues of concern to them
- calls for a UK Charter of Children's Rights.

However, despite what might seem like a wealth of activity, and despite regular outbreaks of public outrage when a child dies or is badly abused, very little attention has been consistently paid to the rights of children in the United Kingdom. Incidents like the recent well-publicised cases of Pindown in Staffordshire, Frank Beck in Leicestershire, or individual child death inquiries – of which there have been some 37 since 1973 – may give a temporary impetus to often short-lived debates about the rights of children, but the situation essentially remains unchanged.

For a great many children, the reality is still that their rights continue to be violated every day, either because they are unaware of them, or because they are powerless to stop any violation. This includes obvious events like the examples of physical and sexual abuses mentioned above, as well as violations which occur as a result of social structural inequalities, like inadequate housing, homelessness or poverty. For example, a recent research study showed that the number of children living in poverty in the UK has doubled in the last 10 years, and it is estimated that over a third of all children now live in poverty (Bradshaw, 1990).

Having ratified the Convention, the UK Government is obliged to implement its provisions with the exception of the five reservations it has entered. In terms of practical action, the Department of Health has been given the responsibility of overseeing the implementation of the Convention on behalf of the Government. In the voluntary sector, the Children's Rights Development Unit was set up in 1991 to monitor progress on the implementation of the Convention, to carry out an external audit, and to draw up a national agenda of reforms relating to law and practice in the UK. Additionally the Unit, which was initially set up as a three-year project, aims to encourage institutions, voluntary organisations, private bodies, local authorities, health authorities and others working with, and for, children to use the Convention to carry out an assessment of their own practices, policies and procedures, and to assist in their lobbying and campaigning work on behalf of children.

Child abuse – an overview

Despite the almost universal agreement that children should be protected from exploitation and abuse, there remains a lack of clarity
about what exactly constitutes abuse. At the extremes of the continuum, some would define a light smack as abusive, while others only
consider actions which are deliberately intended to hurt a child or
where actual physical harm or injury is caused as being abusive.
The range of agencies dealing with child abuse include:

- local authority social services departments who have statutory
  responsibility to investigate and take appropriate action on all
  cases of abuse brought to their attention

- the National Society for the Prevention of Cruelty on Children
  (NSPCC) who have been given similar statutory powers

- the police who are, of course, responsible for investigating
  crimes and prosecuting those who commit them.

Each of these agencies may approach their task differently, and place
a slightly different emphasis on their area of responsibility. For
example, the police may be primarily concerned with gathering
sufficient evidence to pursue a prosecution, the NSPCC might be
most anxious to ensure the child's protection and the Social Services
Department might agree with the need to give immediate protection
to the child, but would additionally be concerned about the
social/structural issues which the whole family might be experiencing, for example, bad housing conditions or poverty. Agencies are
encouraged to work together to ensure maximum levels of co-operation and co-ordination.

The child abuse figures show that large numbers of children in the
United Kingdom continue to be abused, neglected, and deprived,
and that violence against children is widespread. While recent
statistics from the Department of Health report that the number of
children on child protection registers has decreased by 16% from
38,000 in 1992 to 32,500 at the end of March 1993, it should also be
noted that this decrease is partly accounted for by some major
changes in the way that information about child abuse is collected;
for example the removal of the 'grave concern' category from the
register.

The idealised image of the adult/child relationship highlighted
earlier in this chapter is challenged repeatedly every time a child is
hurt or dies as a result of abuse. Inevitably the temptation to place
the blame only on individual adults is strong; however, it is not
improbable that the longevity and endurance of child abuse, including sexual abuse, can be entirely accounted for by theories related to

the individual pathology of evil wicked parents, but is in part also due to the lowly status of children and to the way in which society perceives them and their rights.

While most child protection measures and procedures quite rightly aim 'to protect children from inadequate care, neglect, physical or emotional abuse or other forms of danger in the home', there needs to be more explicit recognition that child abuse is also undoubtedly related to poverty, inequality and other social/structural constraints. For example, Parton states that by 'concentrating only on dangerous individuals we risk ignoring dangerous conditions' and that some attention must also be directed to examining the social, political and legal status of children, within the context of a comprehensive analysis of children's protective rights.

Ad Quote

Placing the names of children who are at risk on child protection registers is just one of the measures that has been developed to protect children from physical and sexual abuse. However, in view of the persistence of all forms of abuse, there is continuing discussion and debate about just how effective registers are combined with growing concern about how their failure to protect children is compounded by the lack of adequate resources.

These concerns were also highlighted in a report, published in 1990, by the London Region Social Services Inspectorate, which revealed that, in London alone, there were 820 children on child protection registers who had not been allocated a social worker to work on their case.

Child abuse statistics shatter the myth of childhood as a golden age of innocence and weakness where children have no responsibilities or anxieties. On the contrary, they substantiate recent research findings which show that it is often children who bear the burden of poverty and hardship in Britain (Bradshaw, 1990).

The role of the state

Under the classification of rights advanced by Veerman, a child's right to protection falls into the 'passive' category where typically, the state defines what the minimum standard should be, identifies all those who fall below this level, and sets up legal and other mechanisms to give assistance and support where necessary. In this context, the state's role has been primarily defined as being to act in the best interests of the child and to remove him/her from danger if necessary. Increasingly, intervention is seen as being beneficial and a key factor in achieving this goal. In this view, the proper physical and emotional care of children became areas of professional concern and the state – through its welfare agencies and the courts, can decide what is in the best interests of the child. In child protection terms, the 'best interest' principle often translates into what is thought to be the 'least detrimental' course of action. This lack of clarity and precision can lead to subjective and value-laden assessments based on individuals' assessment of what is 'right', and to unjustified speculation and discrimination against individuals from communities which not easily fit into the expected models of behaviour; for example, working class and black and minority communities. Children from these backgrounds are more likely to be defined as being 'at risk', placed on child protection registers or be accommodated away from home.

The United Nations Convention does little to clarify the meaning of 'best interest' and, even though many of its articles are based on this principle, the definition is so vague as to give very little real guidance to practitioners. Futhermore, the broad constitutional language used in the Convention is often ambiguous and all-embracing and therefore subject to a multitude of subjective interpretations.

Perhaps inevitably, laws conferring rights often also have gaps, conflicts and ambiguities and, in the case of children's rights, these are pronounced enough to set up a dichotomy in which children's rights *appear* to be ranged against parents and against the state.

In the majority of cases, the state's role in child protection does not conflict with the rights of parents and families, but situations do arise when the interest of parents come into conflict with those of children. This has happened, most notably, in situations where parents abuse and/or exploit their children, and state agencies intervene to protect them. In such circumstances, even though there is no clearly stated hierarchy of rights, the primary duty of the state should be to prioritise protection for the child. This duty is reinforced in Article 19, section 1 of the United Nations Convention which requires states to 'take all appropriate legislative, administrative, social and educational measures to protect the child from all forms of physical or mental violence, injury or abuse, neglect or negligent treatment, maltreatment or exploitation – including sexual abuse.'

In reality, the state's concern for children has often operated simultaneously and in harmony with the, sometimes more muted, rights of parents. But, while parents should always have an opportunity to challenge decisions to remove children from their care, its primary role is to develop effective legislation and social work provision to meet for the care and protection of children.

Hillary Clinton identifies two often complementary approaches adopted by the state for the protection of children who have been subjected to neglect, or physical or emotional abuse.

- Residualism attempts to remedy deficiencies in a particular section of the child population, and services are only provided after a problem has been identified.

- Universalism provides services for the entire child population as part of a broad public and social infrastructure.

She believed that parental behaviour that does not result in medically diagnosable harm to a child should not automatically be allowed to trigger intevention however offensive that behaviour may seem. If state intervention is necessary, the primary role should be to develop adequate legal standards based on the key principles including best interests and the least detrimental alternative for the child. In her view the reasons for intervention:

> Strict legal standards and less state intervention must necessarily underpin a theory that adequately explains the appropriate role of the state in child rearing and provides sufficient checks on the exercise of discretion to ensure that authority is exercised only in warranted cases (Clinton, 1979)

If the state is to be effective in protecting children, there must also be a recognition that protection does not only depend on reactive intervention, but that action must also be taken to tackle the social and economic realities of poverty, bad housing and poor parenting and that more preventive work must also be undertaken with vulnerable children and families. In the final analysis, adults, parents, and the state all have a responsibility to protect and support children as they grow into adults. Society as a whole is empowered to act on their behalf but any action taken should ideally be the same as that which children themselves would have chosen if they were able.

In the United Kingdom, as in other countries, national legislation can play a crucial role in reforming institutions, and professional practice. The Children Act (1989) which is the fifth piece of child care legislation to be passed this century (the others being in 1908, 1933, 1948, 1969) aims to achieve this purpose in relation to the provision of services for children in the United Kingdom. The Act was developed against the backdrop of the Cleveland child abuse scandal in which a number of children were removed from their homes because of suspicions of sexual abuse. When introducing the Bill into the House of Parliament, the Lord Chancellor, Lord Mackay of Clashfern described it as: 'The most comprehensive and far-reaching reform of child law which has come before parliament in living memory'.

The Act aims to balance several different sets of rights:

- those of children to be protected, to be consulted and to participate in decision-making which affects their lives

- those of parents to exercise their duties and responsibilities
  towards their children

- those of the state to protect children who are in need or at risk.

The Children Act, described elsewhere in this book (see Buchanan)
sets out a number of key principles regulating how these matters are
to be handled. While it goes a long way towards explicitly acknowledging children's rights in a number of key areas, the degree of
emphasis placed on the 'best interest' principle helps to ensure that
the power to act remains squarely in the hands of adults. Children
have only been given limited and 'token' rights which, because they
are not based on recognition of their own competence, simply
reinforce their dependence on adults. Because of this, many people,
for example, Mike Lindsay (1989) are beginning to question
whether the Children Act is indeed a 'Children's Charter' as it has
often been described – particularly by Government ministers.

However, despite any criticisms, the Convention and the Children Act can lay the foundation for beginning to alter the prevailing
social and legal constraints on children. In any case, both have far-
reaching implications for relations between children, adults and the
state and both combine aspects of civil, political, economic, social
and cultural rights which aim to protect children and safeguard
their rights.

Children's rights and child protection

The actual number of abused children will probably always remain
unknown and there is very likely an under-reporting of cases, especially in relation to emotional abuse and neglect. Even so, research
has consistently shown that sizeable numbers of children are placed
on child protection registers. A recent National Children's Bureau
review of research on sexual abuse shows that between a quarter and
a third of all children had at least one sexual experience with an
adult before they were 18.

In the period between 1988 and 1990, many official reports and
guidance documents were issued drawing attention to the issue of
child abuse and about the emergence of sexual and ritual abuse in
particular. Between 1973 and 1989 there have been a total of 37
official child abuse death enquiries all of which make general and
specific recommendations for improving policies and practice in
this area.

The debate about the effectiveness and/or appropriateness of child protection procedures is an on-going one, and *Working Together* the most recently published guideline on child protection from the Department of Health explicitly encourages interagency co-operation and recommends that all registered child abuse cases should be regularly reviewed and removed from the register if appropriate.

Until relatively recently, protecting children has remained very firmly in the realms of the adult 'child saving' arena, and children's rights issues hardly featured in the debate.

Where children's rights have been identified as an issue of concern, views have usually been expressed from an adult perspective. For instance, the Department of Health report summarising child abuse inquiries states that, 'on the one hand the emergence of child sexual abuse has led to increased awareness of the rights and needs of children', while in a section entitled 'Parent and Child Involvement' the focus is exclusively on parental and adult involvement, with no mention of how children themselves might be informed about or involved in their own protection.

In its 1992 annual report UNICEF UK addresses the question of whether international initiatives like the UN Convention and the Children's Summit are 'simply rhetoric'. After a fairly thorough analysis, this view is ultimately rejected in favour of the position that, despite any shortcomings, the current convention goes much further than previous Declarations and Conventions in outlining the special and positive rights for children as individuals. It has certainly made a significant contribution to debates about both general and specific areas of children's rights and, in some countries, it is already becoming clear that ratification could indeed represent a solid intent which is already being translated into practical action (UNICEF, 1992).

As regards child welfare and child protection provisions, the Convention provides a critical framework and a practical instrument against which children's rights policies and procedures can be tested. If these were adhered to, it is almost certain that child protection would be less paternalistic, and that increased respect for children's status would result in more opportunities for them to participate fully in matters which affect their lives.

The Covention also outlines the role of governments in ensuring the efficient and effective mobilisation of all social, individual and organisational resources. This is an essential component in any child protection system which tries to ensure that 'the protection of personal integrity goes beyond mere physical security and even emotional security to preservation of the rudiments of human dignity' (Melton, 1991).

On the organisational level, child welfare agencies seem to be generally more aware of children's rights, and many have held meetings, conferences, and seminars to discuss the issues involved. New organisations and initiatives have also been developed to reflect this new consciousness; for example, children's rights and advocacy projects like Voice for the Child in Care, the Children's Rights Development Unit, and the Children's Rights Officers Association. Currently, adults are in the forefront of most, if not all, of these developments, and it is too soon to judge exactly how different these new organisations will be from the traditional 'child saving' approaches of which there is so much criticism.

In particular, the NSPCC is actively engaged trying to develop and expand its approach to address children's rights concerns; for example, it has contributed to the setting-up of the CDRU, and plays an active role in the Children's Rights Officers Association and in campaigning for the creation of a Children's Rights Commissioner. Much of the re-appraisal of the organisation's work will involve attempts to resolve conflicts in a number of important areas including attempts to increase the participation of children as well as parents in discussions and decision-making processes and issues concerning the theoretical, legal, social, and practical context of child protection. In the future, the organisation is also more likely to be confronted with situations where the wishes of the child are at odds with those of the parent and agency. For example, there has been a case, the first case of its kind, in which an 11 year-old girl took her case to the High Court to try to get her name removed from the local authority at-risk register. To date, only parents have been able to take such proceedings but the children's rights principles outlined in the Children Act could, at least theoretically, lead to more children challenging social workers' decisions in this way.

This example clearly demonstrates that, as a result of the Convention and the Children Act, children themselves are becoming more aware of their rights, and more assertive in the areas of child protection. Despite any shortcomings, the Children Act, combined with growing consciousness about the rights of children, has had a major impact on child protection work, as child welfare organisations and individual workers engage with the often complex realities that stem from seeing and working with children as individuals in their own right.

In the final analysis, the Summit goals and the Convention itself set out agreed minimum standards for protection of all children in all nations against abuse and exploitation whether in war, at work, or in the home. They constitute guaranteed criteria against which practical progress can be measured and are a reflection of a growing political and social awareness that children do have basic human rights. In this context a well-supported Convention could be a major instrument for legitimising the concept of children's rights.

In terms of present and future impact on child protection, the Convention has already been influential in 'providing a guidepost to the development of child protection policy' even though there still needs to be major attitudinal change and substantial reform of most existing systems before the full implementation of children's rights becomes a reality for all children.

But, in the final analysis, the Convention is only one mechanism for promoting children's rights and will only be really meaningful in the context of an explicit recognition of the generally worsening position of children all over the world.

If the high hopes generated by the Convention are to be realised, the maximum effort must go into making sure that governments are actually putting the Convention into practice and working to bring about the necessary shift in public consciousness. Since international laws cannot be enforced in domestic courts, success will largely depend on raising public awareness and mobilising public pressure and indignation against the injustices suffered by children.

References

Bentham, J. (1987) *Nonsense on Stilts – Rights of Man*, Methuen Press.
Birmingham City Council, Eduction Department and Low Pay Unit (1992) *The Hidden Army: Children at work in the 1990s: a national child employment study*, London: Low Pay Unit.
Bradshaw, J. (1990) *Child Poverty and Deprivation in the UK*, London: National Childen's Bureau.
Department of Health (1988 and 1991) Inter-agency guidelines on child protection *Working Together*, 1st and 2nd editions. HMSO.
Department of Health (1993) *Children Act Report*, HMSO.
Franklin, B. (1989) Children's Rights: Developments and Prospects. *Children and Society*, 3.1, pp. 50–56.
Franklin, B. (ed) (1986) *The Rights of Children*, Basil Blackwell Ltd.
Freeman, M. D. A. (1983) *The Rights and Wrongs of Children*, Pinter.
Lindsay, M. (1989) Law and Practice, *Children's Rights and the Children Act*.
Melton, G. (1991) Preserving the dignity of children around the world; the UN Convention on the Rights of the Child in International Society for Prevention of Child Abuse and Neglect, *Child Abuse and Neglect*, 15, pp. 343–350. Oxford: Pergamon Press.
Parton, N. (1985) *Child Abuse*, McMillan Press.
Plumb (1972) *In the Light of History*, Penguin.
Rodham-Clinton, H. (1973) Children under the law. *Harvard Educational Review*, 43.
Unicef Report (1992) *The State of the World's Children*.
Veerman, P. E. (1992) *The Rights of the Child and the Changing Image of Childhood*, Martinus Nijhoff publishers.
United Nations Convention on the Rights of the Child (1992), Treaty Series, 44, HMSO.

2 Children's rights to participation and protection:
a critique
Gerison Lansdown

Children lack power in our society. They are amongst its most vulnerable members, and have traditionally been denied basic civil
rights – the right to freedom of expression, to freedom of conscience,
to freedom of association, to privacy or confidentiality and, perhaps
most fundamentally, the right to participate in decisions that affect
them. This denial derives from a view of childhood in which children have been presumed to lack the capacity to exercise those rights
responsibly. Instead, parents have been empowered in law to act on
their children's behalf, and exercise judgement over most of the
moral, legal and practical decisions that affect children's lives. Children are, to a large extent, recipients of adult actions rather than participants in decision-making. However, during the past 20 years,
attitudes towards children have slowly begun to change. The process
of change is a complex one, but perhaps it is possible to identify
three critical factors which have influenced our thinking and attitudes towards children and begun to encourage recognition that
children have rights as well as needs.

First, there has been growing awareness that children are not
always adequately protected within their families, and that parents
are capable of harming and abusing their children. During the
1970s, we encountered the phenomenon of 'baby battering' as it was
then known and, more recently, the existence of widespread sexual

abuse within families of both male and female children has come to light. This awareness has led to a major shift in the legal framework governing the relationship between the state and the family and recognition of the needs for protection of children outside the boundaries of the family. There are now, in general, far greater constraints on the rights of parents and a greater willingness and increased powers on the part of the state to intervene to protect children. The impact of these changes is to begin to afford the child a status independent of his or her parents – to accept that he or she has rights to protection as an individual.

Secondly, we have also recognised that it is neither possible nor desirable for individual families to bear the full costs and responsibilities of children alone. We have seen the development of universal education, and health services, benefit systems to support families with children and the introduction of maternity benefits and some limited day-care provision for working parents. These developments have reflected a growing acceptance of the social responsibility which all citizens carry for children, and a shift away from individualised accountability. The principle of some level of shared responsibility has been integral to much social welfare policy since the war, although the political consensus on this development has been somewhat undermined in the late 1980s with Government policy increasingly pulling back from a commitment to partnership with parents. The developments that have taken place derive from the increasing acceptance that children have social rights: rights to health care, education, housing, and some measure of protection in their standard of living.

Thirdly, we have also witnessed massive changes in the nature of family life. Not only are many children born to single mothers, but divorce rates have escalated considerably. Many children can expect to live through periods of marriage, divorce, single parenthood, and possible remarriage, and many will spend periods of their life looked after by a local authority. Their experience of family is not static or constant. It is no longer possible therefore to subsume the child within the family, and allow her or him to be defined or hidden within it. Children are likely to live in several different formulations of the family, and it has become increasingly clear that it is necessary to acknowledge their rights as individuals if they are to have any control over their lives and to be offered adequate protection and respect for their views. The family can no longer be considered without question as a secure, safe and stable environment for all children, and this change has begun to be reflected in family law.

Additionally, the case for recognising children's rights to greater opportunities for participation has been lent considerable legitimacy by the adoption by the United Nations General Assembly in

1989 of the UN Convention on the Rights of the Child. The Convention, which was ratified by the United Kingdom Government in December 1991 introduces for the first time in an international treaty the principle that children have civil rights. Article 12 of the Convention requires that:

1. States Parties shall assure to the child who is capable of forming his or her own views the right to express those views freely in all matters affecting the child, the views of the child being given due weight in accordance with the age and maturity of the child.

2. For this purpose, the child shall in particular be provided the opportunity to be heard in any judicial and administrative proceedings affecting the child, either directly, or through a representative or an appropriate body, in a manner consistent with the procedural rules of national law.

This Article is explicit in its affirmation that children are human beings who must be taken seriously and respected as participants in their own lives. It is followed by further articles outlining the rights to freedom of expression, thought, religion and conscience, and rights to privacy and information. These principles assert the child's personal integrity as separate from and independent of any ownership by adults.

However, the case for children's rights is not uncontroversial. There has been considerable debate in the wake of ratification of the Convention and following the implementation of the Children Act about the balance between parents' and children's rights. During 1993 there was a profound backlash against the idea that children have a right to greater levels of participation. There is a vociferous and influential lobby amongst politicians, the media and large section of the general public who would argue that it is not appropriate to give rights to children, that the balance has already swung too far in that direction, and that it is more important to give greater focus to the teaching of social responsibility. Children are widely portrayed as irresponsible, incompetent, lacking morality, out of control and without the experience on which to draw for effective participation.

In reality, the changes that have begun to take place have had little real impact on children's status in society. What has happened is that children have become more visible in the public arena. Parents as holders of all rights and responsibilities in respect of children are no longer models accepted as possible or desirable. Children are beginning to be acknowledged as individuals both separate from, as well as part of, the family unit. This shift in thinking has resulted in the reconsideration of traditional approaches to child-care, legal protection, and service provision. But the effect of these changes has largely been to transfer responsibility from the exclusive domain of the family into a wider public sphere. It is other adults with positions of statutory responsibility – the police, the courts, teachers, social workers, doctors – who have powers to contribute to, or impose, decision-making in children's lives, and not the children themselves. Children remain largely locked into paternalistic structures in which adults, not children, are the actors. Public policy as well as family life continues to restrict the rights of children to autonomy, self-determination and to effective participation.

Perceptions of childhood

It is also important to recognise that our perceptions of childhood undergo constant change and are in many ways ambivalent and contradictory. For many adults, childhood is imbued with a rather romanticised notion of innocence – a period free from responsibility or conflict and dominated by fantasy, play and opportunity. Attempts to offer children greater control over their lives is seen as an intrusion into this period, denying them the right to enjoy their childhood. Some adults perceive children as essentially irrational, irresponsible and incapable of making informed choices on matters of concern to them. Yet, for many children of all cultures and classes, the dominating feature of childhood is that of powerlessness and lack of control over what happens to them.

There are widely varying views of the capacity of children to undertake employment, to be left alone, to play unaccompanied, to participate in democratic processes, to choose a religion. And these views are not static, for example, in 1971 80 per cent of seven to eight year-olds were allowed to go to school alone, by 1990 the figure had fallen to 9 per cent. Similarly, with employment, our current legislation deriving from the 1920s sets 13 years as the lower age limit for part-time employment but there is now pressure from the European Community to raise this to 15 or even 16 years. Childhood has been extended considerably during the course of the twentieth century. So the concept of what is a child varies within different cultures, different social groups and at different points in history.

However, whatever boundaries of childhood are drawn, there is broad consensus that children are comparatively more vulnerable than adults, requiring special measures to protect and promote their needs. And it is their need for protection which is used to justify the continued resistance to giving children more control over decision-making in their lives. A self-confirming cycle is established. Children are perceived as lacking competence to take responsibility for their own lives, and therefore as vulnerable and in need of protection. Because they need protection, adults are invested with powers to act on their behalf. Because children are denied the powers to make decisions or fully participate in them, they are rendered more vulnerable to the authority of adults.

Certainly, young children are inherently vulnerable. The very fact of their physical weakness, immaturity, lack of knowledge and experience renders children dependent on the adults around them. For very young children, their survival depends on the quality of care and commitment provided for them by the adults who have responsibility for them. They need shelter, food, education, health care, affection and protection and their survival is dependent on the willingness and capacity of adults to meet these needs. But the inherent vulnerability which we perceive in children is not an objective definition of their capacity. It is only partially drawn from the biological facts of childhood, and owes as much to social attitudes and perceptions which we impose on childhood. This vulnerability in childhood derives from historical attitudes and presumptions about the nature of childhood and is a social and political construct and not an inherent or inevitable consequence of childhood itself. One only has to look at the levels of responsibility accepted by children in many developing countries to see that our elongation of childhood well into the teenage years is neither universal nor inevitable. Similarly, there is evidence that children who experience major surgery, or long-term serious illness develop a capacity for understanding and decision-making which far exceeds commonly held perceptions about children's capabilities.

Children are vulnerable precisely because of their lack of political and economic power, the under-valuing of their potential for participation and consequent denial of civil rights. In other words, it is the structures within which children have to live which serve to render them vulnerable to abuse, exploitation, neglect and disregard for their views, as much as their inherent immaturity, lack of knowledge, ability and experience. Children have, in general, no access to money, no right to vote, no right to express an opinion or be taken seriously, no access to the courts, no rights – except within the framework of the Children Act – to challenge decisions made on their behalf, no right to make choices about their education, no legal right to physical integrity within the family – 'reasonable chastisement' remains a defence for parents to using corporal punishment.

The relationship between inherent and structural vulnerability is heavily determined by cultural attitudes, and there is a tendency in our society to rely too heavily on a presumption of children's biological and psychological vulnerability in developing our law, policy and practice and insufficient focus on the extent to which the presumption of vulnerability creates that vulnerability. Clearly, adults with parental responsibility have a duty to protect children from ill-treatment, and society has a responsibility to ensure that parents do not abuse their powers, but achieving this does not merely imply the imposition of greater powers of intervention on the part of adults. It also necessitates giving children greater powers to challenge and participate in matters that affect them. It is the predominance of a protective model in the construction of our relationships with children which has inhibited the development of appropriate recognition of children's real capacity for participation.

It is useful to look at the position of women as an analogy. Traditionally, women and children have been cast together as weak and vulnerable members of our society. Women were perceived as needing male protection in the shape of father or husband both because of their physical lack of strength and because they were intellectually and emotionally unfitted for taking full responsibility for themselves. This perception of women was used for many years to justify their continued social status as the property of men.

In other words, their presumed inherent vulnerability was the excuse for failing to tackle their structural vulnerability. Once the battles to remove those structural factors began – in the right to vote, the right to own property, the right to custody of children, the right to refuse sex within marriage, the right to physical integrity and freedom from assault, the right to equal pay, not to be discriminated against, the right to privacy – the view of women as being intrinsically in need of protection began to be eroded. Women have a long way to go before achieving full equality with men, but our attitudes in respect of civil rights for women on the principles of equality have shifted dramatically over the past 100 years.

If we are to enhance children's status in society to enable them to participate more fully in matters of concern to them, it will be necessary to achieve a comparable change with that achieved for women. Effecting such a major shift in our fundamental attitudes towards children would necessitate changes in law, policy, and practice in both the public and private spheres.

Rights versus responsibilities

Much of the hostility to the concept of children's rights is rooted in a belief that children cannot have rights until they are competent to accept responsibilities. Their presumed incapacity or unwillingness to do so forms the justification for subsequent denial of rights. Inherent in this linking of rights and responsibilities is a presumption that there are two sides of the same coin – that the exercise of the right must be matched by the exercise of responsibility within the same person. It is possible to argue that there is a relationship between the two but a rather different one. If rights are to be meaningful, there must be a responsibility for ensuring that it is possible to exercise it. Where the right applies to a child, the responsibility for promoting it will usually rest with adults. Children, for example, have a right to life. This right is universal and not contingent on any corresponding responsibilities. The exercise of the right does carry with it responsibilities but they rest not with the child but with the adults who have the power to ensure the child's survival. Children have a right to protection but the responsibility for ensuring that protection rests with first the parents and in the event of their inability or unwillingness, with the state. Children have a right to education but the right can only be exercised if the appropriate provision is available, and that imposes responsibilities on government and local authorities to ensure its availability.

Similarly, children have a right to participate in decisions that affect them. This right imposes responsibilities on adults to ensure that the child has sufficient information with which to make informed choices and that the opportunities are available in which to take part in any decision-making processes.

What is interesting about much of this debate is that the issue concerning responsibility is only invoked in relation to children. In fact, these rights when applied to adults are not contingent on the exercise of responsibility. The right to life, to privacy, to freedom of association, to freedom of religion and conscience, to legal representation, or not to be discriminated against on racial grounds apply irrespective of the behaviour of the adult. The only restrictions that apply are those necessary to protect the rights and freedoms of others.

Some children's rights do relate to special needs associated with youth – such as those which relate to family life or protection from abuse, but many of the rights contained in the United Nations Convention are really better described as human rights. The need for a separate language derives from the past failure to include children explicitly within the scope of human rights – in much the same way as the use of the term 'he' was supposed to incorporate 'she' but in fact has served for years to exclude and marginalise women. So, of course, there are situations where the exercise by children of their rights will intrude on adults' rights in exactly the same way that there are times when such conflicts arise between adults.

The exercise of the right to freedom of expresion can interfere with another person's right to freedom from discrimination, the right to freedom of information can interfere with the right to privacy. These conflicts are an inevitable consequence of individuals having rights and ultimately require state intervention if they cannot be resolved by negotiation. However, where in general we accept the inevitability of conflict between adults in the exercise of rights, we tend to use the fact of potential conflict as justification for denying respect to basic rights when it comes to children. Many of the conflicts that arise within families on a day-to-day level are actually about conflicts between basic rights amongst the members of those families – for example, a conflict between a parent offered and wishing to accept a new job requiring a move and a child wanting to stay put in the same school and with the same networks of friends. Such a conflict has nothing to do with the operation of parental responsibilities or parental rights bestowed in respect of a child. It is a direct conflict between the adult's and the child's rights to exercise a choice over a matter of importance to them. In this situation, the parents' wishes will usually prevail because they are in a position to exert greater power. The child's comparative weakness in relation to economic and physical power, combined with their lack of civil status, would make it hard for them to influence the decision.

Self-determination, participation and protection

There is without doubt an inherent tension between the recognition of the child's right to self-determination, on the one hand, and their right to protection, on the other. Clearly, parents have to exercise difficult judgements about the balance between the need to intervene in a child's life to ensure his or her protection and a child's capacity to make informed choices and to take responsibility for their own actions. The idea that children have rights is seen as profoundly threatening to many adults. It evokes fears of disruption to family life and parental authority, the awarding of rights without commensurate responsibilities, the inability to impose a safe and protective environment for chidren. Some of these concerns also appear to derive from a failure to distinguish between self-determination and participation and the relationship of both of these concepts to the responsibility to act in a child's best interests.

Protection

Adults do have clear responsibilities for the protection and welfare of children. A parent must make an infinite number of decisions and judgements every day in respect of a child. The United Nations Convention of the Rights of the Child acknowledges this responsibility in Article 5 which states that governments must '*respect the responsi-*

bilities, rights and duties of parents ... to provide ... appropriate direction and guidance in the exercise by the child of the rights [in the Convention]'. However, it also recognises the potential conflict in the exercise of those responsibilities by asserting that they must be carried out *'in a manner consistent with the child's evolving capacity'*. In other words, adults do not have unfettered rights to act on children's behalf. The Convention places further constraints on the powers of adults with responsibility for children by requiring, in Article 3 that *'In all actions concerning children, whether undertaken by public or private social welfare institutions, courts of law, administrative authorities or legislative bodies, the best interests of the child shall be a primary consideration'*. This principle provides a test against which adults need to evaluate their decisions and actions in respect of those children. However, it is by no means a straightforward or unproblematic principle to apply.

First, it should be noted that, apart from the Children Act, the concept of the welfare of the child is absent from our legislation. Indeed, even within the Children Act, there is no obligation on parents to act in their children's best interests. Children's welfare is not central to decisions made throughout society. Clearly, many professionals working with children – teachers, nurses, doctors – would argue, with justification, that they operate on a day-to-day basis with that principle as central to their work. However, because they are under no legal obligation to exercise their responsibilities within the framework of a best interests principle, children have no means of ensuring that their interests are heard nor any means of redress in the event of a failure to do so.

Secondly, the operation of a best interests principle should not be seen as inherently beneficial to children. It can be, on the contrary, a powerful tool in the hands of adults which can be used to justify any of their actions and to overrule the wishes and feelings of children. We cannot assume that all adults are well disposed towards children or sensitive or aware of their needs and wishes. There is certainly no evidence to demonstrate that decisions made on the basis of this principle are notably more effective or satisfactory from the child's point of view than decisions made on the basis of any other principle and indeed it is extremely difficult for any adult to determine the best interests of a child. How many parents have been in conflict with each other over what is best for their child – for example, the day-to-day decisions such as bedtimes, staying out, discipline, friendships, which school to attend? Whilst it is necessary for adults who have responsibility for children – or responsibility for aspects of their lives – to pay heed to their welfare in making those decisions, it is also necessary that this responsibility is exercised through a commitment to ensuring that the child's views are an intrinsic part of the process of decision-making. In addition, there need to be clear, explicit and formal channels for children to have the opportunity to challenge the operation of the welfare principle where they consider that it has been wrongly applied or applied without any consideration of their views. Without it, the rights of the child can be subjugated to personal prejudice, an unwillingness to resolve conflict, lack of any consideration of the child's perspective or simply a battle for power in which the adult is invariably the stronger.

Self-determination

As adults, we have the right to self-determination until, or unless, its application begins to restrict or harm the rights of others. Self-determination implies the right to exercise free choices over all matters of concern to us and is central to the right to exercise control over one's life. In order to analyse the conflict which is often posed between parental and children's rights, it is perhaps useful to examine the derivation of the rights involved.

Parental rights are not universal – they exist only in so far as they are necessary to promote the interests and rights of the child and as soon as children are capable of meeting those needs or exercising those rights themselves, then the parental rights recede. They are therefore time limited and highly restricted, and the new concept of parental responsibility introduced in the Children Act more accurately reflects the nature of child/parent relationships. Parental rights, as defined by Lord Scarman in the Gillick judgement, derive from their responsibilities to promote the child's welfare and are limited by that responsibility. The United Nations Convention in Article 5 describes parents' rights and responsibilities in terms of the provision of appropriate direction and guidance to the child in the exercise of their rights, and in a manner consistent with the evolving capacity of the child. Both the Convention and the Gillick judgement, therefore, impose very clear boundaries on parental rights. They exist only in so far as they are necessary for the protection, welfare and promotion of the child's rights. As soon as the child acquires the capacity to exercise those rights independently, the right of parents to exercise their responsibility recedes. Where there is conflict, it is not actually a conflict between the rights of parents and the rights of children. It is perhaps more usefully described as conflict between the adult's responsibility for the protection of the child and the child's pursuit of the right to self-determination, the right to be listened to and taken seriously.

The model we tend to work with, in respect of children, starts with a presumption of protection at birth with a gradual move towards self-determination on the part of a child as she or he demonstrates a capacity to make decisions in her or his own right. In other words, the child has to 'earn' the right to self-determination. The justification for overriding or ignoring a child's wishes is defended on the basis that the child lacks the competence and the adult is charged, at least informally, to act in his or her best interests.

There is an alternative approach which is the model adopted for adults in a democratic and participative society – that is, that we begin with a presumption of self-determination and, only where it is clearly not in the child's best interest, or where it would impinge on others' rights, would it be justifiable to override or deny the child the right. Once the child is competent to understand the implications of their actions and to exercise an informed choice, any rights to intervene on the part of the parent cease. Such an approach places the onus on the adult to justify the intervention rather than on the child to fight the case for control over decisions concerning their own life. Clearly, the smaller the child, the greater the need to intervene, although we have evidence of this philosophy employed with tiny babies. The shift to demand-led feeding from the routine of 4-hourly feeds is an example of allowing the child to determine and control the meeting of need. Such an approach would enhance the right of the child to self-determination without removing the necessary protective responsibilities on the part of adults.

Participation

Self-determination, however, does not mean the same as participation. Self-determination is about giving children the right to take responsibility for their own decisions, and exercise of the right must be bounded by judgements of both competence on the part of the child and the need for protection. But participation is the right to be involved in the process of making those decisions and is fundamental to any basic recognition of children as people. Article 12 is explicit that **every** child 'who is capable of forming his or her own views' must have the right 'to express those views freely in all matters affecting the child'. This right is not qualified in any way. The right to participate therefore is not contingent on a judgement of the competence of the child. Nor is it restricted by adult perceptions of the best interests of the child.

It is a fundamental right that all children should be enabled to participate in all decisions that affect them and that their views must be 'given due weight in accordance with the age and maturity of the child'. Listening to children does not imply that they have control over the outcome of any decision-making process but it does require that their views are respected. It is a simple and self-evidently worthy principle which would, if taken seriously, have a revolutionary impact on the nature of adult/child relationships in this country. Without it children are denied the most basic of principles – to be accepted as people in their own right.

How far is the right to participation respected?

If one analyses current law, policy and practice as it affects children in this country, it very quickly becomes apparent that we are far from complying with the spirit of Article 12 of the United Nations Convention. The Children Act incorporates the principle, requiring that children's wishes and feelings are considered when courts and local authorities are making decisions concerning their welfare. The recent cases of children applying for leave to apply to court for judgements about where they live, and with whom, are positive examples of the application of this right. It is interesting to witness the response to these cases in the media, which have been described as examples of children divorcing their parents. The Children Act has been labelled as a 'Brats Charter' which will herald the break-up of the family. But, whilst the legislation represents an important milestone in the move towards greater recognition of children's rights to participation, there remains a considerable gulf between the law and its effective implementation.

Research published in 1993 reveals the extent to which young people in both residential and foster care continue to feel marginalised from decisions that affect their lives (Fletcher, 1993). Of over 600 young people responding to a questionnaire about their experience of care, nearly all felt that there were areas of their lives where they needed more involvement. Nearly half of those in foster care felt that they had no say in daily decisions. Two in five young people felt that they were not listened to in case conferences or reviews. The National Association of Young People in Care have pointed to consistent failure to involve young people in decisions as broad-ranging as policies within children's homes, children's home closures, placements, contact with families, participation in case conferences, development of child care plans and moves towards independence.

Participation in the education system

Furthermore, the Children Act, although significant, only affects a very limited number of children in very limited aspects of their lives. On its own, it is very far from fulfilling the requirements of Article 12. It is a different matter, for example, when we look at the education system where there is no duty whatsoever in legislation to listen to, or take seriously, children's views. There is no obligation to hear children's views when decisions about school choice are being made and no right for children to be heard even when being suspended from school. Disabled children have no right to be consulted over whether or not they attend a special school, nor about the process of assessment or statementing. There is no formal requirement to hear the views of an individual child concerning any issue relating to their education such as religion, or problems experienced in school such as bullying or harassment. The Education Act 1993 has even given parents the right to remove children up to the age of 18 from sex education in schools.

Schools are not required to introduce formal complaints procedures and children therefore have no access to a publicised or clearly defined route through which to air any grievance or injustice they have experienced. The Children Act imposes a statutory requirement on all social services departments to establish complaints procedures to which children have access. Such a provision is integral to any meaningful process of listening to children and giving due consideration to their views. Whilst it is always preferable for decisions to be made through discussion and negotiation, the right to be heard is an empty protection if it is not backed up by the opportunity to challenge any breach of that and other rights. The introduction of a right for children to have their views and feelings considered in the context of their education also needs to be backed up by the provision of statutory complaints procedures, with an independent element. Only by so doing will children's rights to be given an opportunity to express their views in line with Article 12 of the Convention begin to have any effective impact.

Prior to the introduction of the complaints procedures under the Children Act, there was a great deal of concern expressed that children would abuse the right to complain, and social services would be flooded by scores of frivolous and malicious complaints. Similar concerns were expressed when attempts were made to introduce amendments to the Education Act 1993 for a statutory complaints procedure. In fact, initial research undertaken by the organisation, *Voice for the Child in Care* published in 1992, indicates that over 80% of complaints by children have been upheld and there was, in those cases, serious justification for the complaint. There is no reason to believe that the experience in education would be any different. A joint complaints procedure for children in the health, education and social work departments in Lothian was introduced in 1992 with access to an independent adjudicator in the event of a failure to resolve the problem internally. Certainly, there is no evidence to date that the scheme has been abused or overburdened. Article 12 extends the right of children to express views on all matters affecting them. This means that it is not merely in relation to individual decisions that affect them but also the broader issues that impact on their lives. There are no formal rights for children to participate in matters of school policy or administration, or to be consulted over matters such as discipline, truancy, curriculum, supervision in the playground. Very few schools have school councils and even fewer operate on the basis of mutual respect for pupils and teachers The principle of participation has not been translated into education legislation. It is parents rather than children who the Government perceives as the consumers of education and for whom increased rights to choice and involvement have been pursued. Children have been largely disregarded as individuals in recent education law. Indeed, the right of under-18 year-olds to become pupil governors was abolished by the Government in the Education Act 1988. The Government had the opportunity of introducing the principle of participation into education law during the passage through Parliament of the Education Act 1993, but amendments drafted to introduce a right for children to be consulted on matters of concern to them were opposed by the Government.

Participation in the health service

There is no obligation to listen to children and take account of their views written into health legislation. The Gillick judgement affirmed the right of a 'competent' child to make decisions on their own behalf in relation to treatment, stating: 'The parental right to determine whether or not their minor child below the age of 16 years will have medical treatment terminates if and when the child achieves a sufficient understanding and intelligence to enable him or her to fully understand what is proposed'. However, this principle has been seriously eroded by the Court of Appeal decision in the case of Re W, a 16 year-old anorexic young woman. This judgement sought to distinguish between consent and refusal to consent to treatment. It argues that, in respect of a competent child, both the child and the parent have the right to give consent to treatment. It is only necesary for one party to give that consent for the treatment to be given. Therefore the sole consent of a 'competent' child is sufficient for treatment to be administered. But, in the event of a child refusing to give consent, a parent's consent is sufficient to allow medical intervention.

   In other words, even where the child is seen to have sufficient understanding of the proposed treatment and refuses to agree to it, the parents retain the right to override the child's wishes. This decision has profound implications for the rights of *all* young people to effective participation in decisions that affect their lives. The only exception to this position is in respect of children subject to a child assessment order under the Children Act, who have the right, if they are of sufficient understanding, to refuse medical or psychiatric examination or other assessment.

Participation within the family

Nor is there any requirement to take account of the views of children within the family. The Children Act imposes no obligations on parents to take account of the wishes and feelings of children when making decisions that affect their lives. Indeed, there are concerns that the 'no order principle', which provides that the court only intervenes to make an order where it can be shown to be beneficial to the child, does mean that there is no adequate protection for children whose parents are separating to ensure that their wishes are adequately taken into account. In Finland, there is a requirement written into their equivalent of the Children Act that parents must consult with children in reaching any major decision affecting them, subject to the child's age and understanding. Similar provisions exist in Germany, Sweden and Norway. In Scotland, the Scottish Law Commission in their Report on Family Law (1992) found that there was widespread support for comparable provision here. However, to date there is no such requirement in law.

Children and young people do not feel valued or taken seriously

Children are not consulted and have no opportunities to influence any of the broader policies that affect their lives – decisions about housing developments, road transport, shopping facilities, youth services, environmental policies, recreational and cultural activities. Yet they often have not only very strong views about these matters but also a great deal of relevant and informed opinion to contribute to improved decision-making. We have a long way to go before we could claim to be fulfilling the standards required by Article 12. The Children's Rights Development Unit during 1993 undertook a series of over 40 consultations with young people throughout the UK to ascertain how far they considered their rights to participation were respected. The view which came across with remarkable consistency was that they did not feel they were valued, listened to, or taken seriously. This experience spans the family, schools, social services, health practitioners, the media and politicians. Despite the requirements of the Children Act, it is also clear that children looked after by the local authority continue to experience a sense of impotence and alienation from the system, and that little has improved since the Act's implementation.

We do not have a culture of listening to children. Serious application of the principle of respecting children's rights to participate would require a number of measures.

We would need to ensure that children have adequate information appropriate to their age with which to form opinions. Children cannot participate in decisions if they are not fully informed of the options available to them and the implications of those options. For example, children in a hospital setting need to be informed about who is responsible for telling them what is happening, what the implications of treatment are, side-effects, options that are available, implications of not having the treatment, whether it will hurt, how long it will take.

We would need to provide them with real opportunities to express their views and expore options open to them. A serious commitment to respecting children and their right to participate in matters of importance to them, whether they are in school, in care or in hospital, means it is imperative to make the time necessary to ensure that the child has ample opportunity to explore the issues facing them. Their doubts, anxieties, confusions must be addressed if they are going to be involved effectively. In assessing a young person's competence to take responsibility for decisions, it is important to consider the young person's own views about their competence. The ability of a child to make decisions on her own behalf depends on the child herself but also on how much she is informed and respected by others concerned.

We must listen to those views and consider them with respect and seriousness, and tell children how their views will be considered. They need to understand the process for decision-making, who will be making the decision, when, and what will inform the decision. There is obviously no point in listening to a child's views if you have no intention of taking them seriously. It is necessary to be clear about what aspects of the child's care or education or health or play, he or she can be involved in.

We must let them know the outcome of any decision and, if that decision is contrary to the child's wishes, ensure that the reasons are fully explained.

Children using public services must be provided with effective, accessible and genuine avenues of complaint, backed-up by access to independent advocacy for situations where the child feels they have been mistreated or ignored or abused in any way. In Lothian, the social work, education and health authorities have joined together to produce a children's charter which sets out a shared statement of principles backed up with details of entitlements within each of their services. Every child has been given information about the charter which also introduces an independent adjudicator to whom they can go if they feel that the principles or entitlements are not being respected.

Finally, we must establish systems for monitoring the effectiveness of the processes of consultation, which are informed by children themselves.

Reconciling protection and participation

The following illustrative case highlights the difficulties inherent in reconciling the protective/participative conflict and the challenges that a commitment to respecting children's civil rights can provide.

> A nine year old girl has become withdrawn, tearful and quiet at school. Her work has deteriorated significantly. Over a considerable period of time and after a great deal of effort from her form teacher to ascertain the cause, the child discloses that her father has been abusing her. She pleads with the teacher to tell no-one. Whilst she desperately wants the abuse to stop, she even more desperately wants no intervention as she is terrified of the implications of what she has revealed. The teacher is torn but is obliged to report the disclosure and tell the head teacher who duly reports it to the Social Services Department. What follows is the inevitable interviews with the child and the family, the involvement of the police, and a case conference. It is considered that there are sufficient grounds for believing abuse has taken place although both parents deny it. The child is thought to be at risk and there is serious consideration being given to the necessity of removing the child as the only satisfactory means of protecing her.

Clearly, the procedures invoked in this scenario are designed to protect the child. But, it is worth considering the implications in such a case of the failure to recognise and respect the child's right to influence the decision-making process. We have made progress in that not many years ago it is likely that the child would not have been heard in disclosing the abuse and is even less likely to have been believed and taken seriously. We have therefore improved our capacity to listen to children. However, there is a danger that having taken on board our responsibility to listen to the content of what children are saying, we stop short when it comes to listening to what they want to happen. Our desire to protect takes precedence over all other considerations. It is worth considering what the child's experience might be of the situation described. The implications for her are considerable.

- There is a danger that the child loses all control over the situation. Once the weight of the child protection procedures come into force, the child may be lost in the inexorable processes that ensue. The importance of listening to her, to moving at a pace that she can handle, will not usually be possible.

- She has experienced a possibly overwhelming loss of privacy rendering public what has until now been an intensely private if painful and humiliating experience.

- She may experience the loss of the relationship with her parents with all the associated hurt, rejection, guilt, fear, and loneliness that will bring.

- She may lose her home if, for example, an emergency protection order was sought, and along with her home and everything that was familiar to her, her school, her friends, the very basis of her day-to-day security will disappear.

- She may lose any capacity to trust as she experiences the whole process as yet another betrayal in which her wishes are given scant regard and respect.

If we are to take the child's right to be heard as seriously as we take our responsibilities to protect – and both the Children Act and the Convention are quite clear that we must – we need to examine the impact of the juggernaut of child protection procedures. We need to question and review our preconceptions and understanding of what really is in the best interests of the child. We need to recognise that, in promoting the child's welfare, we must take account of what the child wishes and feels, we must learn to respect the child's integrity and be prepared to consider the possibility of making painful judgements which offer the child, perhaps, less protection but greater control and autonomy over the timing and the outcomes in such situations. It may be that the immediacy of intervention is actually more harmful than allowing the child the opportunity to be helped over a period of time to explore alternative strategies for resolving the problem. Child sexual abuse is not usually life-threatening and has often been going on for some time at the point of disclosure. Insensitive and hasty intrusion may compound the child's lack of self-esteem and self-worth, and actually cause more harm. It may, in some instances, be more to do with the professionals' understand-able concern to protect themselves than to protect the child.

It is possible to explore a number of measures which would give the child greater control over the situation, and a greater capacity for contributing to an outcome with which they feel a sense of owner-ship. There is a need for much greater access to confidential coun-selling. The availability of face-to-face contact in a confidential setting would allow children the opportunity to examine what had been happening to them at their own pace and in the security of the knowledge that they could trust the counsellor. We need to consider the right of the child to an advocate in the child protection process who would be there explicitly to represent their views. Clearly, many authorities do now allow children to be present at case conferences but, without a great deal of effort and thought, the capacity for chil-dren to genuinely participate is limited. Representation would ensure that their views were adequately heard and would lend greater weight to the civil rights of the child in the process. Most importantly, we need to ensure that the child remains firmly at the centre of the process and this can only be achieved by the child's active participation at every stage. The interests of the child are, in these circumstances, at risk of being subsumed to the interests of the professionals involved, the pursuit of criminal prosecutions, and the overriding desire to protect in ways which are defined by the adults and not necessarily by the child involved. We need to review the pre-sumption in favour of immediate action, and be prepared to consider new ways of working to ensure that the child is able to be a partici-pant in the process and not merely a recipient of adult interventions.

A dual commitment to participation

Genuine participation requires a dual commitment. First, it must be accepted that participation is a right and not a charitable gift on the part of sympathetic adults. As a principle, it must underpin all adult/child relationships. Secondly, it must be recognised that, for a right to be meaningful, there must be properly recognised proce-dures for ensuring its implementation with clear means of redress which can be pursued when the right is breached. Until this happens there will be no effective shift in the balance of power between adults and children. Without a shift in that balance, children will continue to be denied participation and we will continue to breach our inter-national obligations under the United Nations Convention on the Rights of the Child.

References

Fletcher, B. (1993) *Not Just a Name: the Views of Young People in Residential and Foster Care*, London: National Consumer Council.

3 Consulting children about the effectiveness of school-based victimisation prevention programmes

Jennifer Dziuba-Leatherman,
David Finkelhor and Nancy Asdigian

In response to growing public and professional concern in the USA about child abuse and other crimes against children, schools and community organisations in the 1980s began to develop and implement programmes aimed at helping children to avoid and to report sexual abuse and other victimisations. While such programmes were not an entirely new concept, since many schools and organisations had long-standing arrangements with local police or other public safety officials to teach children about personal safety, these newer programmes represented a departure in their strong emphasis on sexual abuse and in their use of more innovative and intensive teaching techniques (Wurtele and Miller-Perrin, 1992). Although the programmes vary widely in their format and their content, most contain certain core concepts: helping children to recognise sexual abuse, teaching them to say no to or otherwise avoid overtures, encouraging them to tell an adult about such episodes, and assuring them that such incidents were never their own fault (Finkelhor and Strapko, 1992).

The National Youth Victimisation Prevention Study was a nation-wide survey designed to evaluate the exposure and reaction that young people in the United States are currently having to these kinds of programmes. The study grew out of three primary concerns. First was the desire to know more about how many children have been receiving such programmes. Abuse prevention education programmes have been proliferating rapidly over the past few years (Breen, Daro and Romano, 1991; Kohl, 1993), for several reasons. They address a common concern of parents, educators and children alike. They are relatively inexpensive to implement and maintain (Wurtele and Miller-Perrin, 1992). They can be developed and implemented by ordinary people without a great deal of standardised professional training, although concern about insufficiently trained prevention educators has been raised (Trudell and Whatley, 1988). Perhaps most importantly, almost universally they have produced some immediate results in the form of disclosures from children who had previously been abused (e.g. Hazzard, Webb and Kleemeier, 1988; Kolko, Moser and Hughes, 1989). These advantages notwithstanding, little is actually known about how many children get exposed to the programmes, or about the quality of the programmes they get exposed to. Thus a major focus of the study was to determine which children are receiving the programmes, and to describe the structure and content of the programmes currently being offered.

A second concern involves the utility of the programme. Do children actually learn anything from them? With evidence growing that schools have a hard time teaching children to read, write and subtract – things that are taught every day – observers have questioned whether a few hours or a few days of child abuse prevention education can actually teach anything of lasting value to children (Reppucci and Haugaard, 1989). Is it possible to convey concepts regarding abuse in a way that children can understand? Critics have argued, for example, that concepts such as 'good touch' are very abstract and perhaps even developmentally inappropriate, and that the whole concept of sexual abuse, especially in the family, may be too frightening or too remote to really stay with children (Berrick, 1991; Berrick and Gilbert, 1991). Thus it was of interest to ascertain whether children have been able to actually use any of the advice they have been given in the programmes.

A third goal was to obtain children's own assessments of the programmes. It is ironic that there has been historically, even among professionals in the area of child welfare, a resistance to consulting children directly about matters that concern them. For example, chidren in crisis who have received services are seldom asked about what they thought of their social workers or their legal representatives. While children have recently begun to be consulted about placement decisions, and at least one study has asked children for their views of their court experiences (Goodman et al., in press), these kinds of studies tend to be the exception rather than the rule.

All things considered, it is surprising that the private sector in the USA is far ahead of the child welfare field in this respect. For example, research on children's attitudes abounds in the marketing literature. There are studies of what children like to eat, what movies they want to watch, what kinds of toys they like to play with, what appeals to them in advertisements and what turns them off. Businesses have learned to consult and cater to children because they need to in order to stay competitive. The irony is that the child welfare field, in spite of its pro-child rhetoric, has been comparatively retrograde in not letting children pass judgement on the services provided to them.

The absence of child imput is apparent even in the area of victimisation prevention education, which, overall, has been notably child-centred in terms of both its service philosophy and delivery (Wurtele and Miller-Perrin, 1992). In particular, the prevention programmes appear to have been developed on the basis of clinical interviews with sexually abused children, thus representing adults' conclusions about what children ought to do so as to not end up victimised. In other words, the information imparted by prevention programmes has been based on children's prevention failures, not the successes. Instead, or at least in addition, we need to ask children who have successfully avoided victimisation about the strategies that worked for them. We also need to inquire about children's attitudes towards the programmes, particularly with regard to their interest value, practical utility when applied to real-life situations, and potential for inducing confusion or anxiety. Rather than relying solely upon adult assumptions about victimisation avoidance, the field would be better informed by consulting with the children themselves. This was the third knowledge gap that this study was trying to fill.

Methodology

Study design

The study was conducted through telephone interviews with a nationally representative sample of 1042 boys and 958 girls in the United States between the ages of 10 to 16 and their caretakers. Although many children younger than 10 are exposed to prevention education programmes, we were uncertain, given what is currently known, whether valid interviews with younger children could be obtained and conducted within the study's methodology.

A national sample of households was contacted and screened for the presence of appropriately aged children though random digit dialling. Interviewers spoke with the primary caretaker in each household, asking him or her some questions relevant to child victimisation prevention and explaining the objectives of the study. They then obtained parental permission to interview the child. Speaking to the children, the interviewers again explained the study, obtained their consent, and proceeded with an interview that lasted between 30 minutes and an hour.

The final sample was well matched to US Census statistics for a population of this age: about 10 per cent Black, 7 per cent Hispanic, 3 per cent other races including Asian and Native American. Fourteen per cent came from families with incomes of under $20,000. Fifteen per cent were living with a single parent, another 13 per cent with a parent and step-parent and 3 per cent with some non-parental caretaker.

Pros and cons of surveying children by telephone

Telephone interviewing has perhaps been underestimated as an effective means of surveying young people. Children of this age generally spend a lot of time talking on the phone with their friends, usually with some degree of privacy, often about personal issues. Within their own households, they may be able to be interviewed on the phone much less obtrusively than they would if an unfamiliar adult interviewer arrived on the premises. Moreover, telephone interviews give children a great deal of control over a potentially threatening situation. By simply hanging up, they can always terminate this kind of anonymous interview, something much more difficult in a face-to-face encounter.

Although telephone interviewing sometimes elicits scepticism from those trained in in-person history-taking, it is a well-established epidemiological method (Groves *et al.*, 1988), and is now even used by the US Bureau of the Census for conducting the National Crime Survey (Bureau of Justice Statistics, 1989). It allows access to 94 per cent of US households (Bureau of the Census, 1992). Comparative studies have shown telephone interviews to be as effective as in-person interviews for eliciting information even about such sensitive topics as drug usage and sexual behaviour (Bermack, 1989).

However, this study does not specifically compare the effectiveness of telephone interviewing with in-person interviewing for their respective abilities to elicit candid and accurate information about childhood victimisations. The especially high rates of childhood sexual abuse disclosed in two intensive in-person epidemiological studies with adults have persuaded some researchers of the advantages of that approach for that particular topic (Russell, 1986; Wyatt, 1985).

Telephone interviewing has also been faulted for its inability to access households without phones, households that may contain a disproportionate number of children vulnerable to victimisation and other perils. Off-setting this problem, however, may be the ability of telephone interviewing to obtain much higher participation rates. In-person interviewers have problems gaining access to increasingly crime-conscious households, particularly in high-crime areas, and also to adolescents who are rarely at home and need to be recontacted on numerous occasions before an interview can be completed.

Children's reaction to the survey

The study findings provide qualified support for the use of the chosen methodology. The participation rate was 88 per cent of the adults approached, and 85 per cent of the eligible children in the households of co-operating adults, quite respectable given that the study involved children, a sensitive topic, a lengthy interview and required the consent of two individuals. About half of the refusals came from the caretakers denying permission to interview the children, and half from the children not wishing to be interviewed.

One important issue for this research was whether the children were upset or uncomfortable talking about victimisation and prevention topics. In our survey debriefings, two-thirds of the youths said the interview had been a good experience for them. Only five children reported that it had been bad. The rest indicated neither bad or good. Of the 2000 children we spoke to, 39 said they found something in the interview upsetting. An analysis revealed that, in general, the children who had found something upsetting were more likely to have disclosed sexual and/or family assaults ($X^2 = 10.38$, p<.05), experiences which may indeed be difficult to talk about. But these children were also more likely to attend private, non-parochial schools. From other analyses reported here (see Figure 3.2) we know that private school children are less likely than those in public or parochial schools to receive information about victimisation and sexual abuse; it is possible that they were disturbed by some of the material covered in the interview because they had not encountered it previously.

Adequacy of data obtained from children

Another important question that arises with regard to a study of this sort is whether younger children are truly capable of providing reliable information about their attitudes and experiences. There is, in fact, some evidence that the younger children in this sample had more difficulty with certain portions of the interview. Table 3.1 shows that, when asked to estimate their own risk for a variety of experiences (such as being beaten up by a peer, being sexually molested, getting injured while playing sports), children aged 10–12 responded 'not sure', 'refused', or were simply missing a response significantly more often than their counterparts in the 13–16 year-old range. The same age discrepancy was also noted for a test of knowledge about sexual abuse.

The age discrepancies noted for the expectancy items and the knowledge test are likely due to differences in cognitive capabilities between the two age ranges. Specifically, because children roughly 12 years and younger are less likely to have achieved full capacity for formal operational thought, they may experience more difficulty than older children in responding to hypothetical or otherwise abstract questions, such as those in our expectancy series. At the same time, this developmental disadvantage did not impact children's ability to recall more concrete circumstances such as personal victimisation experiences. Research on event memory suggests that, by the late pre-school years, children are generally able to recall with a good deal of accuracy details of life experiences, particularly those which have personal significance for them (Nelson, 1993; Ornstein, Gordon and Larus, 1992) The findings presented in Table 3.1 provide an additional measure of confidence in the ability of the children in this sample, regardless of age, to accurately describe the nature and content of a prevention programme they attended, as well as their own reaction to, and use of, such programmes.

Table 3.1 Invalid[a] responses to selected item series, by age

Series	Age group		
	10–12 (n=909)	13–16 (n=1090)	2-tailed p
Personal risk for various events (11 items)	1.29%	0.53%	<0.001
Knowledge about sexual abuse (13 items)	2.48%	1.03%	<0.001
Content of most recent prevention programme[b] (9 items)	2.83%	2.34%	0.26
Screener items for victimisations (12 items)	0.25%	0.16%	0.21

[a] 'Invalid' here refers to 'refused', 'not sure', or otherwise missing responses.
[b] Ns are smaller for this series because not all children reported having a prevention programme; this analysis included 627 10–12 year-olds and 781 13–16 year-olds.

Exposure to school-based programmes

Overall, 67 per cent (95 per cent confidence interval = 60 per cent–74 per cent) of children in this national sample reported having received a school-based abuse or victimisation prevention programme at some time, 37 per cent (95 per cent confidence interval = 30 per cent–44 per cent) within the last year. This is an impressive level of exposure and, consistent with other sources (Breen, Daro and Romano, 1991), shows widespread adoption of programmes in recent years by schools.

The younger children, especially those in grades 5 and 6, were the most likely to have received a programme in the last year, and the oldest were the least likely (Figure 3.1). This suggests that schools have been concentrating their attention on elementary age children, a trend consistent with the philosophy of many prevention educators.

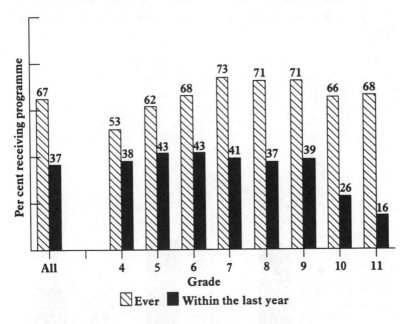

Figure 3.1 Exposure to US school-based prevention programmes

However, few children (only 8 per cent) remembered having received exposure in grades 1 to 3, indicating that most of the training is starting later than many prevention educators recommend. Moreover, there is evidence that training is a relatively recent addition to the curriculum: the proportion of children saying that they had ever received such training peaks for the seventh graders and declines somewhat among the older children. More of these older children had apparently passed through the elementary years without receiving any programme.

The demographic data show the programmes to be extremely well distributed. There were no regional, racial or class differences in children's exposure. There were some differences, however, according to the type of schools. As indicated previously, children who attended private, non-parochial schools (a small 5 per cent of the population) were much less likely to have received a programme than children in public or parochial schools (Figure 3.2); only 19 per cent had received a programme in the last year, compared to 39 per cent of parochial schools and 37 per cent of public schools ($X^2 = 17.6$, p<.05). It is possible that parents and teachers involved in private schools either feel remote from the risk of victimisations, or believe that the teaching of such topics is better left to parents themselves, but we do not have sufficient data with which to fully explore this issue.

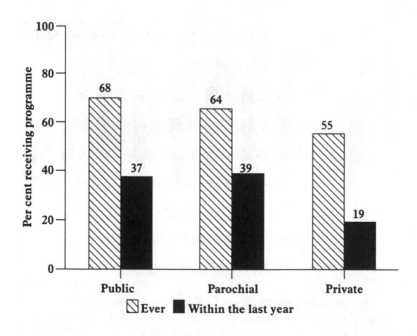

Figure 3.2 Exposure by type of school

In addition to school programmes, a small number of the children (4 per cent) reported having received a prevention education programme elsewhere – the main site being churches. However, most of these children had received school programmes as well. Non-school programmes were the sole programme for a scant 1 per cent of the children, so the findings of this report essentially concern school-based programmes.

Programme content

We asked children many questions about the content of the programme they had received (the one they remembered the best, if they had received several). According to the children, most of the programmes covered most of the topics that educators would like to see included, such as sexual abuse and sexual abuse in the family, the touch continuum, strategies for stopping abuse attempts, admonitions to tell an adult, and reassurances that abuse is never the child's fault (Figure 3.3).

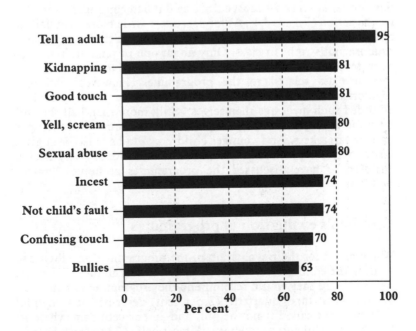

Figure 3.3 Programme contents cited by children

Above all else, the programmes included, or the children remembered, the admonitions to 'tell an adult'. The content on sexual abuse and kidnapping were also among the most frequently mentioned. Among the least frequently covered topics was the problem of bullies. This is unfortunate since, from other portions of the survey, it is clear that being bullied or beaten up by peers was a prime concern for children.

Some of the programme content does get varied according to the age of the children. Sexual abuse and sexual abuse in the family were topics that appeared more systematically in the reports from older children. Some schools may feel this is too highly charged for their younger students. Kidnapping, by contrast, appears to be more stressed with the younger children. It is a widespread notion (but mistaken, see Finkelhor, Hotaling and Sedlak, 1990) that younger children are more vulnerable to being kidnapped.

Prevention educators believe that programmes tend to be more effective when they occur on multiple occasions, when they allow children opportunities to practise the skills they are learning, and also when programmes involve parents, who can reinforce the skills at a later time at home. When asked about these components, 72 per cent of the children said the programme had been more than a single day presentation and almost a third said it had continued over a few weeks period (Figure 3.4). As for practice, a little more than half the children who had received training said that it included a chance to practise skills right in class. Only about one in ten children, however, reported that their parents had been asked to come to a meeting or class related to the programme. (However, children's memories in this regard may be less reliable since they may not have attended such meetings themselves.) Still, more than half the children did end up discussing the programme at home with their parents or caretakers. And younger children, who had also been given more chance to practice in class, were nearly twice as likely as older children to have discussed the programmes at home ($X^2 = 25.8$, $p < .001$).

Children's evaluation of programmes

When asked for their evaluation of the programmes and their usefulness, the children were quite positive. Almost all the children (95 per cent) said they would recommend the programme to other children. Almost three-quarters (72 per cent) described it as helpful. Two per cent called it not helpful and 26 per cent somewhere in-between helpful and not helpful. Almost half (46 per cent) found it interesting, with only 5 per cent describing it as boring and 49 per

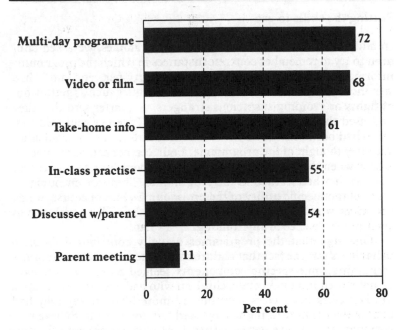

Figure 3.4 Programme features cited by children

cent in-between interesting and boring. When asked whether they already knew the things they were being taught, 17 per cent said they already knew them. The rest said the programme was primarily things they didn't know (5 per cent) or a mixture of things they did and didn't know (78 per cent).

Positive ratings from the children were associated with certain types of programmes. The multi-day trainings and those that gave them an opportunity to practise in class were seen as more interesting and helpful. The topics of sexual abuse, bullies and confusing touch were most associated with the programme being seen as interesting, and all the topics were associated with the programme being helpful. When the programme had information for the children to take home and when it prompted a discussion with parents, it was more likely to be seen as both interesting and helpful. Moreover, interest in the programmes did not wane after multiple exposures; children who had been exposed to three or more programmes actually found the programmes more interesting than those experiencing their first exposure.

Putting the skills to use

In addition to their evaluation of the programmes, we asked children to try to remember concrete instances in which the programme information had proved useful to them. Forty per cent said it had specifically helped them, and they cited examples such as getting out of fights or avoiding suspicious strangers. A quarter said that they had used the information to help a friend. Five per cent said that there had been some time when they had had to say no to an adult and they thought of the programme. Fourteen per cent remembered a time when they decided to tell an adult about something because of what they had learned in the programme. These are encouraging signs of the specific utility of the programmes, but, of course, we do not know whether the young people would have done such things even in the absence of any training.

One sign that the programmes actually contributed to these behaviours was the fact that children who had received programmes containing some specific components seemed more likely to have actually used it. For example, children who had been given a chance to practice skills in class were indeed more likely to say they had used the skills in real life, to have said 'no' to an adult, to have told someone, and to have helped a friend. Also consistent with the philosophy of prevention educators, programmes that were multi-day presentations and those that gave children information to take home had a greater likelihood of actually being put to work. Moreover, the children most likely to have used the skills they had been taught were the ones who had had discussions about the programme with their parents. Children who had been exposed to several programmes were more likely to have used the information to help a friend.

Interestingly, one of the more influential programme components was a discussion about how to deal with bullies. This was among the less frequently covered topics, but when it was included, children were more likely to say they had made use of the programme knowledge. From other aspects of the survey, and other studies, we know that dealing with bullies is the most common kind of victimisation threat chldren deal with (Finkelhor and Dziuba-Leatherman, in press). Apparently, programmes that address themselves to this very relevant concern seem to get utilised more.

On the other hand, some programme components seemed to make little difference. For example, when programmes included exhortations to 'tell adults' it had little effect. Children who had received such exhortations were not more likely than any other children to have actually told an adult, nor did they use the information in any other way. This is probably because children are given this kind of exhortation so frequently from so many sources that one more time does not make a difference.

Another component that made little difference was the identity of the person teaching the prevention programme. A question often debated by prevention educators is whether programmes are more effective when presented by familiar school personnel or by outside prevention educators with special training and extensive experience. Children reported that about half the school-based training (46 per cent) was by school personnel alone. Police officers were involved in about a third (37 per cent) of the programmes and an outsider in about a quarter (27 per cent). But, the identity of the trainer made no difference in children's evaluation of the programmes or the degree to which they utilised the knowledge. Of course, the identity of the trainer is not the same as their skill and specialisation. The outside personnel mentioned by the children were not necessarily people with specialised training. But, these findings support other research (Hazzard, Kleemeier and Webb, 1990) suggesting that whether the trainers come from inside or outside the school makes little difference.

Differences by gender, age, race and social status

In addition to some programme content that made a difference, we also found that there were important differences according to characteristics of children and their families. Not all children felt equally positive about the programmes, and not all children were equally likely to use their skills. First, there were some predictable but also some unexpected patterns in who gave programmes high ratings. On the predictable side, girls tended to find the programmes more interesting, more helpful and full of more new information (Figure 3.5), a finding consistent with a recent evaluation of teen suicide prevention programmes (Shaffer *et al.*, 1991). Boys may have rated the programmes less helpful, interesting and new because they had learned some of this information on their own. But the lack of interest of boys may also have stemmed from bravado combined with the fact that some programmes may have been designed or perceived by the boys as having been designed with girls as the primary audience. Younger children also tended to find the programmes more helpful and containing more new information (Figure 3.6). Older children probably were more likely to have heard the information before, and thus felt more boredom about the training.

But girls and younger children were also more likely to claim to have used the training skills. More girls than boys (31 per cent vs 19 per cent, p<.001) helped friends with the information they got, and younger children were more likely to have used it in some specific

Per cent children saying

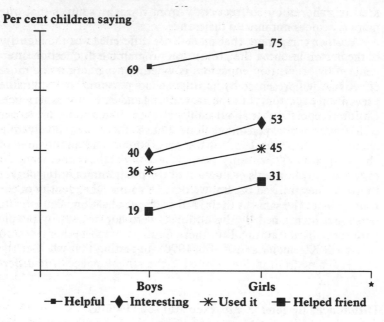

Figure 3.5 Helpfulness and usefulness by gender

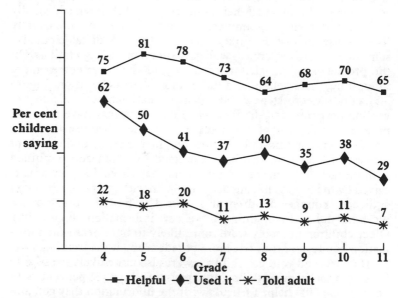

Figure 3.6 Helpfulness and usefulness by child's Grade

situation and have told an adult because of their training. Girls, perhaps, are more prone to helping friends in general, and boys are perhaps more reluctant to show that they needed to be taught any- thing about self-protection, but it may also be that the programmes made more of a lasting impact on girls and younger children.

In addition to the positive response of girls and younger chil- dren, the unexpected finding from this portion of the survey was that black children and children from lower socio-economic status (SES) families were also much more likely to have had positive reac- tions and to have used the information (Figure 3.7). (Our measure of SES here is the educational level of the primary parent; low SES children were those whose parents had not finished high school.) By significant margins, more children of black and of less-educated par- ents found programmes interesting. For example, 67 per cent of the black children found the programmes interesting compared to 43 per cent of the whites (p<.001). The children whose parents did not finish high school found the programmes more useful than the chil- dren of those with a graduate education by a margin of 51 per cent to 26 per cent (p<.001) and more helpful by a margin of 79 per cent to 66 per cent (p<.01). More blacks than whites (59 per cent vs. 38 per cent, p<.001) and more low SES than high SES (51 per cent vs. 26 per cent, p<.001) said they had used the information in specific situations.

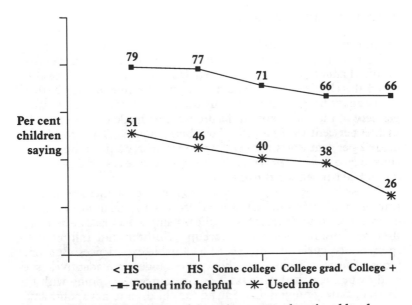

Figure 3.7 Helpfulness and usefulness by parent educational level

The enthusiasm of black and lower SES children for the programmes might, in theory, be explained by the fact that they lived in environments where the information was perceived as more useful and important. However, the study asked parents and children to rate the dangerousness of the communities where they lived and, in multivariate analyses, this did not explain the positive responses of black and lower SES children.

We also considered the possibility that black and lower SES children might be more enthusiastic because the programmes were providing them with information that they were not getting at home. However, this was not the case, either. The black and lower SES children reported that they got information from their parents about sexual abuse just as often as other children. In fact, when we asked the parents themselves about information that they had provided, the high SES parents were the ones who said they had given the *least* information to their children.

Another possibility is that the programmes leave a more favourable impression on black and lower SES children because of their educational approach. If the regular academic programmes are based on individualised competitive learning, the prevention education with its more practical, multi-media, skills-orientated approach may provide a positive contrast for children who may be struggling in other areas. Thus they may rate it favourably and make use of it.

Possible negative reactions

In spite of positive reactions from children and testimony that they had put some of what they learned into practice, the survey also inquired about possible negative effects from the programmes. We asked the children about whether the programme had made them worry about being abused or made them scared of adults. Overall, 8 per cent of the children said the programme made them worry a lot and 53 per cent worry a little about being abused. The programme made 2 per cent worry a lot and 9 per cent worry a little about being abused *by a family member*. And, the programme scared 2 per cent a lot and 20 per cent a little of adults.

These findings suggest that the programmes do increase levels of fear and anxiety in some children. However, the meaning of this can be interpreted in different ways. Fears and anxieties can be bad if they are unwarranted and preoccupy children and inhibit their spontaneity, curiosity and access to valuable experiences. But some types of fears and anxieties about true dangers are adaptive, especially when matched with skills and resources for coping with the dangers. Safety programmes intend for children to have some anxiety and fear about the dangers they warn about. When teenagers are taught about automobile safety, for example, the programmes intend to instill some fear and anxiety about the dangers of speeding or driving while drunk. Similarly, victimisation prevention programmes want to instill some concern about abuse and victimisation. In fact, the children who reported that they had become more worried about being abused may have been trying to convey to our interviewers that they had indeed taken the message of the programmes seriously.

One sign, however, that the anxieties and fears might not be altogether of the benign variety is the fact that they were not evenly distributed among the children. They tended to occur disproportionately among ostensibly more vulnerable children: the younger, the black and those from lower SES backgrounds. Younger children and those from low educated backgrounds reported that the programmes made them worry more about possible abuse. Younger children were also more likely to say the programme made them scared of adults. Three times as many black as white children (21 per cent vs 6 per cent, p<.001) said the programme made them worry a lot about being abused. The percentage of black children who worried a lot about abuse in their families was also higher (6 per cent vs 1 per cent, p<.001).

Once again, we looked for the possibility that these increased worries might be the adaptive responses of those living in the most dangerous communities. However, the higher level of anxieties and fears among black and lower SES children were not explained by living in more dangerous neighbourhoods.

Possibly the most provocative observation about the fears and anxieties is that they occurred among the *same groups of children who also gave the most positive feedback about the programmes and their usefulness*. For example, 92 per cent of the children who said the programme scared them 'a lot' about adults rated the programme as helpful compared to only 70 per cent of the children who said it hadn't scared them 'at all' (p<.01, see Figure 3.8). Similarly, children who were caused to worry 'a lot' about being abused also rated the programme as more helpful than those who were caused to worry only 'a little' or 'not at all' (p<.001). In multivariate analysis, reporting 'worry' was the most powerful predicator of rating the programme as 'helpful'.

In addition, those with increased worries and fears were the ones who had been more likely to actually *use the skills* they had been taught (Figure 3.9). For example, 64 per cent of the children who said the programme made them worry 'a lot' about being abused said they had actually used the knowledge in some specific situation compared to only 33 per cent (p<.001) of the children who hadn't been worried 'at all'. Exactly twice (p<.01) as many children who had been scared 'a lot' by the programme actually told an adult about something as a result of the programme. These signs of very positive responses from the same children who reported worry and anxiety must temper any hasty judgement about what worry and anxiety mean.

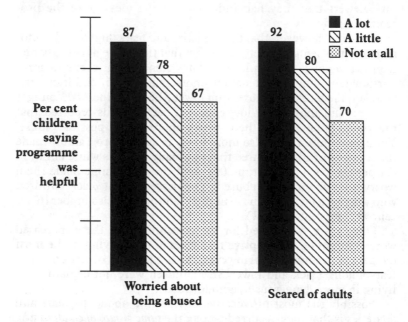

Figure 3.8 Children rating programme helpful by level of worry and fear

One interpretation of the finding, consistent with our earlier discussion, is that the fears and anxieties may have been disclosed by children as testimony to an *appropriate, not bad, outcome*. In any case, these findings point to the need for more careful study of the nature of such effects before adjudging them negative or harmful.

Conclusions

The findings from this study suggest that the majority of children in the US are being exposed to victimisation prevention education programmes. They also suggest that the overall response of children to these programmes is positive, confirming the results of specific programme evaluation studies (Hazzard, Kleemeier & Webb, 1990).

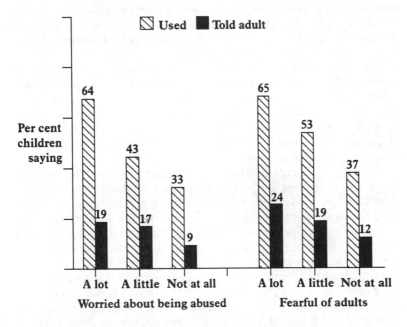

Figure 3.9 Children's use of skills by level of worry and fear

Several points may be concluded about doing service-satisfaction surveys with children. Children as young as age 10 appear to be quite capable of recalling details, via a telephone interview, about victimisation prevention programmes to which they have been exposed, often some years ago. They hold, and can provide to others, opinions about the interest value, usefulness, and emotional impact of these programmes. Clearly, this is information that must be fed back into the design process of these programmes if they are to accomplish their goals of addressing the real-life concerns about, and threats to, the safety of children of various ages.

This type of consultation need not be limited to prevention programmes; the type of policy feedback obtained here could also greatly benefit the design of other services. More research needs to be done to establish a reasonable age cutoff for the use of telephone survey methodology, and also to devise age-appropriate consultation modes for younger children.

There are also some specific prevention policy recommendations from some of the findings. First, prevention education programmes need to do more to ensure that children discuss programmes and their concepts with their parents. It is clear from our findings that, when children have such discussions, they are more likely to use the concepts they have learned. Parental involvement is a goal many programmes already have. But it is not as regular a feature of programmes as some other components.

Secondly, prevention education programmes need to devote more emphasis to dealing with bullies and threats to children from other children. According to study findings, this specific programme component seemed more than others to result in more concept utilisation, probably because of its great relevance to the circumstances of many children. However, it was not a topic that all programmes touched upon.

Thirdly, prevention education programmes need to improve their appeal to boys and older children. The study revealed signs that boys are moderately less enthusiastic about the programmes they have received and make less use of the skills. It is possible that educators and programmes have a subtle bias, communicating more effectively to girls. Or, it may simply be that boys, because of their peer cuture, are a somewhat more resistant audience. In any case, educators should try to overcome the obstacles to reaching boys.

Fourthly, educators and researchers need to better understand and capitalise on the special appeal these programmes have to minority and lower SES youth. The enthusiasm of these youth is certainly a positive sign that the programmes are reaching what, for many educators, is a difficult to reach audience. But, by understanding the sources of this enthusiasm, educators may help improve the appeal of programmes to other groups of young people.

Finally, more research is needed to understand what it means when children report increased anxiety and fear as a result of the programmes. Because they were associated with positive ratings and use of the concepts, this study strongly suggests that such anxiety and fear are not signs that the programme is having some negative effect. What negative effects are occurring may need to be assessed with more subtle and differentiated indicators.

Acknowledgements

The authors would like to acknowledge the Boy Scouts of America for their support of this project, and to thank the following people for their help in this research: Joseph Anglim, Lawrence Potts, Mary Dowd, Charles Morrison, John Boyle, Patricia Vanderwolf, David Bulko, Thomas Edwards, Charles Pressey, Kathleen Kendall-Tackett, Sam Simon, Kyle Ruonala and Kelly Foster. The survey research was carried out by Schulman, Ronca and Bucuvalas, Inc.

Richard Krugman and several anonymous reviewers made helpful suggestions to drafts of the manuscript. Portions of this paper have been published elsewhere.

References

Bermack, E. (1989) 'Effects of telephone and face-to-face communication on rated extent of self-disclosure by female college students', *Psychological Reports*, 65, pp. 259–67.

Berrick, J. D. (1991) 'Sexual abuse training for preschoolers: implications for moral development', *Children and Youth Services Review*, 13, pp. 61–75.

Berrick, J. D. and Gilbert, N. (1991) *With the Best of Intentions*. NY: Guildford Press.

Breen, M., Daro, D. and Romano, N. (1991) 'Prevention services and child abuse: a comparison of services availability in the nation and Michigan'. Paper presented at the National Committee for Prevention of Child Abuse, Chicago, IL.

Bureau of Justice Statistics (1989) *Redesign of the National Crime Survey*. Washington, DC: United States Department of Justice.

Bureau of the Census (1992) *Statistical Abstract of the United States: 1992*. Washington, DC: United States Department of Commerce.

Finkelhor, D. and Dziuba-Leatherman, J. (in press). Children as victims of violence: a national survey. *Pediatrics*.

Finkelhor, D., Hotaling, G. and Sedlak, A. (1990) *Missing, Abducted, Runaway and Thrownaway Children in America*, Washington, DC: Office of Juvenile Justice and Delinquency Prevention.

Finkelhor, D. and Strapko, N. (1992) 'Sexual abuse prevention education: a review of evaluations studies' in D. J. Willis, E. W. Holden, and M. Rosenberg (eds) *Child Abuse Prevention*, New York: Wiley, pp. 150–67.

Goodman, G. S., Taub, E. P., Jones, D. P. H., England, P., Port, L. K., Rudy, L. and Prado, L. (in press) 'Emotional effects of criminal court testimony on child sexual assults victims', *Monographs of the Society for Research in Child Development*.

Groves, R. M., Biemer, P. P., Lyberg, L. E., Massey, J. T., Nicholls, W. L. and Waksberg, J. (1988) *Telephone Survey Methodology*. New York: John Wiley and Sons.

Hazzard, A. P., Kleemeier, C. and Webb, C. (1990) 'Teacher versus expert presentations of sexual abuse prevention programs', *Journal of Interpersonal Violence*, 5, pp. 23–36.

Hazzard, A. P., Webb, C. and Kleemeier, C. (1988) 'Child sexual assault prevention programs: helpful or harmful', Unpublished manuscript, Atlanta, GA: Emory University School of Medicine.

Kohl, J. (1993) 'School-based child sexual abuse prevention programs,' *Journal of Family Violence*, 8, pp. 137–150.

Kolko, D., Moser, J. and Hughes, J. (1989) 'Classroom training in sexual victimization awareness and prevention skills: an extension of the Red Flag/Green Flag people program', *Journal of Family Violence*, 4, pp. 25–45.

Melton, G. B. (1992) 'The improbability of prevention of sexual abuse', in D. J. Willis, E. W. Holden and M. Rosenberg (eds), *Child Abuse Prevention*, New York: Wiley, pp. 168–189.

Nelson, K. (1993) 'The psychological and social origins of autobiographical memory', *Psychological Science*, 4, pp. 7–14.

Ornstein, P. A., Gordon, B. N. and Larus, D. M. (1992) 'Children's memory for a personally experienced event: implications for testimony', *Applied Cognitive Psychology*, 6, pp. 49–60.

Repucci, N. D. and Haugaard, J. J. (1989) 'Prevention of child sexual abuse: Myth or reality?', *American Psychologist*, **44**, pp. 1266–75.

Russell, D. E. H. (1986) *The Secret Trauma: Incest in the Lives of Girls and Women*. New York: Basic Books.

Shaffer, D., Garland, A., Vieland, V., Underwood, M. and Busner, C. (1991) 'The impact of curriculum-based suicide prevention programs for teenagers', *Journal of the American Academy for Child and Adolescent Psychiatry*, **30**, pp. 588–96.

Trudell, B. and Whatley, M. H. (1988) 'School sexual abuse prevention: unintended consequences and dilemmas', *Child Abuse and Neglect*, **12**, pp. 103–113.

Wurtele, S. K. and Miller-Perrin, C. L. (1992) *Preventing Child Sexual Abuse: Sharing the Responsibility*. Lincoln, NE: University of Nebraska Press.

Wyatt, G. E. (1985) 'The sexual abuse of Afro-American and white American women in childhood', *Child Abuse and Neglect*, **10**, 231–40.

4 No one ever listens to us:
interviewing children and young people

Howard Williamson and Ian Butler

Introduction

In this chapter, we describe our experience of one particular research project and illustrate something of the difficulties we encountered in operationalising a project that depended on individual and group interviews with nearly 200 children and young people.

We are acutely aware that children are interviewed for all sorts of evidential, investigative and therapeutic purposes and some of the issues that we raise may have a bearing on interviews of these and other sorts. There is already a literature on the theory and the micro-skills of interviewing children in such contexts (HO/DOH, 1992; Stainton-Rogers and Worrel, 1993) and we do not attempt to cover this ground in these pages. Our concern is with interviewing children and young people for the purposes of social research. There is a full supporting literature already in some areas of research on children; for example, in respect of participant observation (see Fine and Sandstrom, 1988). There is also a full supporting literature on the use of interviews as part of survey approaches to data collection (Marsh, 1988; McCracken, 1988). But noticeably little that addresses qualitative approaches to surveys of children.

Consequently we come to much less prescriptive conclusions than might reasonably be expected. Our observations are offered as part of a continuing commitment to finding ways of hearing what it is that children and young people have to say to us, both individually and collectively, and that will continue to engage our attention for some time yet.

'We will ask the questions...'

If experience were sufficient qualification, then we would all be experts on children and childhood. Indeed, most of us think we are. We have all been there, seen it and done that. Those of us who work with children for a living, might even claim to have got the T-shirt.

As adult professionals and professional adults, we just *know* how to talk to children. What issues can there be around interviewing them?

The first and perhaps the most important issue to deal with is precisely this prior assumption of knowledge on the part of the adult. While other forms of ethnocentrism have been more or less successfully challenged over recent years, the strength of adults' belief in their intuitive understanding and knowledge of children has proved remarkably resilient.

Much has been written already (see Archard, 1993) about the socially constructed nature of childhood and, after Aries's (1960) flawed but extraordinarily important *Centuries of Childhood*, few would argue, in academic circles at least, with the proposition that childhood is a fluid and dynamic phenomenon. That there is no unique or enduring model or experience of childhood is part of the received wisdom on most professional training courses for social workers, youth workers, teachers and others. Childhood manifestly varies across time and between cultures and is differentially experienced according to gender, class and economic status, even within cultures (Hoyles, 1989). Your childhood is not like your children's childhood any more than your childhood was like that of your parents, yet the development of this kind of 'anthropological' imagination in approaching our encounters with children does seem to be very slow to establish itself outside the narrow confines of the ethnographic research community. To others within and without the professional world, such encounters are often considered to come 'naturally'; our contention is that they *must* be considered problematic, in order to ensure that the many grounds for intervention – including those to do with research – are effective, not just efficient.

Yet the problematic nature of interventions with children and young people is self-evident. Our collective attention span, as adults, must be relatively short if we are to judge by how often we seem surprised by what research on children, particularly enthnographic

research, has to tell us. Despite there being no study to our knowledge that reports the social world of children to be a relatively simple
and comprehensible place, we seemed unprepared to acknowledge
the maturity and sophistication that children bring to their understanding of the world and their place in it (Coles, 1967, 1986;
Denzin, 1977). We seem equally unprepared for the realities, sordid
or otherwise, of children's lives, whether this be in terms of sexuality (Fine, 1981, Martinson, 1981), drug use (Adler and Adler, 1978),
aggression (Fine, 1987) or in terms of social and cultural reproduc-
tion (Willis, 1978).

We do not have the space in these pages to explore the social origins or psychological consequences, for adults, of the assumption of
prior knowledge of the lives of children. Nor do we consider the
symbolic and practical importance of the different but related attri-
bution, to children, of relative incompetence. However, we do begin
our account from the premise that children and young people have
something to tell us and that that something will be as illuminating,
reliable, complex and sophisticated as anything that we already
know. Such a conviction has very direct consequences for the ethical and methodological framework that is then put in place around
a particular piece of research, as we shall go on to describe.

We are somewhat sceptical, however, that such a commitment
has found its way into the contemporary discourse around children,
particularly in the sphere of public policy.

As well as the level of personal interactions, it is our contention
that we live currently in a 'deaf ear' policy context, one in which the
voices of the young and their advocates are too often ignored, sup-
pressed or devalued.

We are acutely aware that, while policy documents and scholarly
texts may be riddled with rhetorical – and appealing – references to
concepts such as choice, opportunity, participation, consultation,
justice and empowerment, such language and aspirations are
increasingly dismissed by those at the sharp end of practice as 'all
gesture and no substance'. In teaching, child care, youth work and
related professions, we detect a distinct climate of demoralisation,
stemming from the opinion that policy development bears little
relation to grounded realities in the lives of children and young
people, or to the resources required to provide them with adequate
and appropriate support.

With such perceptions about the current climate, the temptation
is for professionals to use their energies defending their own professional domains, to the further detriment, marginalisation and dis-
empowerment of children and young people. Not all are doing so,
and it is encouraging that a number of social work organisations are
endeavouring to strike out with innovative forms of practice which

do involve children, young people and families as 'partners in empowerment' (Darvill and Smale, 1990). It is in relation to these developments that we are arguing for the importance of developing approaches to interviewing children. For it is a critical time to listen to young people – to secure a real sense of their anxieties, experiences, hopes and aspirations for the future which are not clouded or corrupted by the seductive, but often empirically false, exhortations and claims of the adult producers of public policy.

We cannot escape the conclusion, however, that any social research on children will connect with the broader, contemporary pattern of expectations and norms that govern adult/child relationships and the dominant cultural patterns of interaction between them. Just as childhood is a social and cultural artefact, so too is any research on children, and it is important to explore fully the contemporary context in which the particular project from which we draw our illustrations was set.

Briefly, our project sought to describe, using children's and young people's own accounts, what they understood, theoretically or through experience, to constitute 'significant harm', a concept borrowed from the Children Act 1989 and the contemporary adult discourse on child abuse/child protection, and to go on to explore what might constitute appropriate or desirable support or intervention in significantly harmful situations, as perceived by children and young people. The full results of our study appear in another title in the series of which this volume is part (Butler and Williamson, 1994).

Contexts

The 'web' of factors contributing to shifting ideas about appropriate social work practice and increasing efforts to hear what children are actually saying is a complex one. It includes changing conceptions of appropriate, effective and equitable professional intervention, the public scrutiny of social work services following both inquiries into child protection procedures and the practices of staff in residential child care. Both hinted at the persistent 'deafness' to, or misrepresentation by, adults of the voices of children: they were either ignored or disbelieved. In parallel, there has been a growing 'lobby' on behalf of the voice of children and young people, particularly amongst those in care. In the professional arena, the increasing tendency towards a 'multi-agency' approach has been supported as a method of ensuring the coherence of intervention and avoiding a fragmented and potentially contradictory approach. Such trends have been reflected in recent policy development and legislation.

While such developments have much to commend them, there

remains some difficulty in disentangling the rhetoric from the reality. The political and wider policy framework which surrounds social work practice has, at times, run roughshod over social work endeavour; at other times, it has laid claim to the 'interests of children' when other factors have in fact been setting the agenda. That there is a professional social work tradition of both conformity and dissent, which has sometimes borne little relation to 'evidence' about the needs of children, presents another problem. Distinguishing the 'needs' from the wants of children, and interpreting them without doing 'violence' to them, further confuses the picture.

Nevertheless, current research on the needs of children and young people takes place within what some might view as a dynamic context for social work children's services in both statutory and voluntary organisations. Others might well argue that the wider context of child poverty (Blackburn, 1991), family homelessness, increasing privatised health care, unemployment and declining income support makes social work assistance a marginal exercise in the lives of children and young people. Either way, there is a challenge and contemporary views of the challenge are frequently premised upon a more subjectively defined and 'empowering' view of need.

We should not be deluded or overtaken completely by such rhetoric. The credibility of social work has been firmly shaken by a catalogue of recent events, from the child abuse 'scandals' of Cleveland and elsewhere to 'pindown' in local authority children's homes. Social work services in both the statutory and voluntary sectors have been subjected to scrutiny and criticism from both public and political quarters. The focus has come to be placed disproportionately on methods of intervention in the lives of children; perhaps we need to remind ourselves, and others, that although the intellectual debate about suitable processes should be continued, indeed we hope to make a modest contribution to the debate, there are many children and their families still requiring immediate and everyday support and assistance. They may not even really notice the 'style' with which intervention is effected, however important that may be to the professional world of social work. Outcome is still important, just as process is. Both, it should be added, rest as much in the eye of the beholder as in some neutral objectivity.

None the less, we have declared our commitment to a process which engages with the subjectively held, culturally located experiences and perspectives of young people. We believe this is an important value position to hold as well as a potentially effective (though not always efficient!) and illuminative technical process. Technical efficiency without values can, as Lorenz (1993) has recently reminded us, become a dangerous platform to build, risking collusion with dominant political and ideological agendas which may have little bearing on the recipient's 'best interests'.

It is this 'child-centred' process which is (apparently) currently in the ascendant. Such an approach may be traced back to three distinct contexts, although there is considerable and inevitable overlap between them.

Political and legal

Political and legislative trends have often taken one step forward and two steps back. Even positive developments in this arena have failed to be supported with adequate resourcing. The Children Act 1989 contains many commendable principles but its implementation still leaves many questions unanswered. The Child Support Act 1992 appears to have much more to do with the imperatives of the Treasury and political ideology than with any real sense that 'children come first', the title of the originating White Paper. The recommendations following the Cleveland inquiry were long on rhetoric (about inter-agency collaboration and adequate child protection procedures) but short on specific ideas on practice and even shorter on their rationale and likely effectiveness. At the political level, the balance has (perhaps conveniently) never been struck: social work interventions in the lives of children have either been excessive or insufficient. There has been little consultation with children themselves to gauge the validity of subsequent judgements about the efficacy of social work support.

Professional

The second 'tradition' has been within professional social work itself. In the statutory sector, issues of professional practice have too often been subordinated to organisational restricting, while the valued work of many national voluntary organisations has often been at the margins of crisis intervention. While the voluntary sector has explored a range of innovative practice (such as Family Centre provision and community social work; see Holman, 1983; Phelan, 1983), innovative ideas within 'mainstream' statutory services have largely been ignored or, more often, swamped by the increasing burden of legislative responsibilities placed on social workers. Social workers in both sectors have had to re-examine wider social policy questions such as universality versus selectivity as resources have become more constrained: should there be targeting of client groups, or individual clients, most in need; if so, on what criteria? Radical social work literature has always raised questions about 'whose interests?' (arguing that professional self-enhancement may take precedence over client benefits) and the limited empowering, and sometimes disempowering, effects of social work practice, but recently the possibility that managerial and organisational requirements may hold sway over client interests has entered the mainstream debate (see, for example, Bamford, 1990; Kelly, 1991).

Such an apparently negative picture should not cloud the fact that professional social work services have also genuinely endeavoured to develop practice which is considered to be more effective and relevant to those receiving them (see Furniss, 1991; Rogers, Hevey and Ash, 1989; Morgan and Righton, 1989). Participation, partnership and empowerment have become key words and the legacies of tenants' associations, welfare rights activism and community development have never been completely abandoned; indeed, their principles have at times been resurrected and connected to wider forms of practice (Langan and Lee, 1989; Darvill and Smale, 1990). Nevertheless, once again, the voice of children and their families has often been a mute one in the context of even this level of professional dialogue (though it should be noted that the NSPCC itself has pioneered a professional approach which accommodates 'listening to children', see Blagg, Hughes and Wattam, 1989 and Bannister, Barrett and Shearer, 1990).

Consumerism and citizenship

The third important contextual strand is located not only within social work but across a wide range of public services. Curiously, it finds expression across the political spectrum (from the consumerism associated with the Conservative Right and John Major's Citizen's Charter, to the philosophies of client, or *user*, choice and self-determination associated with the Radical Left in the 1960s, which seemed to lie very low during the Thatcher decade). It is about consumer involvement and participation, ownership, and empowerment. It is about being given, or *seizing*, sufficient information in order to be able to make informed choices. It is about the *right* to pass comment and make judgement on the quality of services provided. The fact that such trends have filtered down from the adult consumer of refuse collection services to children subjected to social work interventions is a welcome development. It creates a possibility that children and young people in quite diverse circumstances will be presented with an opportunity to frame and shape the services which have always been technically in their name through dialogue and negotiation. The commentary and ideas of the National Association of Young People in Care (NAYPIC) in relation to the recent incidents in children's homes, and the influence of other care leavers on some of the provisions of the Children Act 1989, provide examples of the real impact of this changed philosophy. The degree to which rhetoric is converted into reality is always a matter for debate: while some detect tokenism in many contemporary 'consumer-led' initiatives, others are already expressing the view that the pendulum has already swung 'too far the other way'.

The starting point for us, however, was to engage in a process of discovery to illuminate and contextualise the grounded aspirations, hopes, wants and needs of children and young people – in the case of our particular study, in relation to social work support and intervention. This chapter seeks to report how we set about that research task, in terms of securing access to and engaging the interest of children in contributing to it.

Interviewing children

What then are the consequences for those intending to undertake interviews with children that follow from this analysis of the context in which our research was undertaken, a context in which much is said but little is heard and even less considered worthy of close attention?

First, as we have suggested, the exercise must be premised on a preparedness to learn something from people whose views generally do not carry any weight and which takes full account of children's daily experience of dialogue with adults that has too often promised much more than it has delivered. The researcher is not necessarily any more an expert on children than he or she might be on nuclear physicists and should not behave or expect to be treated as such. Nor, necessarily is their rule one of apologist, advocate or interpreter for children. The conventional research rule of objectivity applies.

Taking the comments of children and young people at face value is, of course, hardly unproblematic (Howe, 1990) and mediation has to take place without the process of securing the *unmediated* views of children appearing tokenistic, but there are indications that this can be done (Flekkoy, 1991). What is critical is that the perspectives obtained are grounded in genuine social reality of children's lives and, in order to achieve this, one needs the key to enter their 'social world', which may often be one imbued with secrecy (Varma, 1992). In order to *understand* that social world, one needs to adopt a suitably sensitive methodology (on which very little specifically has been written, though see Waksler, 1991; also Carrington and Troyna, 1988) and to be sure that one is asking the right questions.

In our particular case, the research was designed to be 'illuminative' from the outset – to shed light on the perspectives held by children about, for example, support, neglect and professional intervention. As such, it was important to discuss relevant issues with a broad spectrum of children and young people, some of whom would have had direct experience of certain matters, while others would not. Consequently, some of the 'answers' to the questions posed were based on reality and others on hypothetical situations. Furthermore, some questions were more pertinent to some groups and individuals and, indeed, the research design was premised upon the need to be sufficiently *flexible* to explore, opportunistically, issues raised by respondents in different contexts and with different experiences. A checklist or tightly structured questionnaire would have been patently inappropriate.

The research questions we adopted did, however, suggest a *framework* for inquiry and discussion with children and young people. They sought to explore their concrete experiences with a specific focus on past or present concerns, a description and assessment of family and professional support already received, what kinds of changes would have made things better, and some speculative observations about future anxieties and desirable support should they materialise.

But given the general level of our understanding of the social world of children, it is important that we grounded our inquiries in the concepts that children themselves employed, and we placed a premium on ensuring that in our interviews with children we did not import, uncritically, notions derived from an adult perspective or to draw the framework too tightly. This is more than a plea for the use of age appropriate vocabulary and grammar, although it *is* important to emphasise that apparently unproblematic concepts such as 'safe' or 'bad' do have a generationally different set of meanings and associations for respondent and interviewer.

Opening gambits: creativity and 'style'

Creativity in working with any particular research instrument is also important. We believe that *any* discussion on any issue with children and young people must flow from their experiences. It is hard for them to think the unthinkable. One's framework of questions must be constructed around their experiences, observations and aspirations. One's language, sensitivity (or toughness), and tolerance of tangents must tune in to the individual or group being spoken with. Quite how one copes with the 'dunnos', 'all rights', 'not sures' and 'OKs', *we* dunno – realistically we have to write off some interviews as having provided us with little of substance. No one can force anyone to make a perceptive (quotable?) comment, although one can – and should – try to get to key issues from a number of dif-

ferent angles. One approach might work, when others had seemingly 'failed'.

But it is hardly surprising that it is often difficult to elicit views
and opinions from children and young people – to get them to
express *their* views. Most children and young people are not accustomed to being encouraged to articulate their opinions; they consider them to be unimportant to anyone but themselves, a view often
confirmed by the adults around them in their everyday lives.

One should always try a couple of tacks with the monosyllabic
respondents. Let them discharge their invariable fascination with
your tape recorder; just chat about what it can do. Some shout a few
obscenities into the microphone, but this often gets the ball rolling.
If unsuccessful, make a flamboyant appeal to them: 'Come on, I bet
you're the first to moan that no one ever listens to you. ... well, I'm
right here ready to listen to anything you have to say'. This usually
gets something going, at least for 15 minutes. We are more in favour
of such flamboyance in 'breaking through' to young people than the
more measured approaches recommended for 'rapport development'
advocated, for example, by the American National Institute of Justice. This suggests that in order to empathise with a nervous child's
feelings and indicate the naturalness of such feelings, an interviewer
should say something along the lines of,

> I wonder whether it feels scary to talk to a stranger about stuff that
> is so hard to talk about. (National Institute of Justice, 1992, p. 3)

While we acknowledge below some of the implications of 'stranger
danger' for research, we believe that humour and light-heartedness
– even when seeking to broach serious issues – seems to be the
avenue to which most children can best relate. Serious attention to
their words and viewpoints comes later.

However, it *is* an indictment of the daily experience of not being
taken seriously when they want to be taken seriously, created by
adults for children, that makes children unfamiliar with the niceties
of interview behaviour. That they 'mess about' is a commentary on
that experience rather than on anything they may subsequently have
to say.

On the other hand, of course, one does encounter individuals
who immediately get into full flow and hardly stop for an hour or
two. Their observations are often the most powerful and perceptive.
Qualitative analysis has always to ensure that such incisive comment
is not accorded too much weight, and is properly balanced with the
range of more mundane reactions.

We have introduced, indirectly, the question of personal style.
We would reiterate that humour and self-effacement are useful personal attributes to take into the interview, though they are rarely

mentioned in research methods textbooks. One of us told two timid 11 year-old Nintendo fanatics that the interviewer was a wizard at the game and was promptly handed a joy-stick. Both were past 100 points before the researcher got to 10. They thought it was hilarious that this 'posh git' was so incompetent and suddenly were quite eager to have a chat with him. Similarly, two teenage girls accommodated in the care system had felt somewhat press-ganged into co-operating with a research interview but, after it had finished and they had gone out for the evening, the officer-in-charge said to the researcher, 'you can come again, they think you're a good laugh'. And they had provided by far the best interview up to that point in the research. We are not suggesting, however, that you attempt to 'go native'. It is doubtful whether you could produce a convincing performance either in terms of dress, pose or vocabulary. Age inevitably, unavoidably, creates its barriers and divisions and no child or young person wants to talk to any adult who is patently falsely projecting too youthful an image or persona or self-consciously letting fly with contemporary street *argot*. It is important also, though, to avoid any 'distance' that can legitimately be avoided – to acknowledge that you are not always the expert and be prepared to let the assumption of competence and mastery slip a little with your dignity.

Personal style can affect the actual organisation of the interview process which, in turn, affects the nature of the interview itself. In real settings where contact was made with real young people (schools, youth clubs and children's homes), staff have breathed an obvious sigh of relief that the interviewer had not turned up with clipboard and questionnaire, expecting children or young people to be ushered in at 15-minute intervals. For some, that had been a genuine previous experience of 'researchers'. Some were clearly cautious about us, having received 'yet another bloody memo' to inform that that 'Dr Williamson, who is doing research for the NSPCC' would be getting in touch.

In relation to the 'gatekeeping' professionals through whom we sought access to young people (teachers, youth workers and residential social workers), we stressed our willingness to be flexible. We knew that children and young people are unpredictable. 'Appointments' would be broken. Young people would discover more pressing 'agendas', like going shopping or watching cartoons. Some kids would mess around. Some interviews would be hopeless. [And, of course, some would be brilliant]. In our negotiations with gatekeeping professionals the fact that we understood the context of *their* work, that their workplaces were *not* a laboratory for us to conduct our 'research', put them at ease. And this was critical to win their support.

Authority, responsibility and disclosure

Behind the question of personal style, however, lies the issue of authority. Whereas the task of the ethnographer is to establish the trust (Fine and Sandstrom, 1988) of the group being studied, the task of the interviewer may be perceived as a lesser one of establishing rapport. In reality, this is no more than a matter of degree and the larger issue is the one of authority. Adults are both seen to and in fact do occupy roles of 'direct formal authority' (Fine and Sandstrom, 1988) over child informants in a way that they do not over adult informants, except in the most exceptional circumstances (Goffman, 1961).

We have indicated already how the self-imputed authority of the interviewer might impede the interview process and outcome, but the full force of the issue arises with the emergence, through the interview, of 'guilty' or other uncomfortable knowledge. If one comes to learn during the course of an interview of a continuing situation that might be described as abusive or hear of high risk behaviour or criminal intent, how is one to respond?

In his taxonomy of roles for ethnographic researchers, who have time on their side, Fine and Sandstrom (1988) indicate that the assumption of the 'least-adult-role' (Mandell, 1988) may have some advantages over their own preferred role as 'friend to one's subjects'. Yet, ultimately, theirs is a situational and a personal morality. Where the risk is physical and immediate, Fine and Sandstrom are unequivocal:

> Children can place themselves in danger. In that event, an adult participant observer has a moral obligation to assist them in a way that is 'protective' ... (Fine and Sandstrom, 1988, p. 27)

Yet their general conclusion allows considerably more scope for manoeuvre:

> [It has been] suggested that on occasion it may be necessary to subordinate the self to the role [of researcher] in the interest of research, but, even so, in dealing with children there will be occasions when one's authority should be used to enforce moral imperatives of the self. (ibid. p. 28)

The cultural norm clearly holds that a child's right to privacy and self-determination is a developing one, as is their legal right to independent action but on the basis of a relatively short interview, as opposed to the relatively long acquaintance that a participant observer might have with a child, one has very little to guide one in making a judgement either of the degree of 'risk' or the relative competence of the respondent in any given situation.

Although it is not our intention to discuss the findings from the particular project that we describe here, we did find that young people do identify the clumsy and precipitate handling of disclosure as particularly harmful and do find useful the opportunity to talk over problems with the security of *complete* confidentiality – meaning that further action will *only* be taken with the full consent and knowledge of the child.

Despite the inevitable difficulty of making reasoned situational judgements, and the obvious dangers of employing a purely personal morality, there is little to guide the intending interviewer. The Code of Ethics of the British Sociological Association make no explicit mention of children, for example.

It is by no means clear to us that any extension or amendment to the BSA Code would be possible, given that there seems to be little consensus from which such changes could be developed. That this is an open question is made clear by reference to the situation in the United States. There, building on Federal Regulations (45 Code of Federal Regulations (CFR) 46), adopted by the National Institutes for Health in 1974, the Department of Health and Human Services adopted additional regulations in 1983 (48 Fed. Reg. 9814, 1983) governing research involving children. Essentially, these Regulations permit research on children, only provided that, *inter alia*, parents consent.

Although there is provision under a 1981 revision of the original Regulations to waive parental consent, this is subject to State Law which generally preserves the superior legal and jurisdicial status of parents, a position that most Europeans would now find unacceptable.

Parental paramountcy is implied in Stanley and Sieber's (1992) recent commentary on the Regulations. Here, sympathy is extended to the researcher, who:

> ... does not enjoy spending precious research resources and enduring the attrition of a carefully selected sample in the process of obtaining consent, especially from parents who may disrespect or misunderstand science.

But in order to recognise how much weight such considerations should carry;

> Researchers need only ask themselves what wrath they would unleash on a stranger who tried to usurp their parental role ... .
> (Stanley and Sieber 1992, p.4)

How far we are prepared to proceed in securing the views of children and young people without parental consent and with what degree of guaranteed confidentiality remain acute problems for the intending interviewer as the issue of adult authority in relation to children remains unresolved.

Our approach in the reported research was, through 'gatekeepers', to seek parental consent to their children being interviewed. A letter was circulated through children to parents approximately a week before the day on which it was hoped to interview the children. Gatekeepers, particularly headteachers, often added their own covering letter, stressing the voluntary nature of involvement in the research. The research letter, however, made it clear that unless an active *refusal* by parents was returned, involvement in the research would hinge on consent of the child. Only three such active refusals were received.

There are two core problematics in this approach. First, by using the children themselves as the carriers of the letters to parents, how can we be sure that parents in fact saw them? Our only confidence on this question stems from the fact that there was no *subsequent* comeback from irate or concerned parents after the research interviews had taken place, but this still sidesteps the issue of those parents who show little interest in what their child has been doing at school or at the youth club. (In the case of children accommodated in care, consent was sought through either parents or social workers or, in some cases, both.)

Secondly, we remain unsure what we would have done had a potential respondent sought to *override* an active refusal by a parent. There was only one glimpse of this possible problem when the broad purpose of the research was being outlined in a 'warm-up' ten minutes to a class of nine- and ten-year olds. The one child whose parents had actively refused to allow their participation looked positively disappointed that they could not take part, but the class teacher made it absolutely clear that their parents' decision could not be overturned. Unlike the USA, we do not necessarily have the paramountcy of parental consent enshrined in any code of conduct, but once the strategic decision is made to consult parents it would clearly be ethically unsound to run roughshod over parental refusal, *even if the child still expressed a wish to participate*. An alternative approach which bypassed parents and simply consulted with children would, however, be unlikely to be supported by the institutional 'gatekeepers' on which the researcher is dependent for access to children.

'Gatekeepers'

The presence of an adult whose role in relation to authority remains unclear (the researcher) certainly complicates the lives of those adults who do have authority over and responsibility for children (teachers, youth workers, social workers) and for this reason the importance of securing the support of gatekeepers can not be overstated. The abiding lesson of this particular research project is that one must anticipate substantial difficulties in securing access to groups or to individual children when engaging in qualitative approaches to surveys of young people on even as modest a scale as ours. In our case, the obstacles were formidable.

In part, these could be attributed to the defensiveness of various 'gatekeepers' to children whenever concepts of 'harm' and 'risk' are mentioned. It is invariably equated immediately with 'abuse' and the warning bells this concept signals – partly from a desire to protect children from further unwanted intrusion, but also because these 'gatekeepers' are currently in a 'no win' situation. They have already been on the receiving end of critical political and media responses whatever forms their professional interventions have taken.

In endeavouring to secure access to respondents in institutional settings in the past, we have favoured, from the outset, making informal contact on the ground to ensure that, having negotiated the formal channels, the immediate gatekeepers to children and young people would provide the necessary support. This does, however, pre-suppose that one knows the settings one wishes to cover in advance. In this research we did not. Access routes were, therefore, very much a 'top down' process, starting with a general letter to senior officers outlining the broad thrust and purpose of the work and inviting further exploration of the issues.

Some authorities or departments refused point blank to assist with the research, invariably on the grounds of the current formal pressures they are under.

For example:

I have [now] had the opportunity to consider further your proposals. Unfortunately I do not feel that I am able at this point in time to contribute to your research project. Any involvement would require a considerable amount of preparation and support of individual children, and I am afraid that I cannot prioritise it at this point in time given the considerable pressures already upon my staff.

I am sorry that we are not in a position to assist you

[Source: local authority social services department, October 1992]

Others quite rightly raised a number of key questions to which they required satisfactory answers before deciding to proceed further – these were concerned with wider professional support, confidentiality, parental consent and feedback. Despite the diligence and general supportiveness on the part of these senior gatekeepers, the research was dogged by numerous delays; requests for research cooperation are clearly not considered to be much of a priority in social services, education and youth work departments. We responded to their responses almost by return of post, yet then often had to wait three or four weeks for the next communication.

We recall the feeling of elation when – after four months of painstaking negotiation – one of us finally 'hit the ground' in one authority, paying an informal visit to a children's home to deliver parental consent forms, and actually met with some of the young people who were likely to be participants in the research! The interviewer was seen to actually punch the air in delight.

Such problems do not diminish even if one intends to secure access to young people in less formally 'gate-kept' situations. An important and probably very necessary component of the contemporary construction of appropriate relations between children and adults is founded on the idea of 'stranger danger'. With some justification, children (and, indeed, adults) view with suspicion, if not hostility, approaches to engage in dialogue with adults whom they do not personally know (see Horan, 1987).

Fortunately, given our 'snowballing' approach to constructing a 'sample' (based primarily on age, gender, ethnicity and type of 'setting') we did not have to address the implications these issues could have for sample attrition. We simply had to keep 'plugging away' in order to build up the necessary numbers. For those with more rigid sampling strategies, our rather dispiriting account of the *potential* for sample attrition, resulting from numerous institutional and professional obstacles, needs to be considered with great care.

Sample size might further be affected at the point at which young people themselves give informed consent to the interview process. This issue has been more extensively reviewed in the literature on ethnographic accounts of the social world of children. All we would wish to say here is that most children and young people are often only too eager to talk – *provided they believe that the interviewer is genuinely concerned to hear their stories and provided they are confident that things will not go any further unless they give consent.* Inspiring the trust and confidence of children within a limited time-frame does, of course, pose problems and we have already alluded to some of the methods by which this may be achieved. The important message here, however, is that nothing can ever be guaranteed. The effective 'throwaway' line with one child or group of children which secures the possibility of moving forward may be equally *counter-productive* with another individual or group. Children and young people make quick judgements as to whether an individual (researcher or otherwise) is 'all right' or a 'dickhead', and once such judgements have been made it is difficult to alter them without the unavailable luxury of time.

What became apparent from the comments of the children we interviewed was that they assessed adults (parents, relatives, professionals, researchers) initially in terms of what can only be described as 'maverick' qualities, of which humour was a central part. Being a 'good laugh' was a critical attribute. This is completely understandable when we reflect that young people's lives are routinely about backchat, sharp remarks and flippant asides, often all the more so amongst those experiencing difficult childhoods. What young people sought from adults was some serious listening inside a funny shell – and researchers seeking in-depth views and information were no exception. Whether or not having a certain type of hairstyle, wearing particular types of clothing or being knowledgeable about football or pop music was particularly significant is debatable, but there is little doubt that such factors may, on occasions, have the potential to 'swing' things in the researcher's favour. But such self-presentation has to be carefully managed: a perceived 'biker' image is unlikely to go down well with the aspiring skinhead, unless the researcher can somehow make an appropriate joke about it. This 'management of self', as we have noted, therefore may well demand some element of self-parody, for the critical issue is about 'reading' and then forging the necessary links with the child's personal and cultural interests.

Finally, one issue which was always high on the agenda of senior professional gatekeepers was ensuring provision could be made for children to be interviewed by researchers of the same gender or ethnicity, if they so wished. Contingency arrangements were, in fact, made on this front, but they were not required. All the research interviews were conducted by a white man. Female and black or Asian respondents were always asked how they felt about this. They were quite unanimous in their response: they would make up their own minds and the issue *for them* was whether or not the researcher seemed able to grasp the circumstances and perspectives they were describing. If not, they would exercise their prerogative to abandon the interview – and not one did. We believe that, although the *question* is one which at all times merits careful handling, the answer is not as self-evident as many in the professional worlds of social work and education would contend.

Conclusion

We live in a policy climate in which extraordinary circumstances too often dictate the form of 'ordinary' interventions. The determination of government to re-establish more punitive (and ineffective) juvenile justice measures as a result of a small number of tragic, but completely atypical although media-worthy, events is but one example. We fully concede the interventions with children must acknowledge and take heed of the potential situation and circumstances of a small number of highly disturbed and damaged young people. This applies to research activity as much as to more professional directed enterprise. However, we would also wish to argue forcefully that this minority should not determine the approach taken with most children and young people, whose anxieties and needs are also important and who can – given the right kinds of research intervention – express them articulately and confidently. We risk getting bogged down in the specific issues affecting the most troubled children to the detriment of the general issues which concern the larger body of 'ordinary kids'.

This chapter has attempted to outline some of the factors which we believe should inform an *effective* approach to eliciting the views of that majority. The occasional flippant remarks are not intended as such, for they have a serious bearing on making the necessary connections with potential respondents. It is time that researchers re-evaluated their strategies for talking to children so that they suspend some of the methodological niceties which can be trawled from the textbooks, and substitute them with a range of personal sensitivities which are most likely to secure credibility with those whose views they are seeking to analyse and represent. Listen, and be prepared to learn.

References

Adler, P. and Adler, P. (1978) 'Tinydopers: a case study of deviant socialization', *Symbolic Interaction*, 1 pp. 90–105.

Archard, D. (1993) *Children – Rights and Childhood*, London: Routledge:

Aries, P. (1960) *L'Enfant et la vie Familiale sous L'ancien Regime*, Paris: Libraire Plon, translated by Robert Baldick as *Centuries of Childhood* (1962) London: Jonathan Cape.

Bamford, T. (1990) *The Future of Social Work*, London: MacMillan.

Bannister, A., Barrett, K. and Shearer, E. (Eds) (1990) *Listening to Children; The Professional Response to Hearing the Abused Child*, London: Longman.

Blackburn, C. (1991) *Poverty and Health: Working with Families*, Milton Keynes: Open University Press.

Blagg, H., Hughes, J. and Wattam, C. (Eds) (1989) *Child Sexual Abuse: Listening, Hearing and Validating the Experiences of Children*, London: Longman/NSPCC.

Butler, I. and Williamson, H. (1994). *Children Speak*, London: Longman/NSPCC .

Carrington, B. and Troyna, B. (Eds) (1988) *Children and Controversial Issues*, Lewes: Falmer.

Coles, R. (1967) *Children of Crisis*, Boston USA: Little, Brown.

Coles, R. (1986) *The Moral Life of Children*, Boston USA: Houghton Mifflin.
Darvill, G. and Smale, G. (Eds) (1990) *Partners in Empowerment: Networks of Innovation in Social Work*, London: National Institute for Social Work.
Denzin, N. K. (1977) *Childhood Socialization*, San Francisco: Jossey-Bass.
Fine, G. A. (1981) 'Friends, Impression Management and Pre-adolescent Behaviour' in Asher, S. R. and Gottman, J. M. (Eds) *The Development of Children's Friendships*, Cambridge: CUP.
Fine, G. A. (1987) *With the Boys* Chicago: Chicago Press.
Fine, G. A. and Sandstrom, K. L. (1988) *Knowing Children – Participant Observation with Minors*, Newbury Park CA. USA: Sage.
Flekkoy, M. (1991) *A Voice for Children: Speaking Out as their Ombudsman*, London: Jessica Kingsley.
Furniss, T. (1991) *The Multi-professional Handbook of Child Sexual Abuse*, London: Routledge.
Goffman, E. (1961) *Asylums*, New York: Doubleday.
HO/DOH (1992) *Memorandum of Good Practice on Video Recorded Interviews with Child Witnesses for Criminal Proceedings*, London: HMSO.
Holman, R. (1983) *Resourceful Friends: Skills in Community Social Work*, London: The Children's Society.
Horan, R. (1987) 'The End of Hallowe'en', paper presented to the Association for the Study of Play, Montreal, Canada and quoted in Fine and Sandstrom (1988).
Howe, D. (1990) 'The client's view in context', in Carter, P., Jeffs, T. and Smith, M. (Eds), *Social Work and Social Welfare: Yearbook 2*, Milton Keynes: Open University Press.
Hoyles, M. (1989) *The Politics of Childhood*, London: Journeyman.
Kelly, A. (1991) 'The "new" managerialism in the social services', in Carter, P., Jeffs, T. and Smith, M. (Eds) *Social Work and Welfare: Yearbook 3*, Milton Keynes: Open University Press.
Langan, M. and Lee, P. (1989) *Radical Social Work Today*, London: Unwin Hyman.
Lorenz, W. (1993) *Social Work in a Changing Europe*, London: Routledge.
Mandell, N. (1988) 'The least-adult role in studying children', *Journal of Contemporary Ethnography*, **16**, pp. 433–67.
Marsh, C. (1988) *The Survey Method*, London: Allen and Unwin.
Martinson, F. M. (1981) 'Preadolescent Sexuality – Latent or Manifest?', in Constantine, L. L. and Martinson F. M. (Eds) *Children and Sex*, Boston: Little, Brown.
McCracken, G. (1988) *The Long Interview*, Newbury Park CA. USA: Sage.
Morgan, S. and Righton, P. (Eds) (1989) *Childs Care: Concerns and Conflicts*, London: Hodder and Stoughton.
National Institute of Justice (1992) *New Approaches to Interviewing Children: A Test of its Effectiveness*, Research in Brief, Washington: National Institute of Justice.
Phelan, J. (1983) *Family Centres: A Study*, London: The Children's Society.
Rogers, W., Hevey, D. and Ash, E. (Eds) (1989) *Child Abuse and Neglect: Facing the Challenge*, London: Batsford.
Stainton-Rogers, W. and Worrel, M. (Eds) (1993) *Investigative Interviewing with Children*, Milton Keynes: OU.
Stanley, B. and Sieber, J. E. (1992) *Social Research on Children and Adolescents – Ethical Issues*, Newbury Park CA USA: Sage.
Varma, V. (Ed.) (1992) *The Secret Life of Vulnerable Children*, London: Routledge.
Waksler, F. (Ed.) (1991) *Studying the Social Worlds of Children: Sociological Readings*, London: Falmer.
Willis, P. (1978) *Learning to Labour: How Working Class Kids Get Working Class Jobs*, Farnborough: Saxon House.

5 From the margin to the centre:
empowering the black child
Panna Modi, Caroline Marks and Rhonda Wattley

Loving

Give me your smile,
and I'll give you mine.
Give me your tears,
and that will be fine.

Show that you care,
and give of your time.
Show that you love
and you will be mine.

Sarah Bond, 1993

This poem is symbolised by a picture of a black carer and a child in an embrace, and is a conversation between them.

This chapter looks at social work practice, and at child-care trends and practices in respect of the needs of black children, from an historical and sociological perspective located in a political framework and power relationship. In addition, it looks at some sound practices empowering black children, operating from within the parameters

of a black perspective, and finally it will address issues for a 'way forward' which will attempt to move the needs of black children from
the margin to the centre.

The messages in this chapter attempt to stand to the testimony of
the requirements of the Children Act 1989, Section 22 (5) (C) which
clearly requires the local authorities and voluntary organisations to
give due consideration to 'the child's religious persuasion, racial
origin and cultural and linguistic background', Article 19 of the UN
Convention of the Rights of the Child and the empowerment model
as outlined by MacDonald (1991).

Social work practice and child-care trends – a historical and a sociological perspective

It is necessary briefly to acknowledge and define the 'political'
framework and power relationships within which all services are
designed and delivered. This chapter is written with that thinking
in mind, which is, that

> British society is dominated by white middle-class, professional,
> heterosexual, physically and intellectually able men.

It is this group that dominates political, economic and intellectual
activities to the detriment of other groups.

It is important to acknowledge the work of Maureen Olusola
(1992) who generally confirms the above statements, and has developed a framework of understanding power relationships based on
the 'matrix of domination' which draws on British societal trends
(Jones and Olusola, 1992). In addition, the work of Dr Owusu-
Bempah (1986) further confirms this, and states that upper and
middle class men hold positions of power to the detriment of the
lower classes of people, which also include women and black people
who he has classified as an 'under class' in British society.

Social work perspectives in multi-racial practice

Denney (1983) identifies four dominant perspectives in the social
work literature which have attempted to make sense of the needs of
minority ethnic and black clients: 'cultural deficit' (called the
anthropological approach' in Denney, 1983), 'liberal pluralism',
'cultural pluralism', and the 'structural position'. To this, we now
add a 'black professional' perspective. These, to some extent, constitute a historical progression parallel to that of Government policy,

and also reflect the emergence of the second and third generations of minority ethnic and black communities. Each perspective is a pioneering work of its time, and it is only too easy to criticise with hindsight outside of the historical context. As habitual modes of thought towards black people have, among whites, changed little, we feel that all these approaches have 'something' to offer in helping whites understand the feelings aroused by their current social work experiences (Ely and Denny, 1989).

Before we go on to identify the four dominant perspectives in the social work literature, we want to say something about the above underlined 'something' which is reflected in the reality of current practices related to black children and families.

Goldberg and Hodes (1992) state that, in recent years, it has become starkly evident that racism pervades social life in Britain. Racism is but one form of adversity that ethnic minority families experience; it may be manifested by increased levels of unemployment, poor housing and economic exploitation (Commission for Racial Equality, 1977, 1990). The link between racism and disadvantage is relevant to psychiatrists (Fernando, 1988; Littlewood and Lipsedge, 1989), psychologists (Maxime, 1986; MacCarthy, 1988; MacCarthy and Craissat, 1989), social workers (Ely and Denny, 1987; Ahmed, Cheetam and Small, 1991; Ahmed, 1993; Coombe and Little, 1986; Domenelli, 1988, etc., etc.) and family therapists (Boyd-Franklin, 1989; Ho, 1987; O'Brian, 1990; Pinderhughes, 1982).

Ahmed, Cheetham and Small (1991) have stated that the welfare services failed primarily to deal with these problems appropriately. For example, many Asian mothers have not been helped properly by ante-natal services (Allen and Purkis, 1983). The day-care available to pre-school children of the large numbers of employed black mothers is often of poor quality (CRE, 1975; Jackson and Jackson, 1979; Mayall and Petrie, 1983). Disproportionate numbers of black children are in care, with less chance than white children of reunion with their parents (Ousley, 1981; Batta and Mawby, 1981); House of Commons Social Services Committee, 1984). The care provided by local authorities is often insensitive to diverse ethnic backgrounds and cultural needs (Jones, 1977; ADSS, 1978; Cheetham, 1981; Young and Connelly, 1981). Only recently have black substitute parents been found for black children, and determined efforts made to advance this recruitment (Arnold, 1982; Brunton and Welch, 1983). Schools have met confusion and difficulty in responding to the needs of black pupils and establishing the priorities of education for a multi-racial society (Swann, 1985). Large numbers of black children have been inappropriately suspended from school (CRE, 1985(a)). Welfare services for young offenders have also not operated adequately for black adolescents, and so disproportionate numbers are in youth custody establishments (CRE 1985(a); Pinder 1984; Vita 1986; Taylor, 1981).

Racism has a detrimental effect on the quality of family life for black children and families. Because of racism, black parents may often become more protective towards their children as they reach adolescence, a time when young people strive for increased autonomy and differentiation.

Attempted suicide by overdosing is more common amongst Asians, especially young women, as compared to non-Asian British (Glover et al, 1989; Merrill and Owens, 1986, 1988). It is suggested that there is a link between racism and overdosing. There may be a number of cultural explanations for this, but the one suggested by the authors here is that racism is an attack on the individual which is reproduced by overdosing as an attack on the self. Various forms of self-harm, including self-mutilation, are also other forms of attack on the self. A lot of black children resort to this simply because they are black.

All this is well researched and documented, and social services and social workers have begun slowly to recognise and accept their responsibility for a multi-racial society (BASW, 1982; CCETSW 1984).

Writers such as Pinderhughes (1982) describe black families as being victims of a white-dominated oppressive system.

It is in this white dominated oppressive system that black professionals attempt to empower black children and their families by promoting a black perspective – against all odds, and to enable them to survive and thrive. We will be returning to discuss empowerment issues and the black perspective later on.

Now returning to look at dominant perspectives in social work literature.

Cultural deficit

Fitzherbert (1967) addresses herself to what is still a live issue today: the disproportionate numbers of West Indian children coming into care. She attributes this both to the forms of the lower class West Indian family, and to the inappropriate behaviour of white child-care officers. Fitzherbert was writing about the first generation of West Indians in Britain, whose behaviour derived largely from their countries of origin, and whose difficulties were compounded by their strangeness to this country.

Discussion

Twenty-six years on the work of Barn (1993) based on the Wenford Research Study draws the same conclusions, that black children are over-represented in the public care system. It is argued that lack of preventive work leads to black children being admitted into care much more quickly than white children. Issues concerning preventative work with black families, age, route of entry into care and change in legal status, are considered both quantitative and qualitative terms.

Barn (1993) states that

> while a recognition is made of the disadvantaged position of black families in the area of housing and unemployment and therefore the greater likelihood of such families to need social services help, this study has concerned itself with documenting the ways in which social workers process the cases. It is shown that, while there are no significant proportional differences in the referrals made by agencies such as police and the health services, there are differences in the reasons for which these same agencies referred black and white families. Moreover, the evidence suggests that social workers approached cases of black children and families with a greater degree of negativity than those of white children and families. Such negative attitudes operated to the detriment of black children and families (p 59).

Social workers and others in the caring professions believe that one of their primary roles is to enable their clients and users of their services to alleviate oppression and empower them, thus making them independent rather than dependent on services.

However, Ahmed (1993) argues that somehow black children and families are excluded from this phenomena in practice.

> British society is saturated in oppression. This is based upon race, class, gender, age, disability and sexual orientation (Mitchell, 1989).

For social workers, it is often an easier option to focus on the symptoms of oppression, than on causes of oppression.

Ahmed (1993) states that

> Inclusion of tackling or even addressing black client's oppression [causes of symptoms] is not comfortable for social workers as this requires acknowledgement of racism [one of the main causes] and dealing with it. Acknowledgement of racism shifts the focus from 'disadvantaged blacks' to 'black people being oppressed'. Dealing with racism shifts the focus 'helping disad-

vantaged blacks' to 'tackling oppressors' and redraws a parallel between black people's oppression and oppressors, not between black people and disadvantaged people. The parallel between black people's oppression and oppressors brings the social workers much too close to the 'oppressor' category as part of the dominant society and members of the mainstream institutions. Engrossed in this 'welfare' and 'care' model of social work, most social workers find it extremely laborious. However, the process of owning up to their oppressive role forces them to acknowledge their personal racism and tackle it, however discomforting and distressing it may be. The usual syndrome of passing the buck of oppression to others and blaming institutions, managers and politicians, etc. for racism becomes difficult. It becomes equally hard for them to dismiss the fact that racism does not exist as an external or 'out-of-focus' dimension in social work practice. It then brings into light why social work values, its professional norms and ethics need to be interrogated and scrutinised (pp. 43 and 44).

So much of the work in caring professions, particularly in social work, is done in an individual capacity, that very few or hardly any cases are jointly worked or paired by a black and a white practitioner. Social work practice is primarily conducted in isolation, 'in secrecy', what is exchanged verbally between a client and a worker is primarily a record of the worker, stored in a case file.

Although some departments operate a policy of 'access to client files', not many clients take up the opportunity of reading their files. Therefore for some, their practice is never questioned or monitored closely. There is no guarantee that what is exchanged verbally between a black client and white worker is necessarily an exact record of what really happened!

Trust and self-commitment to anti-oppressive practice is therefore a prerequisite to empowering all clients particularly black clients.

As stated earlier, the Wenford sub-group's study found that social workers did hold negative attitudes towards black families, which frequently influenced their decision-making process.

Local authorities have a duty to attempt to ameliorate the poor situations in families. The borough of Wenford has one of the largest budgets to do preventive work with families. Interviews with key workers revealed that preventive work, where financial help and other assistance is offered to obviate the reception of children into care, was less likely to be done with black children and families. In other words, one black social worker said that

In my team I'm the only black social worker having to work with six other white social workers. My senior is white. In the whole area, all the seniors are white except one who's recently been appointed. So you have to work in a situation where they are predominantly white people, in a situation where white seniors are not looking at how white social workers are dealing with black clients but are monitoring how black social workers are working with white clients. That's a situation you are in. Also, when you get black clients on duty, you are suggesting financial assistance because that's all at the end of the day you are doing. We are not actually doing any preventative work there. We're just kind of giving out Section 1 (1980 Child Care Act, Section 17, 1989 Children Act) payments to the families. Then you hear a colleague of yours shouting across the room – 'repatriation', yeah, this kind of attitude is in the office you know (Barn, 1993, p. 53).

Black social workers will often give accounts of racial remarks made by their white colleagues consciously and unconsciously about black children and families. It is our strong belief that undoubtedly these are fed into their practice with black children and families. For those who challenge this statement, we want evidence of research studies and literature which says: (1) that the reception into care of black children is in proportion to their population ratios; (2) that the admission of black people into mental health institutions is in proportion to their population ratios, and (3) that the reception of black offenders into custodial institutions is in proportion to their population ratios and comparable to the disposals of cases of their white counterparts. The list could go on when considering unemployment, housing, general medical care; racial violence suffered by black people because they are 'simply black' and not guilty of any other offence.

Talking about reception into care or being accommodated by the Social Services Department, the Wenford study highlighted that the most common route for a black child entering care was voluntary.

Amongst child-care practitioners, it is common knowledge that voluntary reception into care means that children have come into care on a short-term basis and with an understanding that as soon as their families are able to care for them again, they will be reunited with their families. Surprisingly, black children who come into care on a voluntary basis often are never returned to their families when they are able to resume their care. They either end up staying in care on a permanent or long-term basis; respecting the original contract of voluntary care. This situation is gradually changing since the 1989 Children Act.

Prior to the 1989 Children Act, large numbers of black children were wards of the courts, in some parts of the country, their lives

totally controlled by the Courts and the Social Services Departments. A lot of these black children had severed ties with their families of origin, and a lot of these children were almost totally cared
for by white foster carers. White practitioners have often alleged that
the child-care practice of black families is often sub-standard, when
measured with their yardstick. The 1989 Children Act demanded
that the Social Services Departments examined their practice
closely, and checked with future needs of those children subjected to
being wards of the courts, of which black children represented the
majority. To date, one is kept guessing about whatever happened to
those black children whose needs slipped between the 1980 Child
Care Act and the 1989 Children Act!

Liberal pluralism

Cheetham's (1972) first major contribution to literature endorses
Roy Jenkins' 1966 replacement of 'assimilation' by a policy aim of
'integration', 'equal opportunity accompanied by cultural diversity
in an atmosphere of mutual tolerance'.

If discrimination could be eradicated, equal opportunity would
develop. Cheetham's work to this mood of consensus-based social
harmony and optimism blends a Weberian perspective with a view
of society as influenced by many élites, each relatively small numer-
ically, operating in different spheres of life. Power is thus diffused
through society and not concentrated in the hands of any one group.
Black people frequently fail to get access to sources of power, owing
to discriminatory practices, which also impinge on many aspects of
their daily lives (Ely and Denney, 1987, p. 78).

Cheetham acknowledges that most immigrants are, to an extent,
identifiable and so can expect to experience discrimination:

> In time their increasing familiarity with the life of the new coun-
> try and their adaptation to it makes many immigrants, and cer-
> tainly their children, indistinguishable from the rest of the
> community. However, those immigrants who are coloured and
> therefore are most easily identifiable may continue to experience
> discrimination and exploitation whatever their personal circum-
> stances and however long their stay in the new country. As a
> result, they and their children can be firmly trapped in a
> deprived environment from which it is hard to escape both
> because they are barred from superior employment and housing
> and because their surroundings provide few opportunities for
> advancement (Cheetham, 1972, p. 5).

Discussion

Denney (1983) says that the pathological – pathogenic model, which assumes an ideology of assimilation and integration, is important here. According to this model, the responsibility for change should be placed on the individual client. However, owing to the dynamics of the client – worker relationship, power is invested in the social worker to decide who is suitable for social work intervention. This means that

> certain racial groupings may be defined as unsuitable for intervention; and black clients such as single mothers, may be deemed to be unsuitable for social work help (Bryan 1992, p. 176).

Sadly, the findings of the Wenford study prove that, because of the lack of preventive work with black families, black children are admitted into care much more rapidly than their white counterparts.

Cultural pluralism

The underlying view of society held by writers in this group is basically consensus oriented, but they acknowledge competition of power between different ethnic groups. The importance of cultural difference and of ethnicity is stressed above all other factors, including perhaps race, and it is the business of cultural pluralists to show how these many ethnicities serve as a support and a buffer against the injustices and misfortunes of a racially inequitable society (Ely and Denny, 1987, p. 84).

Khan (1979) and Ballard (1979) point out that it was no longer appropriate to speak of 'immigrants' and that the policy aim of 'assimilation' was unrealistic, as ethnic minorities were not going to assimilate. At the same time, it was wrong to over-emphasise the influence of the 'traditional' cultural backgrounds of their countries of origin in isolation from the contact and influence of white society.

Discussion

The minorities were sustaining culturally distinctive patterns of social relations, which were the product of their experiences in Britain quite as much as their roots overseas. They were the

> outcome of the strength of childhood socialisation, of interaction with their peer group and a reaction to the hostility and misunderstanding from the majority (Ballard, 1979, pp. 152–3).

This is some way from a straightforward process of assimilation. Ballard (1979) feels that it is too easy to slip into a perception of the cultural worlds of others as an irrational product of sheer ignorance. Instead, they should be viewed as 'systemic totalities'. Practitioners coming into contact with new ethnic groups for the first time need to understand them without being judgemental, and regarding distinctive minority patterns of behaviour as pathological, logical, bizarre or just plain wrong. They should be seen more positively and their strengths acknowledged more positively.

> The provision of 'ethnically sensitive' services should be a normal part of good professional practice, and might also throw a new and more positive light on much that currently appears problematic (Ely and Denny, 1987, p. 84).

Ballard (1979) says that

> any practitioner who does not have a working knowledge of the way in which his clients order, or seek to order, their social worlds, the goals they are attempting to achieve, the style of behaviour they habitually adopt and the kinds of materials, cultural and social constraints under which they are operating must necessarily be professionally handicapped (p. 159).

The structuralist's position

This perspective relates to Marxist analyses in which class and racial divisions form part of unitary state structure at the service of capital. Structuralists locate the 'problem' in deficient material resources, in racists' attitudes and practice within social work agencies, and in the current dominant ideologies of the state.

Discussion

> It is the lack of resources in education, housing and employment which initially create the need for social work intervention at the individual level in the majority of social work 'cases' involving ethnic minorities (Domenelli, 1974).

Domenelli considers that the social worker's role contained conflicting elements: job loyalty as a state employee, wanting to maintain a status quo, versus a liberal helping tradition. The present position requires pressure to be brought about for shifts in resources to take place.

Domenelli challenges the perception that racism exists elsewhere and not in social work. She says that a social worker–client relationship cannot operate in a vacuum divorced from social pressure and influence. 'Social work values' and 'social work knowledge' are expressions of dominant ideologies of the white middle class and therefore there is an imbalance of power between the black children and families and social workers. Domenelli argues that anti-racist social work practice should identify the points at which both workers and clients would have to become involved in effecting change in their agencies and in government services, 'to eradicate institutionised racism and shift power and resources towards ethnic minorities'.

She calls for more 'client-centred, community based' provision – in which the ethnic community's organisations, resources and expertise provide the focus for the programme – and for employment of more black workers, reviews of departmental practices, the reorientation of normal practices and procedures, a re-allocation of personnel and greater involvement of black community organisations, as detailed in the ADSS/CRE Report (1978, pp. 100–2).

Too many black professionals have written too many times, stating more or less the above stated ideas; however, change is very slowly coming. An obvious question we want to ask is, why is change very slow in coming?

Is it because black people have become very clear and assertive about their needs and conversely white practitioners and white agencies also equally have become more clear and assertive about their defence mechanisms?

Brief analyses of the four dominant perspectives in social work attempting to respond to the needs of black children and their families

Having stated and discussed the four dominant perspectives in social work (cultural deficit, liberal pluralism, cultural pluralism and the structuralist position), it becomes very apparent that all these perspectives lend 'something' towards freeing social work practices of racism.

Black children and families have lived in England for nearly 500 years. British white people have ruled, controlled, governed and owned (through slavery) black children and families in many parts of the world. Why is it that they still know, or want to know, so little about their needs? Why is it that black children and families in this country dwell surrounded by legislation which restricts them (British Nationality Act, 1948; Commonwealth Immigrants Act,

1961) as people with equal rights? What is going wrong with the equal opportunities machinery that was invented over 20 years ago?

Practitioners and managers must take some trouble to find the answers to the above questions.

While these different perspectives were being identified and formed, white people were also voicing their fears about black presence in numbers, fears about black men having relationships with white women, fears that cheap black labour would undermine wage rates, and fears that black people would become heavily dependent on the state. Black people have always experienced threats and acts of expulsion, violent assaults and have been, and continue to be, victims of race riots. However, it is also fair to remind ourselves that black children and families have also experienced acts of kindness and have found allies amongst white people who have helped them personally and politically. These acts of kindness have benefited and empowered some black children and their families. However, when weighted against the benefits that white children and their families enjoy, by the virtue of simply being white, they are hardly comparable as being equal.

Racism, discrimination, prejudice and oppression are all issues that are very provocative and have troubled the minds of many people, and people who are affected most by it continue their struggle for equality.

Denial and deflection of racism

Domenelli (1989) says that white practitioners adopt a number of strategies that work against the establishment of anti-racist social work practices; she has identified the following:

1. Racist acts of omission assume racism doesn't exist. Individuals responding on this basis think race is irrelevant in most situations... .
2. Racist behaviour based on denial fails to acknowledge racism in one's own acts or in society... .
3. Racism perpetrated through the dumping approach results in white people placing responsibility for getting rid of racism on black people. ... In practice, this can often mean referring all black clients to a black worker... .
4. Racism depicting decontextualisation strategies accepts that racism exists in society, but refuses to acknowledge that it permeates day-to-day routines. This leads to white social workers recognising intellectually that they are dealing with black people but responding to them as if they were white. Thus, reacting to

black colleagues you work with every day, without taking on
board that they are black, decontextualises them by removing
them for the context of racism with which they work.... .

5. Racism, endorsed by the colour-blind approach, treats black
people as whites, thereby negating black people's specific
experience as black people. White social workers usually express
it as treating all individuals equally without regard to the actual
position from which individuals start. This approach is racist
because it ignores the discrimination experienced.... .

6. Racism operating through the patronising approach involves a
superficial acceptance of black people's specific experiences and
cultures. But, underneath the veneer of equality lies the assumption that white lifestyles are superior, thus adopting a patronising approach ... . This attitude often prevails in white social
workers' understanding of black families' child-rearing practices, where their assurances of their validity are belied by their
taking proportionately more black than white children into care,
believing that black parents offer a sub-standard child care provision to their children.

7. Racism based on the avoidance approach contains an awareness
of race as a factor in social interaction, but avoids confronting
it ... (pp. 12, 13).

These responses, we would suggest, are common to all the groups of
people who experience oppression, and would be exacerbated when
a person is in more than one grouping.

Working towards a black perspective, to empower black children and families

Why is it that white authors and white practitioners are not asked to
define a white perspective? Surely there must be a white perspective? Maybe because a white perspective is accepted as the 'norm',
everybody ought to know it.

A black perspective has no neat and tidy definition, neither is it
just a string of words. A black perspective is more than a statement
against 'white norms', it is an expression of assertion that can be
bound by a semantic definition. The factors that prescribe a black
perspective have a long history of subjugation and subordination.
The circumstances that shape a black perspective stem from the
experience of racism and powerlessness, both past and present. The
motivation that energises a black perspective is rooted to the principle of 'racial equality and justice'. The articulation that voices a
black perspective is part of the process that is committed to replac-

ing the white distortion of black reality with black writing and black experience (Ahmed, 1993, p. 3).

A black perspective should focus on transforming the unequal social relations shaping social interaction between black and white people into equalitarian ones. Additionally, it may also assist white people working from an anti-racist perspective and can build bridges between themselves and black people working towards the same objective from a black perspective. Domenelli (1979, p. 123) argues that white practitioners committed to developing anti-racist social work practice and wishing to work with black children and families need special training to make them:

(a) culturally aware from an anti-racist perspective, that is, able to understand the significance of cultural factors without laying the responsibility for everything that goes wrong at culture's door;
(b) overcome the use of value judgements presupposing the superiority of white British culture and norms;
(c) conscious of the impact of institutionalised racism on their work and commit themselves to fighting it;
(d) explore the impact of white power and privileges in their relationships with black people;
(e) draw connections between racism and the social control elements of social work; and
(f) draw connections between eliminating racism and getting rid of other forms of oppression.

In 1983, the Association of Black Social Workers and Allied Professionals (ABSWAP) was established to facilitate the formulation and articulation of a coherent black perspective on social policy in Britain. This was done by

identifying in which ways overt and covert racism affects service delivery and creating avenues for black people to express community views on service delivery; providing consultative and advisory services; supporting black workers and agencies; exercising influence over training; and providing information services.

In the same year, ABSWAP conducted a survey of the views of black community groups and found that social services were 'enforcement agencies' which broke up black families and aimed to remove black children from their parents. White practitioners were presumptuous, 'nosey', did not understand black people, nor have respect for black families. They considered that black families should be like white families and were not aware of the economic and racist pressures on black families. They were taking black children into care and intentionally severing off family ties, and the effect of this on black children was that they thought they were white. They also pointed out that there was a disproportionate number of black children in care, who were cared for like white children. Child-care policies were 'destroying the black family as a unit' and transracial placements received particular condemnation as perpetuating racist ideologies, by disregarding the difficulties such placements caused for black children when they grew up. ABSWAP called for the development of ethnically sensitive services giving recognition to the strengths of black families and urging local authorities to use them positively.

Classical social work operates with the framework of white middle-class values. This is at variance with the experience of the black families.

Recognising that 'the interest of the black child is paramount', ABSWAP have stressed that standard policy reviews establish whether there are 'significant others' in the child's life being able to meet the child's needs appropriately and efforts must be made to return the child to its natural family as soon as is possible. The 1989 Children Act has also emphasised this point. Committed white practitioners and agencies strive to work towards achieving this, whilst others continue to find excuses for not working with this philosophy and, effectively, black children continue to be marginalised. The ABSWAP document embodies an assertion of black ethnic identities and of black self-respect.

The essential ingredient of any substitute home for a black child should:

1. Enhance positive black identity.
2. Provide the child with the techniques or 'survival skills' necessary for living in a racist society.
3. Develop cultural and linguistic attributes necessary for living in a racist society.
4. Equip the child with a balanced bi-cultural experience thus enhancing the healthy integration of his personality (Ely and Denny, 1987).

Many of the ideas in the document are parallel to those of Ohri, Manning and Como, 1982, expressed in community care. A black perspective can only become functional if black professionals have more power and influence over policy formation and service delivery, thereby striving to eliminate racism.

A black perspective empowers black children by promoting a positive black identity. The concept of identity, particularly in responding to the needs of black children has been a subject of important discussion in the last ten years (Maxime, 1986; Modi and Pal, 1992). Other authors who have written about black and disabled children who have been sexually abused (Kennedy, Dhir and Kelly, 1993) and have stated that the core components of identity are commonly identified as: religion, race, culture and language; disability; sexuality and gender. These are also stated in the Children Act 1989 as 'due consideration should be given to the child's religious persuasion, cultural, racial and linguistic background'.

Maxime advocates that, by the time black children are three, they are very aware of their identity and are most sensitive to racial issues. They are also aware that white is the norm and is sanctioned accordingly; black is usually conveyed negatively. Thus, for some black children, their sense of blackness is repressed or carried around as a big heavy secret. Black children should always be given a message about having a positive black identity and taught pride in their culture. The absence of a strong inner core of positiveness leads to the destruction of self and the black people. A holistic approach that takes account of the 'total child', i.e. all the parts (race, culture, religion, language, etc.) that are involved in the making of him/her can only empower a black child.

Comer and Poussaint (1975) have stated that

> a positive identity ... must be built on an inner core of pride and positive feelings ... or it may fade away under the harsh light of life's realities (p. 17).

All practitioners involved in working with black children and young people have a positive contribution to make in enhancing and nurturing a positive racial identity. This requires educating of self, with sensitivity and receptivity to race.

Assessing black children and families; using the empowerment model

McDonald (1991) discusses the Deficit and the Empowerment Model in her work on assessing black children and families. She states that the Deficit model emphasises the control and authority of the worker. Families are regarded as being 'disfunctional' or having 'deficits'. Black families are pathologised, stereotyped and treated negatively.

She states that the Empowerment model is based on the strengths, abilities and positive contributions a family can make to their life.

We will briefly summarise what she considers to be essential components of the Empowerment model; when working with black children and families (p. 77);

1. Recognition of life experience
2. Understanding black experience
3. Sensitivity to cultural pride
4. Positive self-image
5. Knowledge of family/support system
6. Positive role model for black children
7. Redress of power imbalance
8. Work against racism
9. Social worker's action to work towards redressing power imbalance and provide appropriate services to black children and families.

Way forward

The machinery of Equal Opportunities has been in operation for 20 years; however, the task of eradicating racism from social work practice is far from being completed. Black children and families continue to be over-represented in care and custody situations; conversely this is not reflected by black professionals also holding more powerful positions. As long as the black professional and black community is under-represented in decision-making processes which have direct implications for black children and families, they will continue to be victims of white dominated oppressive social work practice. It would be wrong to accuse all white practitioners and agencies of lacking commitment to eradicating racism in social work practice. There is some sound practice in different pockets of the country where black children and families have been empowered and where they also have as good an access to service delivery as their white counterparts. This good practice is not standardised and we are concerned about those black children and families who do not fare as well from accessing services as their white counterparts.

Ahmed (1993, pp. 26–8) has suggested that, in relation to accessing resources to black children and families, the usual social worker's assumptions for black children are:

(a) There are not enough numbers of black foster or adoptive parents because black families do not come forward to provide this service.
(b) Absence or limited numbers of black carers is due to the fact that they do not fulfil the requirements laid down by the authorities.

(c) In black culture, concepts of fostering, adopting and caring outside the family network are not accepted.

(d) Social work time and resources are already stretched to their limits so that promotional work of finding black families and carers and additional work of providing support and assistance to newly found black resources are not possible, however desirable.

Social work assessment needs to face up to the consequences of these assumptions and preempt them. The needs of aforementioned children and others like them can then be truly assessed. The following checklist aims to provide a framework for social work assessment of black clients.

Checklist of assessment of needs of black clients

1. Have you acknowledged the fact that all assessments of black clients require recognition of racism and its effects whether covert or overt?
2. What steps have you taken to examine your values and perception of black families critically?
3. How do you ensure that your assessment is not based on negative stereotypes of black families?
4. Are you able to identify the root cause of your anxiety in applying your assessment methods and skills without blaming black clients?
5. How do you respond to black clients challenging or criticising your assessment – constructively or defensively?
6. Are you confident to share your assessment openly with black clients and their families?
7. Do you usually define the needs of black clients or ensure your assessment is based on their experience and reality? How do you ensure your assessment is based on their experience and reality?
8. Do you assess strengths of black clients, their families and communities as well as their weaknesses, problems and needs?
9. What have you done to ensure your assessment responds to different and specific needs of black clients, not just 'special' needs?
10. Can your assessment make clear distinctions between clients' possible control of personal problems, and external constraints beyond their control? What are the distinctions?
11. Is your assessment sensitive to cultural implications, expectations and aspirations? Make a list of cultural implications, expectations, and aspirations.

12. Are you restricting your assessment because you think there are no resources which justify a partial account of black clients' needs?
13. Do you fit in black clients' needs in your assessment or vice versa?
14. Have you made passing and/or irrelevant comments which may distort your assessment and misguide social work action?
15. Is your assessment capable of incorporating effective short- and long-term planning and evaluation?
16. Do you challenge and include critical assessment of racist procedures and practices of other institutions and professionals involved with black clients whom you assess?
17. What steps have you taken to check whether your assessment is influenced by a pathological, liberal or safe approach?
18. Are you fully aware of any racist outcome your assessment may have on black clients? Identify and list any possible outcomes that may be racist.
19. Do you actively seek and/or use advice and guidance from black expertise?
20. Can your assessment advocate for change and race equality? How?
21. Can your assessment empower black clients? How?
22. How do you evaluate your assessment of black clients and the outcome of your assessment on black clients?

Conclusions

It is never easy for black professionals to write about black children and families in relation to social work practice. They are only too aware of how black children fare in comparison to their white counterparts when accessing a service delivery. Black professionals are also trapped in a political framework governed by power relationships, where they too are at the bottom of the pile in terms of having control and influence in designing and delivering services to black children and families.

How can black professionals empower black children and families when they do not feel empowered? This is a question black practitioners too often have asked their white managers?

Despite the oppression experienced by black practitioners, they continue to empower black children and families, working from a black perspective and having a commitment and a belief that black children too have as much right as their white counterparts to receive an equal service. Black practitioners and the black commu-

nity have never asked for anything over and above their white counterparts.

In this chapter we have attempted to look at social work practice
and child care trends from an historical and sociological perspective,
based within a political framework and power relationships. Therefore, we have looked at the four dominant social work perspectives
and discussed how service delivery affected black children and families. We have also discussed Domenelli's (1989) work on white
people's attempts to deal with racism, and finally we arrive at the
core of the chapter where we attempt to discuss the issues and
realities of working towards a black perspective endeavouring to
empower black children and families.

We have found it necessary to cover a lot of the old ground to
give practitioners a snapshot of the overall context of social work
practice in relation to the black children and families, both from the
macro- and micro-level. At times, it feels like working through trea-
cle, chipping away quietly. However, we hope and believe that, if
black South Africans have rid themselves of Apartheid, we too can
work towards eradicating racism from social work practice. This is a
vision every black professional must hang on to and strive to work
to.

Reminding ourselves of current service delivery to black children and families – despite the changes in the legislation, service
delivery to black clients is very variable and ad hoc: primarily
dependent on the consciousness and goodwill of the practitioners. It
is becoming increasingly apparent that, amongst the caring professions, particularly social work, primarily it is still operating at the
two extremes in relation to black children and families. Either they
seem to have a liberal or a safe approach, anxious not to be labelled
racist, so keen that they tend to shy away from their duties of protecting the black children from abuse, or they do not hesitate to
remove black children from their families, who according to them
are not suitable parents, and whose child-care practices are perceived as being sub-standard. And, while the caring profession is
swinging like a pendulum between these two extremes, it is continuing to remain in a state of flux, whether in terms of intervention or
inaction (Ahmen, 1989; Modi and Pal, 1992).

While, on the one hand, professionals are paralysed in trying to
sort out their standpoint and appear to be 'politically right on' black
children, on the other hand they become more interlocked and
embedded in their oppressive practice. The professionals who
should be helping them become more distant, and the struggle to
empowerment becomes a mere figment of their imagination.

Milner (1975) states that racism is an irrational and unjust attitude towards another race which is often accompanied by stereotyp-

ing. This is often made easier when there are visible physical differences between groups.

A child is a sensitive being; its inate characteristics and behaviour are moulded by the way it is nurtured. Through this, it learns about its identity – who am I? ...; it learns about acceptance – How do I fit in?

Positive daily interaction between the care-taker and child helps it to develop physically, emotionally, intellectually, etc. All that it recognises, its perception of the world, are dependent upon the way it is treated and the experiences which are available to it. Black parents and carers must therefore provide their children with positive messages about their identity. These should also be reinforced by others with whom the children have significant relationships, e.g. teachers, social workers the children are likely to come into contact with.

A child is dependent upon its environment, and learns to trust through understanding its surrounds. If the child and environment are in communion so that the child's needs are met and satisfied, it develops into a 'wholeness', a happy, secure, enriched and valued person.

If the environment works against the child, racially, culturally, socially and educationally, the child becomes disorientated, trust is destroyed, self-image is shattered, and conflict arises.

Too many black children have been damaged by white agencies and by systems that do not work in communion with their needs. Practitioners must therefore re-evaluate their practices in relation to black children and families. How and why is it that agencies fail black children and families? How is it that agencies empower black children and families?

The UN Convention on the Right of the Child says that all children have:

The right to affection, love and understanding
The right to adequate nutrition and medical care
The right to full opportunity for play and recreation
The right to a name and nationality
The right to special care, if handicapped
The right to be among the first to receive relief in times of disaster
The right to learn to be a useful member of society and to develop individual abilities
The right to be brought up in a spirit of peace and universal brotherhood
The right to enjoy these rights, regardless of race, colour, sex, religion, national or social origin

White practitioners and managers must ask themselves whether black children, too, equally enjoy all the rights as do the white children?

References

Ahmed, B. (1989) 'Protecting black children from abuse', *Social Work Today*, 8 June.
Ahmed, B. (1993) *Black Perspectives in Social Work*, Jo Campling, Venture Press.
Ahmed, S. (1991) 'Cultural racism in work with Asian women and girls', in Ahmed, S., Cheetham, J. and Small, J. (eds.) *Social Work with Black Children and Families*, London: Batsford/BAAF.
Ahmed, S., Cheetham, J. and Small, J. (1991), *Social Work with Black Children and their Families*, London: Batsford/BAAF.
Allen, R. and Purkis, A. (1983) *Health in the Round*, Bedford Square Press.
Arnold, E. (1982) 'Finding black families for black children in Britain' in Cheetham, J. (Ed.) *Social Work and Ethnicity*, Allen and Unwin.
Association of Directors of Social Services and Commission of Racial Equality (ADSS/CRE) (1978) *Multi-racial Britain: The Social Services Response*, London, Commission of Racial Equality.
Ballard, R. (1979) 'Ethnic minorities and the social services: what type of service' in Kahn, V. S. (Ed.) *Minority Families in Britain*, London: Macmillan.
Barn, R. (1993) *Black Children in the Public Care System*, London: Bradford Press/BAAF.
Batta, I. D. and Mawby, R. I. (1981) 'Children in local authority care: a monitoring of racial difference in Bradford, *Policy and Practice*, 9 (2) pp. 137–50.
Bond, S. (1993) *Child Education*, Scholastic Publications Ltd.
Boyd, Franklin, N. (1989) *Black Families in Therapy: a Multi-system approach*, New York: Guilford Press.
British Association of Social Work (BASW) (1982) *Social Work in a Multi-cultural Britain*.
Brunton, L. and Welch, M. (1983) 'White agency, black community' in *Adoption and Fostering*, 7 (2).
Bryan, A. (1992) 'Working with black single mothers: myths and reality' in Langan, M. and Day, L. (Eds) *Women, Oppression and Social Work Issues in Anti-discriminatory Practice*. Routledge.
Central Council for Education and Training in Social Work (CCETSW) (1984) *Teaching Social Work in a Multi-racial Society*.
Cheetham, J. (1972) *Social Work with Immigrants*, London: Routledge and Kegan Paul.
Cheetham, J. (1981) *Social Work and Ethnicity*, Allen and Unwin.
Comer, J. and Poussaint, A. (1975) *Black Child Care*, New York: Pocket Book.
Commission for Racial Equality (1975) *Who Minds?*
Commission for Racial Equality (1977) *A Home From Home*.
Commission for Racial Equality (CRE) (1985) (a) Report of the Formal Investigation into the Suspension of Black Pupils in Birmingham, London.
Commission for Racial Equality (1990) Annual Report.
Coombe, V. and Little, A. (Eds) (1986) *Race and Social Work: A Guide to Training*, London and New York: Tavistock.
Denny, D. (1983) 'Some dominant perspectives in the literature relating to multi-racial social work', *British Journal of Social Work*, 13, pp. 149–74.
Domenelli, L. (1979) 'The challenge of social work education', *Social Work Today*, 10 (25).

Domenelli, L. (1989) 'Anti-racist social work', in *A Challenge for White Practitioners and Educators*, London: Macmillan Educational.

Ely, P. and Denny, D. (1989) *Social Work in a Multi-racial Society*, Gower.

Fernando, S. (1988) *Race and Culture in Psychiatry*, London: Croom Helm.

Fitzherbert, R. (1967) *West Indian Children in London*, Bell.

Glover, G. Markes, F. and Nowers, M. (1989) 'Parasuicide in young Asian women', *British Journal of Psychiatry*, 154, 271–2.

Goldberg, D. and Hodes, M. (1992) 'The poison of racism and the self-poisoning of adolescents', *Journal of Family Therapy*, 14 (1), February.

Ho, M. K. (1987) *Family Therapy with Ethnic Minorities*, Newbury Park, CA: Sage.

House of Commons Social Services Committee (1984) *Children in Care*, 1, HMSO.

Jackson, B. and Jackson, S. (1979) *Childminder*, Routledge and Kegan Paul.

Jones, C. (1977) *Immigration and Social Policy in Britain*, Tavistock.

Jones, J. and Olusola, M. 'Power and oppression in child sexual abuse'. Paper presented at the Children Risk Conference, Bergen, Norway.

Khan, V. S. (Ed.) (1979) *Minority Families in Britain*, London: Macmillan.

Kennedy, M. Ohir, B. and Kelly, L. (1993) 'Recognising identity in the ABCD pack – abuse and children who are disabled', The National Deaf Children's Society, NSPCC: Way Ahead – Disability Consultancy and Chailey Heritage.

Littlewood, R. and Lipsedge, M. (1989) *Aliens and Alienists: Ethnic Minorities and Psychiatry*. 2nd edn, Harmondsworth: Penguin Books.

MacCarthy, B. and Craissat, J. (1989) 'Ethnic differences in responding to adversity: a community sample of Bangladeshis and their indigenous neighbours', *Social Psychiatry*, 24, 196–201.

MacCarthy, B. (1988) 'Clinical work with ethnic minorities', in F. N. Watts (Ed.) *New Developments in Clinical Psychology*, 2, Chichester: British Psychological Society/Wiley.

McDonald, S. (1991) 'All equal under the Act', *Race Equality Unit – Personal Social Services*.

Maxime, J. E. (1986) 'Some psychological models of black self concept – social work with black children and their families', in Ahmed, S., Cheetham, J. and Small, J. (Eds) reprinted 1988, 1990, 1991, Batsford, BAAF.

Mayall, B. and Petrie, P. (1983) *Child Minding and Day Nurseries*, Heineman.

Merrill, J. and Owen, J. (1986) 'Ethnic differences in self-poisoning: a comparative study of Asian and white groups', *British Journal of Psychiatry*, 148, 708–12.

Merrill, J. and Owen, J. (1988) 'Self-poisoning among immigrant groups', *Acta Psychiatrica Scandinavica*, 77, 77–80.

Milner, D. (1975) *Children and Race*, Hammondsworth, Penguin.

Mitchell, G. (1989) 'Empowerment and opportunity', *Social Work Today*, March.

Modi, P. and Pal, J. (1992) 'Beyond despair – child sexual abuse and the black community', in *Confronting the Pain of Child Sexual Abuse*, pp. 66–76, FSU Publication.

O'Brian, C. (1990) 'Family therapy with black families', *Journal of Family Therapy*, 12, pp. 3–16.

Ohri, A., Manning, B. and Corno, P. (1982) *Community Work and Racism*, London: Routledge and Kegan Paul, Children Act 1989, HMSO.

Ousley, H. (1981) *The System*, Runnymede Trant.

Dr Owusu-Bempah, J. (April 1986) 'Oppression, exploitation and discrimination in a racist, sexist and classist society', *Newsletter of Leicestershire Racism Awareness Consortium*.

Peter, E. and Denny, D. (1987, reprinted 1989) *Social Work in a Multi-racial Society*, Gower.

Pinder, R. (1984) 'Probation work in multi-racial society'. A research report for the Home Office Research Unit.

Pinderhughes, E. (1982) 'Afro-Asian families and the victim system', in McGoldrick, M., Pearce, J. K. and Giordano, J. (Eds) *Ethnicity and Family Therapy*, New York:

Guilford Press.

Pitts, J. (1986) 'An eye for an eye: young black people in the Juvenile Justice System', in Mathews, R. and Young, J. (Eds), *Black Youth, Sage Swann Report, 1985. Education for all.* HSMO.

Swann Report (1985) *Education for All*, London: HMSO.

Taylor, W. (1981) 'Probation and alternatives to custody in a multi-racial society', CRE.

Young, K. and Connelly, N. (1981) 'Policy and practice in the multi-racial city', Policy Studies Institute.

6 Young people with a disability:
aspects of social empowerment
Peter Appleton

Introduction

In their book *Out of Sight* Steve Humphries and Pamela Gordon document the experiences of disabled children in Britain in the early part of the twentieth century. Two themes persist throughout the book. One is the children's segregation and isolation. The other is the courage and fortitude of the children, and their families.

In the 1980s and 1990s in Britain and the United States, some disabled children are experiencing a different sort of isolation. It is the isolation of feeling different, feeling lonely, and feeling anxious about what adulthood will bring. The feelings of isolation are more hidden, because schools have integrated, leisure and recreation facilities are available, and prejudice appears to be on the wane. But, if you talk to children with disabilities (Madge and Fassam, 1982), or observe them at play (Guralnick, 1986), it is clear that we are a long way from true integration. By early adulthood those with physical disabilities are likely not to have a partner, to have few friends, and not to have appropriate communication aids and advice (Thomas, Bax and Smyth, 1989). However, one is also struck by the sheer resolution of many children and families. Most disabled children want to be in an integrated school setting, despite its problems, and many parents during the 1970s and 1980s battled with local authorities to gain a place in mainstream school for their child.

This chapter is concerned with the social empowerment of children and adolescents with disabilities. Many of the issues I deal with arose out of a recently conducted interview study of 79 young people with spina bifida (Appleton *et al.*, 1994), and the service development experience which ran in parallel with the research.

Although empowerment can be taken to refer to a young person's autonomous plans, decisions, wishes, and actions, it is crucial to remember that this occurs in a social context (Bronfenbrenner, 1979). Children's capacity to plan, and develop autonomy, derives from loving and caring relationships with parents and other important adults in the social network (Bowlby, 1984; Bronfenbrenner, 1979). It also derives from satisfying relationships with peers – from a feeling of social acceptance by peers, and from friendships (Harter, 1986; Parker and Asher, 1993). It also derives from what Bronfenbrenner calls mesosystem linkages – the capacity of the various settings the child lives in to link together to:

> encourage the growth of mutual trust, positive orientation, goal concensus, and a balance of power responsive to action on behalf of the developing person (Bronfenbrenner, 1979, p. 216).

In our study, and in our service development plans, we were able to address a number of key questions about disabled children's own points of view, in the context of their social relationships – in particular:

1. what aspects of self were personally important
2. how competent the young people felt in various aspects of their lives
3. the benefits and costs of social comparison with peers
4. the role of gender
5. the importance of an adult confidant
6. the developmental role of co-operation across settings.

Defining spina bifida

For the purposes of our study (Appleton et al., 1994) spina bifida was defined as

> open or closed myelomeningocele, with or without associated hydrocephalus, with or without ventricular drainage. All patients had measurable functional impairment of locomotion, continence, intellect or physical parameters associated with the spina bifida.

Spina bifida is a disorder of the development of the brain and spinal cord. The normal process of covering the spinal cord with bone and skin fails, leaving an area of exposed nervous tissue. These nerves are not fully developed, and damage after birth and during surgery further reduces function. This may result in paralysis of limbs, loss of sensation, or bowel and bladder incontinence. Within the brain, the normal flow of fluid may be interrupted causing hydrocephalus, the accumulation of fluid.

Much of the physical damage of spina bifida can be corrected. The defect in the back can be closed. The hydrocephalus can be drained via an implanted valve. Surgery may improve deformities and promote mobility and continence. However, the underlying injury to the nerves cannot be healed or replaced, and residual impairments persist. Some young people experience memory and concentration problems, difficulties with numeracy, and problems with considered thought. There may, in addition, be long periods of missed schooling due to health problems and hospitalisation. There is a raised risk of depression in adolescence. The degree of disability is very varied – from none at all to combinations of all the above.

Case finding childen with spina bifida

The children and young people in the sample were aged between 7:0 and 18:11. The diagnosis was confirmed in all cases with the young person's own medical advisors and/or by review of the medical notes. Case notes were obtained in order to clarify points in the history and on cases not seen clinically.

For case-finding we utilised hospital records, community child health records, voluntary society records and national family fund records. Some of the young people previously unknown to hospital services had recently moved into the area, and others had 'mild' conditions that nevertheless met our criteria for impairment. We eventually had a list of 104 families in the research geographical area who had a child with spina bifida.

Approaching the families

Each of the families was approached and offered the opportunity of a home visit to explain the nature of the research, for them to make a decision about whether they wished to participate. 17 families chose not to participate and 8 children had to be excluded from the study either because they were very severely intellectually impaired or because the family was experiencing severe family distress at that particular point in time. This left 79 cases in our sample.

An able-bodied comparison sample

For each of the 79 young people a comparison subject individually matched for age, gender, classroom and housing neighbourhood was obtained. The comparison subjects had no known chronic illness, disability, or special educational need.

The interviews with the young people

The psychological interviews were carried out in a confidential setting within the school, college or workplace. The interviews took up to 4 hours and were frequently broken up into manageable portions of time depending on the child's age and preferences. The interview consisted both of free-wheeling discussion with the young person, and standardised questionnaires. Standardised questionnaires included those by Renick and Harter (1988) and Harter (1985).

How internally consistent or reliable were the children's questionnaire responses?

The children with spina bifida responded as consistently and reliably as their able-bodied controls on the questionnaires, which were carefully chosen and piloted for their applicability to childen with specific learning difficulties (data reported in Appleton et al., 1994).

The results

I will review our findings, and service development discussions with disabled young people, under the six categories introduced earlier, i.e. personally important aspects of the self-concept, feelings of competence, social comparison with peers, gender, the role of an adult confidante, and the importance of cooperation across settings.

Quotations are given from young people with spina bifida who participated in the research, and from interviewer research reports. Details have been anonymised, but the age and gender of the young person are as given.

Service development discussions were held with teenagers with a range of different physical and sensory impairments, drawing on their views about need, and about the findings of the research.

Personally important aspects of the self-concept

Central to the young person's sense of self, and motivation, is the range of experiences which are personally valued – experiences that are salient, and occupy attention and feeling. Working individually, it is possible to discover areas of personal importance through discussion and through provision of developmentally appropriate opportunities. However, in a survey, the research questions have to be carefully circumscribed and, in our study, we wanted to know whether the range of self-concept areas rated as important by able-bodied young people were also rated as important by disabled young people. The reason for addressing this question will emerge below.

In our study, all children were asked to rate how important each area of their self-concept was to them personally, using the well-standardised format of the *Harter Self-Perception Profile for Learning Disabled Children*. The areas were:

1. being accepted socially by peers
2. academic ability
3. athletic ability
4. showing good behaviour
5. one's physical appearance.

Interestingly, on average, there were no significant differences, comparing able-bodied young people with young people with spina bifida. That is, no area was less important to the disabled group. One theory of stigma (Crocker and Major, 1989) suggests that disabled people can reduce the impact of feeling different, by devaluing the importance of that aspect of themselves that feels different. For instance, physically disabled people could protect self-esteem by denying the importance of physical appearance and physical capacity. We found no evidence for this theory in our study.

> I think that looks are terribly important because you can go a long way on your looks. People make impressions based on looks … boys take one look at you and they either fancy you or they don't. I guess that I just don't think that I am that attractive … I'm a bit too scared to ask anyone whether they think I am attractive. (Girl, age 16)

Academic opportunities and mainstream peer opportunities were also valued:

> I'm not fast at reading but I enjoy reading and like to take my time over it because then it makes more sense and I enjoy it more. I worry a lot about maths because I don't understand some of the pages in my maths book and if I ask teacher then it means

that I get stuck on that page and shall be on it for quite a while. I think it is important to be good at school things like maths and reading because you need them if you want to get a job. If I get a good job then I will be able to buy a house and a car. (Girl, aged 11)

I know I am slow at answering these questions but it's my head you see ... I have to have time to work things out. I have been educated in ordinary schools throughout my life and I'm glad of that. It wasn't always easy but it taught me a lot ... it taught me how other people without disabilities would react to me and it also taught me about how to react to them. (Girl, aged 18)

Some other issues specific to disability emerged from the interviews:

Kids need to be told the logical reason why they are in a wheelchair ... this crap ... oh, you are there because you are God's little girl is potty ... children can understand a lot more than you lot think. It's unfair to tell them lies, particularly when they have to cope with that handicap for the rest of their lives. (Girl, aged 17)

One thing that I remember about hospitals that made me really angry is that I was having a medical and my dad was carrying me and he sat me down on a chair. The doctor then asked me if I could move my legs and yet he could damn well see that I couldn't move my legs. That is the reason that I went to see him! My mom still feels angry because doctors ask such silly questions when they already know what the answer is. (Girl, aged 11)

How competent did the young people feel?

If the disabled young people felt that all areas of the self-concept were just as important as did the able-bodied controls, how competent did the disabled group feel?

Young people with spina bifida felt, on average, less competent in most academic areas (especially maths), less socially accepted, and less athletically competent, compared with the self-ratings of able-bodied controls.

Because they felt that these areas of self were important, there was evidence of discrepancies between levels of importance and self-rated levels of ability. In our study, for those areas that individual young people placed particular importance on, young people with spina bifida experienced considerably larger discrepancies (between level of importance and level of comparison) than did their able-

bodied comparison group. In turn, we found that larger discrepancies were associated with lower overall self-esteem.

> I wasn't good at school ... those questions show that don't they?
> I don't like myself for it ... I mean that you are supposed to be
> good at school that is why you are there. After each essay I never
> got as good marks as the other children no matter how I tried ...
> it's been explained to me that there is something wrong with my
> head but it doesn't make it any better. I thought that I had passed
> my maths exam ... I even told my Dad ... he would have been so
> proud you see ... but I found out that I had failed. Everyone said
> that it didn't matter but it did to me but that didn't seem to
> matter to them. (Girl, aged 18)

A number of young people experienced bullying (see Madge and
Fassam, 1982) –

> People skit me all the time. Sometimes they shout 'spastic',
> which really upsets me. (Girl, aged 13)

We have a general picture of the disabled young people feeling that
they do not match up to the expectations that they are setting for
themselves. So what is the origin of the self-expectations?

Peer social comparison – a catch 22?

Children from age 8 upwards know what features of themselves they
want to compare with others, who they want to compare with, and
for what purposes (Harter, 1986; Dweck and Leggett, 1988). Children are able to make very fine discriminations between their own
competencies, and personal characteristics, and those of others
whom they know, or imagine.

In our study, the majority (>70 per cent) of young people with
spina bifida compared themselves with able-bodied peers, when
comparing themselves on social acceptance, academic ability, good
behaviour, and physical appearance. Even for athletic ability, a
majority of the disabled group compared themselves with able-
bodied young people (59 per cent). Not suprisingly, this choice of
comparison group was strongly associated with being in mainstream
school – of the 49 disabled young people in mainstream school 43
compared themselves with able bodied peers on intellectual ability,
whereas only 4 out of the 16 in special school chose to make the same
comparison.

One way of looking at this finding is that one objective of educational integration has been achieved. Young people with a physical
disability think of themselves as in the same social-world-of-com-

parison as able-bodied peers. Most of those we interviewed wanted to remain in mainstream school.

However, there was a cost to this. The disabled young people, by routinely comparing themselves with able-bodied peers, felt relatively less competent and less socially accepted.

In our service development discussions with disabled young people, we have sought views about these findings. Most disabled young people we have talked to definitely want to be in mainstream school (see also Madge and Fassam, 1982). They feel that it is inevitable that, as they mix on a day-to-day basis with able-bodied peers, they will compare themselves. They also want to break down barriers further, especially in integrating athletics and gymnastic activities. However, they place great value on also meeting with groups of other disabled young people – to discuss and compare common experiences. These include self-care and personal aspects of the disability, and the feelings of being different that many feel.

It is important to remember that all young people experience multiple comparison or reference groups – the school peers may not be the same individuals as the youth club, or athletics club peers – and that multiple reference groups, across settings, provide useful developmental preparation for adulthood.

> Human development is facilitated through interaction with persons who occupy a variety of roles and through participation in an ever-broadening role repertoire. (Bronfenbrenner, 1979, p. 104)

Gender

It is now well known that able-bodied adolescent girls feel less happy about themselves than boys. This applies to overall feelings about the self, specific evaluations of academic competence, and in particular physical appearance (Allgood-Merten et al., 1990). The findings in our able-bodied sample confirmed this.

However, we also found that, for physically disabled girls, there is a 'double jeopardy'. In statistical terms the self-perception effects of gender add to the self-perception effects of disability (Appleton et al., 1994). Particularly in the areas of physical appearance, academic competence, and athletic competence, both gender and disability contribute to high discrepancy scores between 'importance' and self-rated competence, making girls with spina bifida more vulnerable to lower self-esteem that boys with spina bifida.

Girls with spina bifida assigned greater importance to physical appearance than did able-bodied girls and boys.

If I could be someone else then I think that I would choose to be a tall, thin, long blonde-haired model ... a bit like Madonna in her early years ... before she went ... funny ... you know. (Girl, aged 17)

The disabled girls experienced great sensitivity about their looks, and their physical difficulties with continence and mobility. Boys, although concerned, were apparently less affected than girls. It seems likely that the ever-present emphasis on physical appearance in our culture, which affects all girls, has an especial impact on disabled girls. Negative body perceptions may be frequently cued by mobility difficulties, toiletting arrangements and difficulties, and skin and self-care problems. It is difficult to forget your body when you are a teenager who looks and feels different. Being in a mainstream school, comparing self with able-bodied peers, underscores the difference.

Young people's feelings about their body are more closely tied to overall self-esteem than are any other aspects of the self-concept (Harter, 1986). This was found to be especially so for girls with spina bifida (Appleton et al., 1994), and is therefore a stong indicator of priority for therapeutic help (see also Varni and Setoguchi, 1991).

A surprising finding was that disabled girls felt less supported by parents than did disabled boys, or the able-bodied young people.

My parents are OK, they try to help, to understand, but it's difficult for them and I can't tell them what is inside – I get so angry sometimes. (Girl, aged 14)

I don't get on well with my parents at all ... my mother has always treated me as though I am a burden. I feel guilty all of the time about lots of things. I often think that I would be better off dead ... I feel fat and loathsome. (Girl, aged 17)

A number of girls in our sample expressed a need to talk about depressive feelings, but expressed also the feeling that they didn't want to talk to their parents, either because parents would find it too painful, or because they 'wouldn't understand'. One 18 year-old disabled girl had contemplated suicide after the death of a friend with spina bifida. She felt guilty because she had survived, couldn't talk to her parents and had no close friends. A 12 year-old girl who strongly disliked her own body, and was called 'spastic' by peers at school, felt she couldn't talk to her parents. Disabled girls do appear to be acutely aware of the chronic stress their mothers experience in looking after them, and consequently may 'protect' their mothers by not confiding their own anxieties and concerns. From the general developmental epidemiological literature it is known that parents are less tuned in to depression and anxiety in daughters, than in sons

(Verhulst and Koot, 1992). Whether this is also true for disabled girls is not known.

It is important to emphasise that the processes involved are complex, and parents under stress may feel just as trapped as the young person with the disability. Interventions to support parents are just as important as those to help young people (Sloper and Turner, 1993). In the early years, support for parents is critical as they are the primary resource for the child's development.

An adult confidante

Both our research and service development discussions point to the need for a confidante for some young people with a disability. The need may be greater for girls, or girls may more readily utilise such a person. While the confidante could of course be a parent, it may be that the person would have to be outside the nuclear family:

> My relationship with my mom and dad is difficult ... my handicap makes me angry ... and I hit them sometimes ... it doesn't make me feel any better ... I'm still angry. My handicap affects them and they start shouting at each other. (Girl, aged 12)

> My mom doesn't listen to me and my dad doesn't want to talk to me. Sometimes when I talk to my mom she turns around and walks away from me ... it makes me feel awful ... I go upstairs and stay in my bedroom. Mom doesn't let me see friends ... I'm not allowed out and I end up spending time in my bedroom. Everyone in our house is too tired to take me out. My mom is always watching the television and doesn't want to go out ... she watches videos ... and she watches every programme on the TV. (Boy, aged 7)

> I feel depressed all of the time ... I haven't spoken to anyone about it. I don't know who to talk to ... I mean who can help me? (Girl, aged 17)

> It had taken a long time to come to terms with the death of her friend and during this time she did not confide in anyone. I was the first person she had told. Since then another friend had died, but she said that the second time she found it a bit easier to cope with, because she was not so close to this girl. She felt that, although her parents cared for her, they did not understand her and did not want to listen to her problems. (Interview Report on Girl, aged 18)

> Yes, I do feel like killing myself ... if no one wants to be around me ... then what is the point of going on? If I feel like this in a

few years time then what will I feel like in the future? I began to
start to think about killing myself about a year ago ... I don't
think of it very often but when it does I just can't stop thinking
about it, particularly when things go wrong for me. I understand
that you would rather not keep that bit of what I have said a
secret and I don't mind talking to someone about it. I would talk
to Mrs. Smith about it. I don't know if I would actually kill
myself ... it depends on how bad things got. (Girl, aged 14 years)

Perhaps the most important aspect of social support is the **perception** that someone is emotionally available, someone who will listen,
will accept you for who you are, and will accept you whatever happens (Sarason, Pierce and Sarason, 1990; Bowlby, 1984).

We have returned to the theme of isolation. For young people
feeling different, less competent, anxious about the future, and anxious about their parents' capacity to understand, there is a clear need
to break the wall of isolation, and enable the young person to disclose, unburden, and be helped to envisage opportunities.

Only connect

We have described young people's expressed wish to mix with both
disabled and able-bodied peers. This is one indication of the importance, for human development, of participating in multiple settings.
We have also described the importance of an adult confidante who
may empower the young person to take development forward on the
basis of what motivates the young person, what emotional and social
barriers require overcoming, and how settings can be linked up.
Finally, the centrality of support for the parents was emphasised.
Bronfenbrenner sums up these aspects of psychological development as follows:

The developmental potential of participation in multiple settings will vary directly with the ease and extent of two-way communication between those settings. Of key importance in this
regard is the inclusion of the family in the communications network (Bronfenbrenner, 1979, pp. 216–17).

Echoing this we were told:

I'm not challenged enough by work or my parents. I sew
wedding dresses and do embroidery and things but as soon as I
try and do something like lifting the iron Jim my boss gets upset
and tells me it is something that I can't do. I know everyone
thinks that they are doing it for my own good but they think I
can do a lot less than I can actually do and it gets on my nerves.

> At school they taught me to do simple things like make a cup of tea for myself but my Mom and Dad won't even let me make a cup of tea at home. I do it when they are out because I think what they don't know won't hurt them. Trouble is, if they found out then they would never leave me alone. (Girl, aged 18 years)

What struck us during the research was the agency-centredness of much work with children. Even discussion about inter-agency work tends to focus on how agencies can work together rather than how they can jointly facilitate children's development in the environmental settings the child lives in – the various school settings, the various activities at home, youth club or other peer activities, and any other regular settings.

When entering a new setting, it must be remembered that it is the young person, not a professional, who is the primary link.

> He went to an able-bodied sports club every Friday night and played basketball for a disabled team on Saturday. He said 'I love sport and travel all over the country doing it'. I asked him how his interest had first started and he said 'I just thought that I would join a club and it started from there. I sat outside the club for ages just trying to pluck up the courage to go in but I'm glad that I did. Before I joined I sat in the house doing nothing in particular and since joining it my life has changed and I get out of the house a lot more. I have got a lot more friends too' (Interview Report on Boy, aged 15).

If a parent or peer also participates in a number of settings, they function as supplementary links. For instance, bringing a friend home from school requires facilitation by parents, and co-operation from the friend. Or, to take another example:

> I try to lead as normal life as I can ... I've got a job ... a newspaper job. I've just started it. The woman in the paper shop nearly died when I applied for it but she gave me a trial and saw that it was possible for me to carry the papers in my wheelchair. I'm just doing one delivery a week at the moment but I'll be able to do more in the school holidays and things when I am more used to it. I get £2.92 per week but I only keep £2 of it because I give 92p to my mate because he comes and helps me with the difficult bits ... it's things like gates with funny catches that are hard but I'm sure that it will come with time. (Boy, aged 15)

By adapting to a variety of people and situations, social skills develop in scope and flexibility (Wadsworth and Harper, 1993; La Greca, 1993; Inderbitzen-Pisaruk and Foster, 1990). Supplementary links can scaffold this process.

Bronfenbrenner (1979) suggests that the developmental potential of settings is enhanced if the role demands in the different settings are compatible, and if the roles, activities, and relationships in which the young person engages encourage the development of mutual trust, a positive orientation, goal consensus between settings, and an evolving balance of power in favour of the developing person.

This is the substance of young people's social development – finding their feet in new tasks, and new social challenges. For disabled young people, impairments not only restrict physical access to new settings (which is the obvious effect), but also restrict the natural ease with which primary and supplementary links can be set up. Personal links betwen the various school settings, leisure settings, and home-life, become more important to establish, to ensure that developmental social opportunities are being afforded, and scaffolded, with the appropriate balance of power to the young person.

Inter-setting links between the various home and school settings and perhaps the most important linkages to examine, and this process should begin from school entry, and be based on links established during preschool development (Appleton, Meredith, and Everitt, 1994).

Teenagers with disabilities, like most teenagers, want to establish themselves in a variety of community leisure facilities. Agencies may initially underestimate the importance of this clear need, which begins gradually during middle childhood, but becomes central to social development during adolescence. Whereas in school, teenagers can become established in social routines which may not challenge their personal development, leisure activities with peers carry challenges which require the young person to develop new social, cognitive, and physical skills. Feeling socially accepted in a peer group is just as important for self-esteem in teenagers, as having close friendships (Harter, 1986).

A great deal of work is still necessary by agencies to 'decentre' from their own definitions of 'settings' (e.g. schools, clinics etc), and 'functions' ('inter-agency co-operation', 'key workers' and 'care co-ordinators'), and to start again from the point of view, and the day-to-day environmental opportunities, of young people and parents.

Concluding remarks

This research study was with young people with spina bifida. Because the sample was geographically defined, and did not have any major selection biases, the findings should be of relevance to services for young people with spina bifida in other areas of the UK. Whether the findings are of relevance to other physical disabilities, such as cerebral palsy, is not known. However, certain principles have emerged from both the research study, and from discussions with service users, which may have general applicability, but it must be emphasised that there is a great need for well-designed outcome studies in child disability, examining whether services are effective. In this chapter I have cited models from mainstream child development research, such as the work of Bronfenbrenner (1979) and Harter (1986, 1991), which are useful in designing therapeutic interventions.

The key messages from work reported here, and the theoretical background, are as follows:

1. Children and young people will tell you what is important to them, and there is good reason to suppose that interventions are more likely to be effective if they match the developing self-concept (Harter, 1991),
2. by occupying a variety of roles, in a variety of settings, and comparing themselves with both able-bodied and disabled peers, young people's social development should be promoted,
3. social and psychological isolation can be overcome by facilitating and scaffolding developmental opportunities across a variety of roles, and settings, with an evolving balance of power in favour of the young person.
4. an adult confidante, who is emotionally available, able to understand what is important to the individual young person, and able to acknowledge and understand the barriers to social development opportunities, will be important for all young people with a disability; for some young people it will be a parent – for others it should be some other trusted figure,
5. girls can be more vulnerable to negative feelings about the body, and negative feelings about parental support.

The themes introduced at the beginning of this chapter – of social isolation, and courage – have come full circle, and are as relevant to modern-day children as they were to disabled children earlier this century. Children and young people wish to take up developmental opportunities, make close adult and peer social ties, and feel control over their lives. There is much specialist knowledge which can be made available to young people in their environments, and there is much yet to be learned about how best to support young people in achieving their full place in society.

Acknowledgements

The research reported here was done in collaboration with Vicki Böll, Colin Elliott, Nick Ellis, Pat Jones and Philip Minchom. Funding was from the Association for Spina Bifida and Hydrocephalus. The interviews with the young people were conducted by Colin Clerkin, Trish Gilroy, Val Lawson, and Ann Llewelyn.

References

Allgood-Merten, B., Lewinsohn, P. M. and Hops, H. (1990) 'Sex differences and adolescent depression', *Journal of Abnormal Psychology*, **99** (1), pp. 55–63.

Anderson, E. M. and Clarke, L. (1982) *Disability in Adolescence*, London: Methuen.

Appleton, P., Minchom, P., Ellis, N., Elliott, C., Böll, V. and Jones, P. (1994) 'The self-concept of young people with spina bifida: a population-based study', *Developmental Medicine and Child Neurology*, **36**, pp. 191–197.

Appleton, P., Meredith, K. and Everitt, G. (1994) Inter-agency cooperation for entry into primary school for children with special needs. Paper given at Welsh Office/Department for Education/Council for Disabled Children Conference on Code of Practice for Special Educational Needs, Cardiff.

Bowlby, J. (1984) *Attachment and Loss: Volume 1. Attachment*, Second Edition. London: Penguin.

Bronfenbrenner, U. (1979) *The Ecology of Human Development*, London: Harvard University Press.

Crocker, J. and Major, B. (1989) 'Social stigma and self-esteem: the self-protective properties of stigma', *Psychological Review*, **96**, (4), pp. 608–630.

Dweck, C. S. and Leggett, E. L. (1988) 'A social-cognitive approach to motivation and personality', *Psychological Review*, 95, (2), 256–273.

Guralnick, M. J. (1986) 'The peer relations of young handicapped and nonhandicapped children' in Strain, P. S., Guralnick, M. J. and Walker, H. M. (Eds) *Children's Social Behaviour: Development, Assessment, and Modification*, London: Academic Press.

Harter, S. (1985) *Manual for the Social Support Scale for Children*, Denver, Co.: University of Denver.

Harter, S. (1986) 'Processes underlying the construction, maintenance, and enhancement of the self-concept in children', in Suls, J., Greenwald, A. G. (Eds) *Psychological Perspectives on the Self*. Volume 3, London: Erlbaum.

Harter, S. (1991) 'Developmental differences in the nature of self-representations: implications for the understanding, assessment, and treatment of maladaptive behaviour', *Cognitive Therapy and Research*, **14**, (2), pp. 113–142.

Humphries, S. and Gordon, P. (1992) *Out of Sight: The Experience of Disability 1900–1950*, Plymouth, UK: Northcote House.

Inderbitzen-Pisaruk, H. and Foster, S. L. (1990) 'Adolescent friendships and peer acceptance: Implications for social skills training', *Clinical Psychology Review*, **10**, pp. 425–439.

La Greca, A. M. (1993). Social skills training with children: where do we go from here? *Journal of Clinical Child Psychology*, **22**, pp. 288–298.

Madge, N. and Fassam, M. (1982) *Ask the Children: Experiences of Physical Disability in the School Years*, London: Batsford.

Parker, J. G. and Asher, S. R. (1993) 'Friendship and friendship quality in middle childhood: links with peer group acceptance and feelings of loneliness and social dissatisfaction', *Developmental Psychology*, 29, 4, pp. 611–621.

Renick, M. J. and Harter, S. (1988) *Manual for the Self-Perception Profile for Learning Disabled Students*, Denver, Co.: University of Denver.

Sarason, B. R., Pierce, G. R. and Sarason, I. G. (1990) 'Social support: the sense of acceptance and the role of relationships', in Sarason, B. R., Sarason, I. G., and Pierce, G. R. (Eds) *Social Support: An Interactional View*, Chichester: Wiley.

Sloper, P. and Turner, S. (1993) 'Risk and resistance factors in the adaptation of parents of children with severe physical disability', *Journal of Child Psychology and Psychiatry*, 34 (2), pp. 167–188.

Thomas, A. P. Bax, M. C. O. and Smyth, D. P. L. (1989) *The Health and Social Needs of Young Adults with Physical Disabilities*, Oxford: Blackwell Scientific Publications Ltd.

Varni, J. W. and Setoguchi, Y. (1991) 'Correlates of perceived physical appearance in children with congenital/acquired limb deficiencies', *Journal of Developmental and Behavioral Pediatrics*, 12 (3), pp. 171–176.

Verhulst, F. C. and Koot, H. M. (1992) *Child Psychiatric Epidemiology*, London: Sage.

Wadsworth, J. S. and Harper, D. C. (1993) 'The social needs of adolescents with cerebral palsy', *Developmental Medicine and Child Neurology*, 35, pp. 1015–1024.

7 The Dolphin Project:
the impact of the Children Act
Ann Buchanan

Nobody tells me anything (Young man in residential care. September 1991)

14 October 1991 saw the implementation of the Children Act 1989. Many called this the most radical child-care legislation to hit the statute books for over 40 years. It was designed to change the face of child-care policy and practice. The Department of Health spent over eight million pounds on an impressive implementation programme. This was to ensure that all those who were in one way or another involved in giving or receiving services were aware of the important principles underlying the Act. A central tenet of the legislation was that the child's welfare was 'paramount' (Children Act, Section 1), and that 'the ascertainable wishes and feelings of the child concerned' considered in the light of his or her age and understanding, should be elicited (Children Act, Section 1 (3a)).

I was visiting a residential establishment in September 1991, when I met the above young man. Throughout the country, there was a buzz of excitement as people were attending training courses on the new legislation. This young man had been 'in care' for many years. I asked him what he thought about the new Children Act. He asked me to explain what it was, and after hearing my brief explanation, he remarked with the resignation familiar in many young people being looked after 'No one tells me anything'.

This young man was the inspiration for our project. It seemed important that young people whose lives were most affected by the new legislation should have the opportunity of saying what they felt about the changes. As our team was based at the University of Southampton, we adopted the University's symbol the Dolphin, for our project.

During 1992, 45 young people being looked after in three local authorities, Birmingham, Berkshire and Hampshire, took part in the Dolphin Project. In each area, there were two groups of young people who met in non-stigmatised settings. Each group met on three occasions for two hours. The groups were lead by Ann Wheal, an experienced inner-city teacher and youth workers together with Daphne Walder another teacher and home tutor. In Birmingham, where many young people came from black and ethnic minority groups, the project was also led by Sue Macdonald who, as a black youngster, had been in care herself. I myself then met the carers of the young people at separate meetings. All the meetings with the young people and carers were recorded, and questionnaires were also completed. Some 40 hours of recordings were later transcribed. This and other available data was then analysed and central themes arising from the six groups extracted. Full details of the project, its methodology and its findings are described elsewhere (Buchanan et al, 1993).

This chapter is about the impact of the Children Act on young people who are being looked after. It is based on findings from the Dolphin Project and, as this book is about participation and empowerment, it seems appropriate that, as far as possible, the words of the young people themselves are used to express their views. The first section gives an overview of what the Children Act 1989 hoped to achieve, and in particular what it hoped to achieve for young people who are being looked after by local authorities. The second section highlights what the young people themselves knew about their rights under this legislation; while the third section explores what they felt about a range of issues relating to the Act. In the fourth section, young people give their views on a range of other issues that they felt were important to them and which in one way or another effect their participation, empowerment and future citizenship. The final section draws together some of the key messages from the young people, and considers how those who have been looked after can take up their rightful place as valued citizens after the experience of being in care.

What the Children Act 1989 hoped to achieve

In the 1980s, with legislation relating to children and families scattered throughout the statute books, it was recognised that a fundamental review was required of both public and private child care law (DHSS, 1985; DHSS, 1987). Coincidentally there were tragedies in the child protection field leading to the deaths of Kimberly Carlisle, Jasmine Beckford and Tyra Henry (Department of Health 1991). This led, on the one hand, to anxieties about the effectiveness of child protection procedures, while the events in Cleveland on the other hand, epitomised the need to balance this protection duty with the rights of parents to challenge state intervention. It was from the Cleveland inquiry that came the famous remark from Lord Justice Butler-Sloss (1988) which became central to the drafting of the Children Bill:

> ... the child is a person not an object of concern. (Butler-Sloss, 1988)

Here was recognition that the child or young person might have wishes and feelings relating to a situation, and that these wishes and feelings should be considered when decisions affecting that child are being made. There was also the suggestion that the child might be as well equipped to know what was in his or her best interest as those trying to help.

The Children Act 1989 in England and Wales cannot be separated from the international movement supporting children's rights. It has been said that 'The children's rights movement is a social movement with no clear beginning and no obvious end in sight' (Hawes, 1991), that it started as long ago as the seventeenth century in the early efforts to improve the lot of children and young people, and that it came of age with the adoption by the UN General Assembly on 20 November 1989 of the United Nations Convention on the Rights of the Child (United Nations, 1989). The Convention is not enforceable by law, but it does provide internationally accepted minimum standards which can be used to persuade those in authority to meet them. In the United Kingdom, the Convention was ratified in December 1991, just after the implementation of the Children Act. In many ways, the Children Act 1989, incorporating as it does many of its principles, is the United Kingdom's answer to the Convention. Some, however, would say the United Kingdom has still a long way to go before it meets all the requirements (Newell, 1991).

The relationship between parental rights and the rights of children under the Children Act 1989

The Children Act 1989 brought into force a new concept of parental responsibility, which means:

> All the rights, duties, powers, responsibilities and authority
> which by law a parent of a child has in relation to the child and
> his property. (Children Act 1989, section 3.1.)

Under the Act, parental rights are placed firmly in second place
behind the welfare rights of their child, and the emphasis is moved
from parental rights to parental duties and responsibilities. The Act
is, however, quite explicit that it considers it better for children and
young people to be brought up by their families as far as this is consistent with their welfare, and indeed it places a specific duty on
local authorities to promote the upbringing of children in 'need' by
their families (Children Act 1989, section 17).

Although the Children Act places considerable emphasis on consulting the child [Children Act 1989, section 1(3), and 22(4)], the
child's wishes and feelings are not paramount. It is the child's welfare which is paramount. The Lord Chancellor in presenting the legislation made it clear:

> The Act does not make the child's wishes absolutely determina-
> tive of the matter, it puts the child's wishes at the forefront of the
> circumstances to which the court shall have regard. That is a
> valuable position for those wishes [but he adds that] where a
> child was sufficiently mature his or her wishes would probably
> rule the matter.

He acknowledged that, before the 1989 Act, it could be said that the
law erred too far in the direction of protection and was on the whole
unreceptive to the autonomy of adolescents. The Children Act was,
he felt, the first English legislation in which children's rights were
taken seriously and not identified exclusively with the concept of
welfare. One of the golden rules laid down by the Lord Chancellor
was that the Act should be read as a whole. When read as a whole,
the importance of involving children and young people in all decisions that affect their lives, and of helping create the conditions that
enable them to be involved in these decisions is emphasised. Information is central to this participation. Under Schedule 2 paragraph
1(2) of the Children Act, the local authorities have to publish information about the services they provide and take steps to ensure that
those who may benefit from the services receive information. This
applies as much to children and young people as anyone else, and
applies equally to those who do not speak or read English.

The expectations of local authorities when looking after children and young people

Under the Children Act 1989 a child or young person is looked after if he or she is being provided with accommodation [Children Act 1989, section 22(1)] or in 'care' (Children Act 1989, section 31). A local authority has a responsibility to provide accommodation for any child under 16 years of age, where there is no person who has parental responsibility for that child, or where he or she has been lost or abandoned, or where the person who has been doing the caring is unable for whatever reason to provide suitable accommodation.

Children over 16 have also to be provided with accommodation where their welfare would be seriously at risk without it. Other children may be accommodated if it is felt it would safeguard or promote their welfare. When a child is in accommodation, any person with parental responsibility for the child can at any time remove the child from the accommodation.

A child is looked after under a Care Order following a court hearing which proved:

> That the child concerned is suffering, or was likely to suffer, significant harm and that the harm or likelihood of harm is attributable to
>
> i)	the care given to the child, or likely to be given to him if the order were not made, not being what it would be reasonable to expect a parent to give to him; or
> ii)	the child is being beyond parental control. (Children Act 1989 Section 31(2))

It is important to remember that the court cannot make an order unless:

> It considers that doing so would be better for the child than making no order at all. (Children Act 1989, Section (5))

When a child or young person is being looked after by a local authority, whether accommodated or there under a Care Order, the local authority has certain clear duties towards that child. The first duty is:

> To safeguard and promote his welfare (and the second is) to make such use of services available for children cared for by their own parents as appears to the authority reasonable in his case. (Children Act 1989, Section 22(3))

The following comments from young people were taken during the Summer of 1992. In the intervening period, the Children Act has no doubt brought major changes in child-care policy and practice, but the views of the young people given here remind us how far the local authorities have yet to go before they live up to the expectations of the Children Act 1989.

The Dolphin Project: what the young people knew about the Children Act 1989

Most young people in the project had not heard of the Children Act. Although some authorities had special information leaflets and guides for them, very few young people had seen them. There is some evidence that, since 1992, many young people being looked after are better informed. Information is the key to participation and empowerment, and indeed the young person's right, and yet many of those who have responsibility for young people have enormous anxieties in this area.

> *I had never heard of the Children Act, so when I got your letter I went to the library to find out what it was.*

> *The Children Act has been brought in ... and the children did not know about it. Social workers ... have they heard about it?*

> *I want to read the script of the Children Act from start to finish.*

Closely related to what young people knew about the Children Act 1989 was what information young people had about their legal status. Almost all the young people had come into care before the Children Act. They knew broadly whether they were being 'looked after' on a voluntary basis or under a care order. They were generally less clear, and in most cases less interested, about what type of order and the implications of that order, but felt they had a right to know. Young people 'of sufficient understanding to make an informed decision' were not always being informed of their right to refuse a medical, psychiatric or other assessment.

> *My legal status? I have been to court ... they did not consider my wishes and feelings ... they gave me twenty-one days ...!*

> *Legal status: I am certainly not married!*

> *What is the age you can ask the court to change things? When can you leave care?*

> *Ward of court means every time I need a hair cut I have to ask the court. Care order just means I have to ask the social worker!*

> *If they have care and control and a ward of court on you, you are sunk.*

> *I have all my papers at home ... I asked for everything to be photocopied and they did. Everybody has a right to know their legal status.*

> *Medicals ... do you have to have them? They thought I was mad basically ... taking me to all these medicals.*

According to what I have been told, my mother still has full parental rights over me now it is changed to 'being accommodated'...

The anxieties from both young people and carers about lack of information also referred to their specific rights and responsibilities under the Act.

Specific duties under the Act: the impact on the young people

Under the Children Act 1989, local authorities have a range of specific duties to young people they are looking after. These are clearly outlined in the Children Act 1989, Guidance and Regulations, Volume Four. Young people's views on just a few of these duties are expressed here.

Religious persuasion, racial origin, cultural and linguistic background

Section 22 of the Children Act 1989 specifies that 'due consideration' should be given to the child's religious persuasion, racial origin and cultural and linguistic background. In the Dolphin Project, particularly in areas where the population was predominantly white, carers had concerns how this could be implemented in practice. However, in one area, considerable efforts were being made to give 'due consideration' to race, religion and culture, but sometimes not all the young people 'owned' and understood the purpose of plans being made.

They tried to make me learn my language ... I don't want to learn it ... none of my other family speak it ... What I am trying to say is that they should have asked me if I wanted it in the first place ... I do stick to my culture ... I don't eat, I have always done that, my family does that.

They tried to force me to go to the Mosque ... come on they said, you are going today. What is the use of taking me when I am just going to walk out.

He got into trouble with one of the teachers because he was racist, and he only got into trouble because the teacher was racist (a complaint was made). The teacher had a very bad reprimand.

Young people with disabilities

The Children Act 1989 has specific responsibilities to help young people with disabilities lead as normal a life as possible. Only one such person took part in the project. This young person needed braille paper for writing short stories which was her hobby. She also needed braille paper for her homework. She was accommodated in a setting with other young people without disabilities. Unfortunately, the carers did not know what services she was entitled to and as a result she spent her own pocket money on her braille paper. Joining the Dolphin Project was very empowering for this young woman who then went on to take responsibility for making her life go the way 'she wanted'.

Planning meetings and reviews

Central to the care of young people being looked after were the decisions taken at planning meeting and reviews.

Before a child or young person is accommodated, the local authority has a duty to draw up a plan in writing with the child and parents, and this plan has to be scrutinised within four weeks of the placement. The purpose of the plan is to promote and safeguard the child's welfare and should include, after consultation with the child and the parents, a list of the child's identified needs (including needs arising from race, culture, religion or language, disability, health), how those needs will be met, the aim of the plan and timescale, the proposed placement, arrangements for seeing and being reunified with parents, the extent to which the child and his parents have been consulted, arrangements for dealing with disagreements or complaints; future educational plans for the child and dates of future reviews (The Children Act 1989, Guidance and Regulations, Vol. 4, 2.17–2.20, pp. 41–42).

Local authorities are required to review the case of a child within four weeks of his or her first being looked after, then within three months of this review; thereafter not more than six months after the previous review. Parents and children should participate in the review, and there should be consultation with all those involved. In addition to those matters considered in the original plan, the review should consider whether the current placement is appropriate, whether it meets the child's needs; whether there is a need to appoint an independent visitor and where appropriate plans for reunification with parents or plans for aftercare (The Children Act 1989, Guidance and Regulations, Vol. 4, 3.1–3.26, pp. 58–64).

However, many young people who took part in the project were not able to participate in their reviews, and consequently felt it was a waste of time attending. They also felt intimidated by large meetings. Sometimes they would have preferred not to have certain people there but felt unable to say so. They felt things were better where they had a quiet discussion before their review with their social worker/key worker and where planning meetings and reviews were held at times convenient to families and the young person.

How can I speak ... they are talking about my family ... I can't talk about what I want with them there.

I have been to one ... I did speak but I did not say everything I wanted to say. I couldn't really say it in case I upset my key worker.

When I found out things did not change, I did not bother to go.

It is better to talk to your social worker first, you can tell her what you think.

It is just a waste of time ... they are always making the decisions aren't they? They are not speaking to you, they are just telling you what you have to do.

Can I take someone else along to my review?

[At reviews] when you have something to say, they do not give you enough time to get it out.

If you had a choice of where to have the review/planning meeting, I think it would be better out in the community away from the children's home.

They say they will let you know and then they don't, not until the next review.

A key issue at planning meetings and reviews were young people's views about contact with their family.

Contact with families

The Children Act makes is absolutely clear that children should have contact with their families, unless there are reasons specified by the court why this should not happen. This contact should not only be promoted at planning and review meetings but by letters, telephone calls, exchange of photographs. It is acknowledged that contact with a child's family is important even when there may not be any possibility of returning home. However, the local authority also have a duty to give due consideration to the child's wishes and feelings about seeing their parents, and other members of his or her family and family friends. (The Children Act 1989, Guidance and Regulations, Vol. 4 4,1–4.41, pp. 65–73).

Young people in the project welcomed the greater efforts that are to be made under the Children Act 1989 to keep families together. A number of young people were bitter that, in the past, they had been removed from their families unnecessarily. The dilemma in the partnership relationship is, whose views should rule the day? Those of the parents or those of the young person? The project highlighted the wisdom of listening to the young people. Most young people knew whether or not they wanted contact with their family, and wanted their views respected, even if this might involve an element of risk to them. When their views were not respected, they sometimes found other means of achieving what they wanted.

We should try hard to stick with our families.

For a start I don't think children should be taken away. Like now they try to keep you with your parents as much as possible. We did not have any help at all, we were just whisked away that was it.

You should be allowed to go and see your family unless you are in danger. But if you are not in danger, I think you should be allowed to see your family when you want to. At the moment my social worker is saying no, but I am still going behind her back and going to see them.

At the end of the day everyone has to have contact with their family ...

Under the Children Act you are supposed to stay near your parents and family ... but if you have been sexually abused (you get moved away).

When they tell ME it is a good idea to see my family, I tell them where to go.

If there is a family they should be put together ... in my case ... that would have helped us to stick together ... now we are separated we are all split up ... if they did some rearranging they could keep most of the families together.

There was this girl ... a really lonely girl ... very timid and shy ... they said they couldn't get her a place with her sister. She moved with my foster mother ... she played up ... then they put her to live with her sister ... Now that could have been done all along because there were beds. I asked the social worker and she told me they did it to see how they would act if they were apart.

They are children and when they take you away from your Mam at such a young age it does affect you badly ... why are social workers doing this?

I have been away for so long I don't want to go home. My Dad used to be battering me every day, and I don't want that any more ... I can't put up with all that.

Young people being looked after, and separated from their families, are very isolated, especially when things are going wrong for them.

Problems, disagreements and complaints

An essential criteria in empowerment is the facility to make a complaint if the young person feels this is necessary. Section 26(3) of the Children Act 1989, requires the responsible authority to establish a procedure for considering any complaint made to them by any child who is being looked after by them, or who is not being looked after by them but is in need. Further details on how this should be implemented are given in the Children Act 1989, Guidance and Regulations, Vol. 4, 5.1–5.56, pp. 74–87.

In this study, the complaints procedure was better known than most parts of the Children Act 1989. Most young people had heard about it, and some had made use of it to good advantage. This seemed to be where they were supported in making their complaint. Others did not bother because they felt they could not get the help they needed, or as it was part of social services, they thought they would not get anywhere.

> I knew that it wasn't right, but I didn't know what it was, and I didn't know what to do about it. Everybody should know about the complaints procedure.

> Complaints procedure? They are not around ... I had to ask. You have to ask for them ... They don't have them on display.

> People who live independently (age 16 plus) aren't told about the complaints procedure. I haven't been told anything.

> When you complain, they are supposed to come back and tell you.

> I made a complaint once, but I don't know what happened to it.

> Complaints procedure? I don't need it!

Aftercare

One of the major anxieties for young people being looked after was what would happen to them after they left care.

An important new right for young people under the Children Act is that local authorities not only now have a duty to prepare young people they are looking after for the time when they cease to be looked after but they also have powers and duties to provide aftercare advice and assistance to such young people. These powers and duties extend until a young person is 21 years old (Children Act 1989, section 24). In certain circumstances, for example, if the local authority has made a grant to help a young person continue with education or training, this may extend after 21 until he or she finishes their course. Preparation for leaving care is clearly outlined in the Children Act, Guidance and Regulations, Volume 4 and includes helping young people to develop such skills as cooking, budgeting, to learn about personal and sexual relationships, how to apply for benefits, and acquire a knowledge of services and resources. Young people leaving care not only have a right to advice and information but may, in certain circumstances, receive assistance in cash or in kind, and if he or she cannot return to their family, the local authority has a statutory duty to ensure accommodation is provided for such single homeless young people whom they assess as vulnerable. (The Children Act 1989, Guidance and Regulations, Vol. 4, 7.1–7.102, pp. 97–113).

Young people who took part in the project, especially those soon to leave care, were sceptical about the promises of the Act. They did not feel they had the necessary preparation for leaving care and they did not know how to achieve help if they needed it after leaving care.

Aftercare ... I don't want to think about it.

Aftercare ... is that like 'afterlife' ... reincarnation!

At home I started cooking at nine. When I was in care I did not start until I was 13.

Can I change a plug? ... we are not allowed to do any of that at the home. We get an electrician in.

Social services ... they can't just leave me because I would get into a lot of trouble.

Money is the biggest problem on leaving care.

I visited my old home (residential establishment) and it was quite painful when I was told to go away. No one told me that I would have nothing. I can't afford to eat, let alone pay for train fares (to visit DSS office). That's why I want to join the army.

I think I am ready to be out of care ... but it makes you frightened ... even though social services are a load of c–p there is security that there is always somebody there. They said I was capable ... and although I've been in care nine years, they can't just put me out.

The Children Act 1989, Guidance and Regulations, Volume 4 outlines in considerable detail the possible needs of young people being looked after, and ways in which these needs may be met. However, some things that were especially important to the young people were sometimes given a lesser priority in this Guidance.

Empowerment and participation, issues important to young people

The importance of choice

Many young people are at a disadvantage in the decision-making process because they have not had the experience or the opportunity to develop the necessary skills to participate. Guidance and Regulations on the Children Act do specify that all children need to be given information and appropriate explanations so that they are in a position to develop views and make choices. But, young people who took part in this study felt it was important that they had *more* opportunities to make real choices in their lives. Not just big choices about where to live, and who to live with, but choices about the day-to-day running of their establishment, involvement in making up the rules of the establishments, running residents meetings, involvement in how services should be provided when they left care.

> *I did not want to go to boarding school ... don't let them trick you, that's what they did to me.*

> *We did not really have a choice. I was split from my brother and sister.*

> *The only choice I have had is where I would live when I left the children's home.*

> *Life story work ... I said no, I did not want to do it ... but my brother had to do it. It is not fair. They wrote 'when you were five your mother died.' Then my social worker said she wanted me to see a psychiatrist ... to help me get over my grief ... I said I had got over it ... she said I had not got over it properly ...*

> *Choices? yes I do get choices and I like this (choosing food, involvement in residents' meetings, etc).*

The choices young people have in many cases is related to how much money you have or how much money you can anticipate that you may have at some time.

Allowances

Although money is, for most of us, central to our lives, it is strange how often the importance of this is overlooked when working with young people in care. Money, and knowing how much you can expect, is power. Money matters, in one way or another, generated more discussion in this project than anything else. Young people needed to know about their likely allowances in order to make choices in their day-to-day lives, and to plan their future. Young people were severely disempowered by the arbitrary way many decisions relating to pocket money and other allowances appeared to be made.

You need to know about money.

They don't tell you about pocket money.

We all get the same ... no matter what age you are.

We spend most of our pocket money on hair things and the like ...

I went to Germany and I got some money ...

You can apply for money ... but you don't always get it. Aunt and Uncle get a small allowance for me ... things like trips and a new bike ... that is not out of the money they are given ...

Can you get a grant if you go to college?

I have to have some special paper for braille ... do I have to pay for this out of my money? I have to pay £1.35 for the paper ... for homework and for general writing ... I like writing stories ...

Some kids get more than others. I was a bit spoilt because I helped.

If you don't ask you don't get it. They don't tell you what you are entitled to ... they are just saving money.

It ought to be written down the money you're entitled to.

It would be fairer if there were set allowances ... but some kids have special needs.

Overcoming the stigma of 'care'

One of the major concerns that came up in all the Dolphin groups was the stigma of being in care.

All young people complained of the considerable unequal opportunities as a result of being looked after. Some of this inequality was related to the crippling effects of being an 'object of concern'. They were often distressed that 'special allowances' were made for them at school and elsewhere because they were in 'care'. Empowering young people who are being looked after may mean treating them like any other young person; in particular, having similar expectations for their behaviour and achievements.

When you say you are in a children's home, people think you are a tramp or something.

When they know you are in care, they let you off when you have been bad. I want to be treated the same ...

You say you are in care and lots of people feel sorry for you. I hate that feeling, because it makes you feel really awful.

Fostered? With me I say it is my family ... it avoids problems.

Tell them about care ... not for their sympathy ... but so they can know how we really are.

Perhaps related to this stigma is the difficulty many young people found in developing valued relationships.

Relationships

This topic was brought up by young people in all the groups. Meaningful relationships give purpose to life. Many young people who have been in care and who may have moved around from placement to placement may not have had the opportunity to make and keep friends. The Children Act Guidance and Regulations note that the capacity to form satisfying relationships and achieve interdependence with others is crucial to the future well-being of the young person. Empowering young people is therefore about helping them to form other relationships and other contacts.

I find it hard to explain, but because I have been brought up in children's homes I find it really hard to form relationships. It is probably because I have been brought up in care, and have kept moving around.

I have nothing in common with anyone who has not been in care ... I am 17 going on 40 ... how can you sit there and talk about cars all night ... the biggest problem they have had is how to get the newest BMW.

Many young people make their best friends at school. For some young people being looked after, this was not possible.

Education issues

Children who have been looked after by local authorities often need extra help and encouragement, and opportunities to compensate for early deprivation and for educational disadvantage. Local authorities are specifically reminded that, in looking after young people, they should have regard to the importance of continuity of education and that they should provide educational opportunities and support (Children Act 1989, Guidance and Regulations, Vol. 4, 1.105–1.114, pp. 21–22). However, up to a third of young people who took part in the Dolphin Project were out of school/further education/work training. The number of children in residential care who are out of school overall may be even higher. In each area, education was raised by young people as a matter of concern. In all areas there were young people 'being looked after' who were missing out on schooling, not getting sufficient help in returning to school, and some young people were not getting the necessary peace and quiet to do homework. Many of the young people we spoke to wanted much more support and help in their education. In some residential establishments being out of school was the 'norm' rather than the exception. A young person who is in care needs a powerful advocate to ensure equality of opportunity, and that means equality of access to education.

I have missed loads and loads of schooling. I want home tutoring.

I'm not at school at the moment ... I don't fit into normal comprehensive ... there is no help or encouragement to go back to school.

No-one listens when I tell them I am bullied.

I passed into grammar school ... I misbehaved (and was suspended) it was all this moving about (in care).

I went back to the fifth year again because I moved around in care. I have been out of school for four months.

There is no quiet room at X ... If you want to be quiet you have to go to the toilet.

I get no help with any form of homework.

I wish I had stayed at the same school because every children's home I went to I changed school. One day I woke up and thought I am not getting anywhere. The teacher said you are a 'no hoper', you will leave school with nothing ... but ... [he is now at college].

Bullying could be a reason why a young person did not feel able to be at school, but bullying was also a problem in residential establishments.

Bullying

Empowerment in child protection is also about protecting young people from significant harm after they come to be looked after. Local authorities have a duty under the Children Act to safeguard and promote the welfare of those they are looking after (Children Act 1989, Section 22(3)). However, the level of bullying in residential establishments mentioned by some young people in the project, and the apparent inability of the staff to contain this, fell far short of the principles of the legislation.

I am not being disgusting, but the kids run riot in XX home.

*When we were getting bullied, my Dad said something to the head.
That home had a reputation for that ... it is closed down now.*

There is so ... much aggro in there and the kids were really horrible.

*I was at this children's home. The kids used to pick on my brother ... I
used to stick up for my brother and then I would get the shit kicked out
of me ... we complained but they did not do anything.*

*You really do have to stick up for yourselves in some children's homes
... you really do.*

*My brother was lying there and someone else was punching him bad ...
and a member of staff standing there doing nothing. I said ... you
should be sorting this out ... she said I am not going to get hurt and I
had to threaten her so she would help my brother.*

*I've had a really hard time ... I've been picked on and bullied ... . If
you tell the social workers you are known as a grasser and get even more
... .*

*I have seen him coming down in the morning crying ... it is so bad ...
now like today ... he did not want to eat ... he did not want to work ...
he is not usually like that.*

Citizens of the future

The young people who took part in the Dolphin Project will, like
other young people who have been looked after, go out into the
world to become tomorrow's citizens and parents. The young people
we spoke to did not feel they had been adequately prepared for these
responsibilities.

At the start of this chapter we summarised some of the core principles in the Children Act 1989; the paramountcy of the child's welfare; the status attached to the child's wishes and feelings and the
duty of local authorities to safeguard and promote his or her welfare
while he or she is being looked after. Most of the young people who
took part in the Dolphin Project had originally come into care
before the implementation of the Children Act 1989. The irony is
that many of them were originally placed in care to protect them
from harm. They were disadvantaged before they came into care
(Bebbington and Miles, 1989). They were further disadvantaged by
having been in care.

But, what was exciting about the Dolphin Project was, as we have
seen, that the young people had very positive and relevant things to
say about how their lives could be improved. From the many things

they said, perhaps their two most important messages were to hear what they were saying, and to give them the information they needed in order to make the decisions that affected their lives.

Hearing what young people are saying

The starting point is finding ways to hear what young people are saying. Young people who are being looked after become expert at saying what they are expected to say. They are highly selective with whom they share their innermost wishes and feelings. In our research, we found they shared different types of information in different settings. For example, the information that came from the group settings was very different from the information given on the questionnaires. In the relaxed group settings, young people were prepared to share with us very sensitive issues, for example, their distress at being bullied and their attempts to end their lives. They would never have given this sort of information in a questionnaire and even in one to one interviews it would be unlikely to emerge. Young people were empowered by such groups and valued them for the opportunities to share common experiences with other young people in care. 'I never knew other people felt the same way', was a common response. They wanted such groups to be more readily available. Happily, we were able to arrange for the groups to continue in each of the three authorities. In Birmingham the Children's Rights Officer gathered up the nucleus of the Dolphin Project for regular group meetings. In Berkshire, a similar group was set up. In Hampshire, the local authority set up its own *Listening to Children Project* (Buchanan, in press), and some young people joined forums for planning services. It is hoped that such groups can become commonplace.

Young people told us that, for one-to-one discussions, they generally chose their carers, because carers were around and know them better than their social workers. Some carers, however, felt that they did not have the skills to communicate effectively with young people particularly if they were severely distressed. But, come what may, carers are undertaking this important role, and it is imperative that their skills are recognised and developed.

The need for information

All the necessary information is in the Children Act 1989 and in the accompanying volumes of Guidance and Regulations. But how many carers have read the Guidance and Regulations cover to cover, let alone the Children Act? Information is power; when young people are growing up, developing the skill of using information and making decisions is an essential training for citizenship. In the Dolphin Project, carers felt anxious about sharing information with young people because they were concerned that 'things would get out of control'.

The courage of the Dolphin carers who facilitated us speaking to 'their' young people needs to be acknowledged. At the Dolphin meetings the young people were very eager for information and took away some £80 of Children Act leaflets and Children's Legal Centre documents. To our surprise, most of the young people used the information they received, responsibly. But, they did make appropriate demands on the system. A young woman with visual impairment refused to have her review until her advocate could be present. Another young person insisted on attending a child protection conference and yet another found a way to persuade her mother to let her live with her.

Information is not something that can be handed over in a book. It needs to be available when it is needed and opportunities need to be made for issues to be discussed. Carers who took part in the project were anxious that, if the young people had information and they did not, this disempowered them as carers and misunderstanding arose. For effective participation, information had to be freely available to all parties.

During the last year, the Dolphin team at Southampton has been developing a handbook for residential and foster carers which will meet some of these needs both to communicate and to share information. The funding for this work has come from Central Council for Education and Training in Social Work. It is to be called *Answers: Handbook for Residential and Foster Carers* and will be published in March 1994 by Longman. The aim of this book is to act as a 'talking tool' (Wheal & Buchanan, in press) which carers and young people can use together. It contains a wide range of basic information about the Children Act, as well as practical information such as how to get a job. It also contains a number of paper tools for eliciting worries that young people may have. Readers are referred to specific pages of the Children Act 1989, Guidance and Regulations for further information on specific topics.

Answers is only a start, but it is hoped that other people will find further ways of hearing what young people are saying, and of sharing the information with them which is their right. In the long run, this may lead to the Children Act 1989 having the impact that was intended, and the young people who are being looked after receiving both the quality of service to which they are entitled, and the preparation they deserve in order to become valued citizens of the future.

Acknowledgements

The Dolphin project would not have been possible without those who took part: first, the young people who had the courage to come along; secondly, the residential and foster carers who gave us the benefit of their knowledge and experience and finally, the three local authorities: Berkshire County Council, Birmingham City Council and Hampshire County Council who took the risk of letting us talk to young people they were looking after. I would also like to acknowledge the skills of our group facilitators, Ann Wheal, Daphne Walder and Sue Macdonald who made it feel OK to come along to the Dolphin Project.

The young people themselves took part in the hope that, by sharing their thoughts and experiences with us, this would help other young people who were looked after by local authorities in the future. It is in this spirit that this chapter is written.

References

Bebbington, A. and Miles, J. (1989) 'The background of children who enter local authority care', *British Journal of Social Work*, 19, pp. 349–368.

Buchanan, A., Wheal, A., Walder, D., Macdonald, S. and Coker, R. (1993) 'Answering back', Report by Young People Being Looked After on the Children Act 1989. CEDR, Department of Social Work Studies, University of Southampton.

Buchanan, A. (in press) *The Children Act 1989: Partnership in Practice.* Avebury.

Butler-Sloss, E. (1988) *The Cleveland Report.* London: HMSO.

Department of Health (1991) *The Children Act 1989: Guidance and Regulations, Residential Care*, Volume 4. London: HMSO.

Department of Health (1991) *Child Abuse – Study of Inquiry Reports 1980–1989.* London: HMSO.

Department of Health and Social Security (1985) Review of Child Care Law. London: HMSO.

Department of Health and Social Security (1987) *The Law on Child Care and Family Services.* London: HMSO.

Hawes, J. M. (1991) *The Children's Rights Movement. A History of Advocacy and Protection.* Boston USA: Twayne Publishers, Hall & Co.

Newell, P. (1991) The UN convention and Children's Rights in the UK. *National Children's Bureau*, London.

Race Relations Act (1976). London: HMSO.

Sex Discrimination Act (1985). London: HMSO.

The Children Act (1989). London: HMSO.

United Nations (1989) *The Convention on the Rights of the Child.* UNICEF.

Wheal, A. & Buchanan, A. (1994) *Answers: Handbook for Residential and Foster Carers*, Longman.

8 Issues for children and young people in local authority accommodation

Chris Wilson

> My foster parent is in a fight with the Social Services over my banding and whether I claim benefit when I'm eighteen in a few weeks' time. If they can't sort it out, I've been told I've got to leave on my birthday, and the baby is due in two weeks. I've got no say in it. Michelle

> I had six foster homes in two years and now I've been in one I really like for two years. But they took me out the day after Mum [foster] smacked me when I nicked money from her purse. I haven't got a bed now and there's three other kids in this house and my Christmas presents are waiting in my bedroom. I want to go home. [Christmas was in two weeks] Andrew

The first young person was caught up in a dispute over which she had no control. The child focus was temporarily lost, and the young person concerned was slipping between the safety nets.

Andrew was the subject of an over-zealous child protection procedure which was fundamentally affecting his delicate emotional balance, having suffered abuse most of his life. All agencies were doing what was 'best for him', but his current circumstances were now reflecting something very different for him.

Neither of these young people had the information, or confidence to use it, that might have, first, restored a child focus to the situation, or, secondly, presented the Social Services Department with an experience from which to develop better ways of handling such situations for other children in the future.

Michelle, from both her background and years in care, had never possessed either the information or the necessary confidence, and had felt power differentials acutely.

This young person, castigated for her dependence on care, was only one of a handful of young people independent enough to seek advocacy help in a power-play situation in which she was no more than a pawn, whilst being surrounded by caring professionals who only had her best interests at heart.

The caring establishment

These young people were part of a caring establishment that had already accepted the moral framework of the UN Convention on the Rights of the Child, particularly Articles 12, 13 and 17, and understood the legal framework particularly of section 17, 22, 26 of the Children Act, 1989. The local authority concerned had a separate children's complaints procedure and a policy that states that it 'actively encourages comments and representations concerning the delivery and nature of its services'.

In other words, the rights to complain as a process were in place, together with the moral and legal basis for establishing a child's right to participation, but was it empowering children in residential care to speak and be heard? In the words of Gerison Lansdown from the Children's Rights Development Unit, would it

> ensure children in residential care have information appropriate for their age with which to form opinions? Would it provide them with meaningful opportunities to express their views and explore options, and would professionals listen to those views and consider them with respect and seriousness? (Lansdown, 1993)

Experience of children speaking about their care would suggest otherwise, and encourages the view that children and young people looked after are subject to a particular caring services bureaucracy and dynamic that reflect Social Services Departments' individual and institutional views of children's rights issues. Most other professionals have a more distinct role than Social Services Departments. Social Workers complain with conviction that they are a catch-all service whose roles overlap with education, psychology, health, and the law. Particular policy failures in these areas are the stuff of social workers' cases, and society does not seem to award social workers credibility in their intervention in these ambiguous roles.

Achievement of credibility in the present climate is felt to lie within fast and consistant assessment and intervention. For that, you need a complex and consistant set of procedures; particularly in high profile areas such as Child Protection. Policy, resource priorities, and practices can become firmly dictated by these procedures. In fact, many comment that child-care generally appears to be driven by child protection procedures. Eventually, emphasis becomes focussed on processes rather than outcomes for children.

Quality services

Kieron Walsh (1991) commenting on quality in public services, argues that, as the market-based approach of the public services is extended to professional services, such as Social Service departments, there is a need to develop more sophisticated approaches to quality specification, primarily because of the shifting values of society.

> It is difficult to conceive of the production of high quality of public services without considering the role of the client. User-evaluation will always be an element of the analysis of the quality of public services (Walsh, 1991).

Quality attempts appear presently to be top-down mechanisms intended to ensure that good service is produced in the first place. However, again Kieron Walsh writes that

> it is arguable that it is not possible to state and monitor the quality of human services as it is for products, and quality assurance is missing because of the shifting nature of consumer evaluation. Expectations rise and we compare our experiences with others. We must adapt to constantly shifting evaluations.

There are indications from children that evaluation does not happen and their lives in residential care are driven by control mechanisms in the form of 'correct processes'. These cannot look at outcomes unless constantly shifting evaluations are made of children's views. As these are largely absent, we have only processes and not outcomes.

For example, it was more important that Andrew and the fostercarers family were the subject of blanket and separate child protection investigation and conferences than looking at the possible outcomes for them. Professionals could have worked back from the type of incident to look at procedures that were available and appropriate for that situation. The principle now appears to be that bases must be covered, and that those bases must be somehow capable of evaluation. There becomes greater emphasis on inspection services and audit, and much more comprehensive complaint procedures. Letting a case generate its own laws becomes dangerous practice because, very likely, such an approach will miss out essential items on the checklist of procedures.

This is a modern and ever-increasing pressure that causes particular anxiety in social workers talking to children. It is a pressure that most would concede is highly necessary in the complex environment in which case planning takes place.

However, it is entirely possible that the sum total of the checklist boxes do not amount to a child's concept of his or her reality. And what is child focus anyway? Is it that which the child wishes and believes is right, or is it what professionals believe is best for them? In the climate described above, it is clear that there are extreme pressures to follow the latter view, and, if it all goes wrong, there is an expectation that the child will be able to complain to the new comprehensive inspection services.

The role of advocates

In reality, it is not surprising that few do complain. An independent or internal children's advocate's most difficult task is to establish effective and meaningful links with the individuals and teams who make up the services. These links must have a distinct purpose and credibility that are, in practice, difficult to establish; based as they must be on education of the social workers to see advocacy in an unthreatening way, rather, as primarily a remedy for what is structurally a highly expressive situation for children and secondly as a practice filter that should be integral in every caseworking situation. In fact, it should mimic the way equal opportunity plans should operate.

Given the dynamics of the social work situation, it is easy to see why case workers might perceive advocacy as both a threat and a discomfort. With ever-increasing complex situations to assess, and ever-decreasing budgets, they work within tight resources and practice parameters towards assessment and proposed remedies or caseplans; that is, processes. Anything that introduces more variables into a highly elastic situation requires more work, more resources, more fine judgement, and less power over desired or correct processes and procedures.

The often missing variable is what the child wishes and will be committed to. Therefore, making the child's agenda outcome more likely is often professionally difficult. It requires a cultural shift to see that filtering practice to uphold children's views is not about inherent criticism of current practice but of an attention to a much neglected area. Professionals should not feel threatened by children's views or advocacy services.

There is little doubt that children's rights on the general Social Services agenda is either largely absent or tokenistic. For example, in England and Wales, comprising over 100 local authorities able to employ advocates, the Children's Right Association lists nine internal Social Services advocates and eight jointly or semi-independently funded external advocates. Client children and young people exist as professional cases which professionals have ownership of, and responsibility for. Many workers therefore have strong views about apparently non-case-related, semi-independent interventions by perceived quasi-inspectorial agencies. This possibly applies whether it is by an outside agency or an internal 'arms length' unit. Potential case criticism and non-therapeutic intervention are seen negatively therefore, by powerful gatekeepers.

Perhaps there is a further restriction in that, as accommodated children's views are partial, in the sense that they are only related to Social Services Department experiences, Social Services Departments tend to believe they own and pay for such views. That, translated, means their views are not for general consumption.

The low numbers of children in residential care who take up children's advocacy services reflect both these service dynamics and their surrounding by authority figures who traditionally know what's best for them. They have received partial, pre-selected information, if at all, and usually that information has not been contextualised for them. After experiencing months or years of such a system, they have not the information or the confidence to have opinions. Those opinions they do have affect outcomes very little. It is a remote power agenda they become used to having no influence upon.

The isolation of accommodated children

Perhaps a further factor is the relative isolation of accommodated children and young people. Placement is carried out on a case-by-case basis, dependent on the availability of homes, and on the services of particular fostercarers who, in rural communities particularly, are scattered geographically. Young people are not generally aware of other young people accommodated elsewhere, or of the support that might be available from them. Very few authorities make extensive use of general groups, although they may be involved in small, usually semi-therapeutic groups of children with similar backgrounds of abuse. There seems little enthusiasm for large-scale grouping which may very understandably be first about a fear of contamination, and secondly about concern for reinforcing children's views of themselves, not as individual people, but as abused children.

Many professionals believe that children are not interested in such groups in any case. However true that might be, the reasons may have more to do with children having no conception of what groups are or could do for them. They are not used to being heard in any case, and why should a group make a difference to that.

> I have left care now, but I got a lot of help from Julie. Her dad abused her, like mine did, but I didn't meet her until my last year. I used to get angry and shout a lot because I thought this had only happened to me. My foster mum used to talk to me but she didn't understand like Julie did. We didn't speak much about it because we both [Julie] knew. When it went bad at home [foster], they wanted to put me in another, but Julie and me got together and said we wanted our own place now. In the end they found us a place and came to see us instead. It is working out really well. I couldn't have done it without Julie, and I think about the other girls in my place and how it would have been a lot better if we could have got together before (Andrea).

In Andrea's case, and for many other children in foster care, having no peer group support actually prolonged her view of herself as different, and had the effect of destroying any mechanism for obtaining her and other's group views of services. It denied them the chance to generate sufficient self-confidence to express those views. Of course, it also denied the Social Services Department the chance of any testing out of their services with young people.

Having said that, it appears that the situation may be structurally different for young people in residential homes. In recent years, there has been a move away from residential provision nationally following the publicity and notoriety of particular homes where abusive care regimes have been in operation. This, combined with the significant expense of large establishments, queries about standards of residential social work training and the emphasis on local authority permanence planning programmes, has caused some authorities to abandon the concept altogether.

However, evidence indicates that children in small family group homes have the opportunity of peer group support which reduces isolation and builds confidence. Equality of care standards is also more likely as the young people are more aware of comparative care standards and can also resolve group problems faster than individual ones. Perhaps such homes are more able, structurally, to attract the attention of inspection services when problems are building than in foster homes where often examination of care standards appears less critically examined until after a serious event has occurred.

It is worth noting that the children in small family group homes are often there because they chose that facility, if it is available, rather than foster-care because it lessens the conflict of loyalties between their own parents and foster parents. By doing so, they are exercising their belief of what is right for them in a positive way. However, there are very few family group homes compared with the number of children looked after in the UK.

Large residential institutions, although rapidly declining, still represent a significant part of residential provision in this country, and there is no indication that isolation, although in a different form, is less of a reality for children accommodated within them. It is generally accepted that young people in such institutions suffer considerably more stigma than their fostered counterparts. This can lead children, who may already be blaming themselves for abuse and for being there at all, to see themselves as different at best, and second-class as worst. Despite the protestations of such institutions, it is inevitable that childen are less individualised, more subject to blanket rules and restrictions, and more competitive for attention than in other care provisions. They are often just as geographically isolated from their families as fostered children, and have had less choices about the nature of their placement.

A combination of this internalising of negative feelings of self, less personalised attention, less family support, degrees of institutionalisation, and much geater bureaucracy, does not encourage a young person to seek information or express views with confidence. Children's agendas are clearly less likely and less able to be met within large residential institutions despite the best efforts of staff within them.

In a sense, isolation is yet another structural hurdle for children in shaping future service provision. It also exacerbates all the dynamic facts mentioned earlier, including protectionist attitudes, fear of practice criticism and process rather than outcomes. Lastly, it reinforces artificial passivity in young people and contributes to institutional inertia.

Children's rights services

Responses to this situation are slow in appearing. They consist of mainly semi-independent and small-scale internal or external children's rights services, if there is any provision at all. These tend to reflect high-level cautious vision in Social Services Departments rather than worker-level informed demand. These services are entering an area at the very beginning of recognition of the desirability of such services, and without universal approval or the correct structures in place.

There can be no denying that the slow chipping away by single advocates within the caring services who continue to show little enthusiasm to get informed, is an exhaustingly slow and intensely conflictual battle. It is one which will reap very small numbers of children who wish to be represented, and therefore there is always the danger that its inherently conflictual nature may be a cumulative burden that neither social services nor advocate will wish to bear. Perhaps then, in this context, it might seem strange strategy that we see the mission as attempting first the children's rights reform of Social Services Departments. This is an institution with the most oppressive power over children, the least motivation in practice to make a cultural shift, the most power as gate-keepers to prevent intrusive outside intervention, and the most adept at translating intrinsic inertia into the acceptable language of evolution. Such reform is being attempted without a change in current Social Services Department structures, without the cultural shifts necessary for consensual approval, and by a handful of single advocates. Perhaps the nautical equivalent is attempting to pull a supertanker off its present course with a piece of thread.

The question now is, are institutions paying lip service to a 'politically correct' ideal that is ahead of its time? In many local authorities this is highly likely, but children are oppressed and without civil rights now. There can be no waiting for the institutions and society to decide when chidren's rights have come of age.

Such arguments are not about hopelessness, but about turning the rhetoric of 'we want to listen to children and will pay for the privilege', into a form of practice reality within such institutions. Without reality there can be no effective strategy. So what is the way forward?

Moving forward in terms of children receiving residential care requires not only a study of the reality of contemporary Social Services Department practice, but an understanding of existing caring service strengths on which to build. Despite the criticisms of culture, structure and climate made in this paper, there are considerable positives to be understood and used.

It is an old adage that one should see the advantage in every apparent disadvantage. Social Services Departments are used to change. Some might think that often there seems no period of development and consolidation between Social Services organisational changes, as there are so many changes. If that is the case then the integration of a children's rights filter should be more viable than in a traditionalist agency. In fact, they have been known to change extremely fast once the political correctness of a potential change is accepted. Structurally, personnel turnover in Social Services Departments is reasonably active, and this factor alone does not allow people to be rooted in past practices.

However, the biggest positive may be the social workers themselves. Their constant battle against the ambiguity of their role encourages a sense of professionalism and duty despite their difficulties. I have personally known very few local authority workers who were not caring, or had not what they believed to be the best interests of their children at heart.

This is not meant to be patronising, but perhaps pointing out that I believe social workers would prefer not to deal with hopeless situations past the point of effective recovery. They know as well as anyone that more informed, more confident children have fewer problems because they are less vulnerable to adults who try to take advantage of their lack of knowledge about the world they live in.

John, in residential school, became suspicious of a master who was continually hanging around a boys' dormitory on various pretexts. He knew it was not right, but was listened to by management who stopped this master's practice before anything happened.

Social workers know that less-vulnerable children also mean fewer problems for themselves, and that few chidren will use information as destructive weapons. Even if they did, they would have as much right to do so as adults.

It may, therefore, be only a matter of education rather than persuasion to integrate children's rights filters. Training in Social Services Departments is taken very seriously by both workers and management. That again bodes well for the future, and the eventual move from 'interest' courses to mandatory may not prove too difficult a hurdle.

Ways forward

In fact, the way forward can only be in education; of children, of workers, of institutions, and of the community. It must lie in the application of scarce resources to preventative programmes of education both inside and outside the community which will result in cultural shifts. Such shifts may worry both the management and workers of large institutions when they begin to realise that neglecting children's rights will be seen in the same light as racism; that is, it's just unacceptable.

However, if we are looking first to change within large institutions given the arguments that have gone before, what can single children's rights officers do?

First thoughts are to the accessibility of information and procedures for children. This is not about the rhetoric of child-friendly 'cultures', but about a significant reduction in Social Services Department internal bureaucracy through the production of a local agreed standards document. Children and young people seeking decision-making find different ideas and different standards from the plethora of professionals who have some partial involvement with them. Decision-making becomes delayed and depersonalised, and every small matter travels up and down the professional levels. It may bear no relation to the young person's agenda by the time it is imparted to them. 'I'm sorry, it seems to be the policy and I can't do anything about it.' Such statements could be avoided if an agreed standards document were in force. If it had already been distributed to children in residential care, the problem might not have arisen in the first place. A clear standards document outlining the basics of what children can expect from care levels in foster homes and what, in residential institutions should be mandatory as a basis for empowering children in residential care.

Perhaps second thoughts should be about children's isolation in residential settings. It is now a government requirement that there should be an independent volunteer visiting service for children with poor or discontinued links with their families. Again, given the arguments elsewhere in this chapter, the question must be asked whether that is a sufficient remedy for the need for peer group support and confidence building of residential young people. Is the philosophy that children don't see themselves as accommodated but fully integrated into a foster family; and getting all the support they need there? Or should it be that accommodated children are receiving a similar service that should stand quality comparison with similar peers' experiences; and where group problems are more likely to be resolved quickly and effectively than if each goes it alone. My contention is that it is clearly the latter. That all children who wish it should have not only a visiting service but, through it, be able to meet in group settings, facilitated by Social Services Departments. Such settings would have a legitimacy not only to resolve problems but shape future service provision. They would groom young people to have the confidence and backing to present and use their new information.

The present situation is open to abuse in that it depends wholly on trust in, and information from, a whole variety of different people. I've no evidence that this trust is abused to any great extent, but if we call abuse the persuasive preselection of a particular option for a child, then there is little doubt that it happens. In Andrew's example, illustrated earlier, he was not told that an investigation could have been carried out in his existing foster home. If he had known that, he might have argued for that outcome or appointed someone to argue on his behalf at a much earlier stage.

Travelling forward further, and looking particularly at the single internal or external advocate role in a local authority, there is a need for maximum impact. Children are scattered geographically in most authorities, and it is desirable to physically integrate the advocate role within the agencies most associated with children, and in the local communities. Clinics based regularly in local health or education establishments may go some way towards increasing accessibility for scattered young people and making links with other services. These links benefit children in that they offer possible independent medical, legal and educational service opportunities that become options for young people. It is in this area that a discussion is needed about the existing style of reactive advocacy.

One can see that, in the current environment, it should be reactive. Advocates would be invading a child's privacy by holding information about them prior to any use that they wish to make of the service. That information would almost certainly emanate from Social Services Departments and therefore could not illustrate a holistic view of the child or young person. Rather, it would outline problems that pathologise and label a child and their family.

However, many feel that children with little information or confidence may need encouragement to use advocacy services, and that there should be proactive measures such as inviting advocates to scrutinise existing disputes between children and the department. They feel this should be the case particularly when dealing with young people in residential care. In many ways this is a Catch 22 situation, which is not capable of resolution in present circumstances. Linking advocates to other services who serve children in residential care may go some way towards a resolution, but it can be a dangerous position for a Social Services-funded advocate.

Opportunities for young people to pop their head out of the care network and perhaps come across a clinic advocate whilst they receive a legal or medical service are rare. But if they do, the experience allows a young person to meet others and align themselves with a non-residential reality.

Travelling further down the road to penetrating inertia with single advocates, there should be a concentration on service gaps in local authorities. This is where there is little professional 'ownership' or gate-keeping, least argument about non-therapeutic intervention, and young people are only marginally receiving a service. Such a gap frequently occurs with children about to leave care or for those who have technically, although not completely, left care.

Having said that, there are recent moves by some local authorities to resource this area more fully. It may be possible, more by default than design, to gather groups of young people and offer facilitation towards support/consumer groups, or perhaps even skills courses. Many local authorities will argue that they offer comprehensive leaving care packages, but often the reality is very different. It is particularly noticeable that six months to a year from leaving care, young people are often at a very low point and struggling on all fronts. Groups of these young people who are emerging from the care chrysalis and looking at an independent reality often have the most to say about their past care regimes. Their input, facilitated and organised, could energise local authorities to engage in a cultural shift that would introduce more radical visions of children's councils deeper within the residential provision. This should not be a radical vision, and it says a great deal about institutions who still believe that it is.

Without doubt, the greatest strides forward for children's rights in residential care must come from the education of professionals' attitudes towards seeing children as groups of people, not as cases, but as multi-dimensional and potentially self-activating people who have rights, and not just needs. Others working in this field and writing in this book have spoken about the challenge of moving from a needs model to a rights 'model'. This proposition seems particularly apt for work with children in residential care.

The question is whether professionals are ready to undertake this challenge in the current social work climate. There is not yet universal evidence of institutional management moves to provide mechanisms to listen to the views of children in residential care.

Furthermore, should not organisations be taking a more global view of children in need than those receiving services?

It is about calculated risk taking and investing in community education projects resourced sufficiently to have an impact on children's lives. Workers within such projects could act as local ombudsmen examining the ability of all child-related institutions to take on board children's views, forming children's focus groups, and taking up individual young people's issues. With a combined services backing they would have both a strong local voice, and work closely with all community institutions. Advocacy would be for all children with the establishment of community clinics. There would be a raised media profile on children's issues and, on an individual basis, the representation of children caught up in adult bureaucracy. Such projects would educate parent's groups, and, of course, represent children who are receiving the services of accommodation by the local authority.

A step further, or perhaps simultaneously, is the possible establishment of a Children's Commissioner to monitor the effectiveness of all services provided by councils and public bodies concerned with the care of children and young persons. This debate is currently under way and on the 20 January 1994, Lord Elis Thomas spoke concerning a Local Government (Wales) Bill in the House of Lords and the need for a Welsh Commissioner.

> The proposal for a complaints service to look at the needs of children in each principal council is for a local children's commissioner or a local ombudsman. This would be in the form of a representation or advocacy service and would relate not only to the functions of the principal councils but also to the associated functions of the health authorities and NHS trusts. That gives the opportunity for a comprehensive advocacy or representation service within each authority area.

He went on to describe the New Zealand model where the commissioner has the functions of

> monitoring and assessing the policies of any department, persons, or bodies which provide a service for children. The commissioner has the power to encourage the development of policy and services, to promote research, to enquire generally into the matters relating to children, to receive representations from the public and to increase public awareness.

Perhaps the primary difference between children's advocacy services and the commissioner would be the establishment of a statutory voice for children who cannot vote and who are very low on the political agenda. In a sense, the voice comes with the 'commissioner' territory, together with an immense ability to both co-ordinate children's welfare in and out of residential provision, and secure the right balance of resources for children from local authority funding.

These are not radical visions or even difficult ones to put into practice. They do, however, have the potential for making an external cultural shift that stimulates large institutions such as Social Services Departments to realise that they have no choice but to truly integrate children's views into their services.

Children are an oppressed group by the virtue of being children. Children who are residentially placed are 'protected', isolated, ill-informed, and mostly not listened to. Children who are from a different ethnic background, or who have a disability or a learning difficulty, suffer multiple oppression. As the tariff rises, so their ability lessens to get help from largely tokenistic advocate services.

It has been accepted for many years that children and young people who have the information and the confidence to shape more of their lives equate to less vulnerable children who are less likely to suffer abuse at the hands of adults. Must it not then be the case that adults' awareness of children's rights and the education of children are the central pillar of large-scale prevention and the eradication of the need for post abuse (and eventually advocacy) services?

References

Elis Thomas, D. (1994) *Hansard* 20th. Jan. p. 824.
Landsdown, G. (1992) NSPCC Research and Policy Forum, Cardiff.
Walsh, K. (1991) *Public Administration*, **69**, pp. 503–514.

9 Approaches to empowerment and participation in child protection

Ilan Katz

Until fairly recently clients' participation in decision-making was not a priority in social work, and clients' views of the social work process were not considered to be particularly valid indicators of social work effectiveness (see Marsh and Fisher, 1992). This resistance has been linked to 'professionalism' in social work, and the early use of psycho-dynamic and systemic theories as the basis of practice.

Some authors believe that task-centred and behavioural social work, because they are based on contracts, provide an alternative to the psycho-dynamic and systemic approaches. Clients have greater say in the content and outcomes of the work, and the contract is an open document so there is no 'hidden agenda'. However, behavioural approaches can be manipulative, relying on rewards and positive reinforcement. Similarly, tasks can be determined by workers rather than clients, so client participation is not guaranteed in these models.

The social welfare systems in which social work has functioned have also discouraged client involvement. In child protection, client participation in case conferences and reviews focussed on clients' rather than on professionals' actions. Professional accountability has been dealt with separately in supervision and appraisal. Clients have had no input into these processes.

In the 1960s, Arnstein (1969) advocated that members of the community should have more control in the funding and development of community programmes. Participation was seen as a 'radical' aspiration. The recent interest in participation, however, includes a 'new-right' agenda which aims to break the entrenched power of 'inefficient' public sector professionals (Braye and Preston-Shoot, 1992). This parallels a move towards more openness and accountability of public agencies to their consumers, and is allied with a concern for 'quality services' in which the main component of 'quality' is 'customer satisfaction'. It is arguably this combination of left and right political impetus which has led to a consensus that participation is 'a good thing' (Rojek et al., 1988). Nevertheless, current frameworks of partnership and participation are couched in individualist rather than collectivist terms, often in the language of consumerism (Croft and Beresford, 1990). The Children Act 1989 provided an individualist legal framework for client participation in the child protection system. Partnership with parents and ascertaining children's wishes and feelings are key principles within the Act.

In contrast to professional practice, research into clients' views has a relatively long history. The most celebrated early British study was by Mayer and Timms (1970). It was followed by a number of others, for example, Maluccio (1979). Phillimore (1981), Sainsbury et al. (1982). These authors found that most clients felt satisfied with their workers. However, clients and practitioners perceived the objectives of the work differently. Clients did not feel powerful in the practitioner/client relationship.

It is unclear whether these samples were representative of social services' clients, including children and young people, especially of those involved in child protection.

In the 1980s research focussed on ways of involving clients in decisions. The main areas were:

- access to information (for example, Ovretviet 1986; Shemmings, 1991)

- parental attendance at child protection conferences (McGloin and Turnbull, 1986; Shemmings and Thoburn, 1990; Thoburn, 1991)

- clients' perceptions of casework (Maluccio, 1979, Magura, 1982).

Studies have consistently found that both clients and practitioners have valued access to information and shared recording. Ovretviet (1986) and Shemmings (1991) showed that virtually all of clients agreed with provision of access. Practitioners initially resisted but subsequently felt that shared recording was effective and did not detract from child protection issues.

Research has shown some resistance by practitioners to parental participation in child protection conferences. Even so, more than 70 per cent felt that parental participation was helpful in making effective decisions and did not detract from the conference's ability to carry out its tasks (Lewis, 1992).

The two major factors determining successful parental involvement were first, preparation of both parents and workers, and secondly, the chairperson's ability to involve parents meaningfully in the discussion. All the studies found that full participation in conferences was necessary. Parents felt it was better not to participate than to attend only part of the conference.

The research has been less focussed on partnership in the casework process itself than on participation in child protection conferences. Marsh and Fisher (1992) found that most practitioners thought they were working in partnership with families but that the latter rarely felt that they were being treated as partners. Marsh and Fisher's study follows previous work on agreements (Corden and Preston-Shoot, 1987; Aldgate, 1990) in advocating that successful participation in casework depends largely on using written agreements.

Marsh and Fisher found that there were five principles guiding successful involvement in the casework process:

- investigation of problems must be with the explicit consent of the potential user

- user agreement or statutory mandate are the exclusive basis of partnership-based intervention

- intervention must be based on the views of all relevant family members and carers

- services must be based on negotiated agreement rather than on assumptions about the behaviour and wishes of users

- users must have the greatest possible choice in the services that are offered.

They consider that a task-centred approach to social work is a prerequisite for achieving partnership.

Thoburn et al. (1992), focussed their research particularly on participation in child protection conferences. Their findings agree with Marsh and Fisher that participation can be effective, but that proper training, preparation and resources are essential. These authors point out that participation is more difficult to achieve than most practitioners believe. Thoburn, for instance, comments that clients are not involved in service planning, and there is a long way to go to true participation.

Little research has been conducted about children's involvement (Westcott, 1995). Barford and Wattam (1992) pointed out that involving children in child protection is more difficult than involving adults. The Department of Health has addressed this issue and has emphasised the difficulty of involving children meaningfully in decision making.

Westcott's research project with two NSPCC teams involved interviewing practitioners, parents and some children in eleven cases. She found that there was a large gap between workers' and clients' perceptions of the work. Her findings indicate that clients were concerned about their relationship with the practitioner and what s/he could provide for them materially, but that practitioners were concerned mainly about changes in the family and their own effectiveness. They were less concerned about their own feelings towards the family and the family's feelings towards them.

The common themes emerging from the research are that practitioners are much more likely than clients to believe that their work is participative. Clients are generally satisfied with their practitioners, but do not feel powerful in the relationship.

During the 1980s the NSPCC opposed full parental and child participation (Dale et al., 1986; Bedford, 1986; Morrison et al., 1990). Following the Children Act, however, the NSPCC developed practice standards which include participation. The project reported here aimed to investigate current NSPCC practice relating to client participation by identifying areas of good practice and showing how practice relates to policy and theory, specifically around children's participation.

The evaluation involved face to face interviewing of practitioners, parents and children using a semi-structured interview schedule. Practitioners from NSPCC projects interviewed the worker, child(ren) and parent(s) involved in a case from another team, the aims being to:

- consider children's, parents' and practitioners' perceptions of participation in decision-making

- discover the degree of participation in a range of NSPCC projects

- focus on the role of written arguments

- identify methods for furthering effective participation

- develop a methodology for peer evaluation by practitioners.

The use of practitioners as evaluators of their peers was new to the NSPCC and seems not to have been used before in any evaluation of social work practice. Ten practitioners from nine NSPCC projects were involved in the evaluation. Peer evaluation was adopted because of the lack of resources to pay researchers and the wish to involve practitioners and to provide them with evaluation experience.

Each evaluator received one briefing day. Interviewing and writing-up were expected to take another day. At the briefing day the practitioners received an evaluator's pack containing interview schedules for children, parents and practitioners; and an evaluator's questionnaire; separate letters to parents and children explaining the purpose of the study and their rights to confidentiality and to decline to answer questions; and guidelines for practitioners on setting up, conducting and recording the interview. The intention was to give them as complete a guide as possible to evaluation interviewing without requiring them to study research methodology.

Interview schedules contained questions about client participation in the casework process. The questions were based largely on areas identified by Marsh (1983), Thoburn (1992) and Westcott (1995) as being key areas of concern around participation in casework – ie written agreements, the referral process, recording and attendances at decision-making meetings.

Practitioners, parents and children were asked questions covering these areas. Evaluators concentrated on important decision-making points. Practitioners were asked for their perceptions of the extent to which parents and children had participated in decision-making, and about the theoretical and policy influences on their practice.

Because the evaluators were seen as more than information gatherers, they were also asked to judge the degree of participation and discuss the effects of theory, policy and practice on participation in the case, recommend further research and comment on how practice had facilitated or limited participation. There were no set rules about recording interviews.

The ten families involved were clients of nine NSPCC projects. Nine were single parent families headed by the mother. Children interviewed were aged from nine to sixteen years. Three families had been involved with the NSPCC for over one year, three between four months and one year and the remaining four between three and four months.

The families were chosen by colleagues in the evaluators' teams according to the following criteria: they agreed to participate; the NSPCC had worked with them for more than three months; work was ending or had been completed; and the practitioner considered at least one child capable of responding to the interview schedule.

Validity and reliability

Ten evaluators, each conducting one set of interviews, posed problems of validity and reliability. Validity was tackled by basing the questions on previous research findings.

Reliability was more difficult to address. The interview could not be standardised because of the large number of interviewers, their inexperience in research methods, the short briefing/training period, the fact that they only conducted one set of interviews, the wide variety of clients and the variation in the ages of the children. However, as the evaluators were practitioners experienced in interviewing parents and children, problems of rapport, phrasing of questions were minimised.

The interview schedules themselves posed some problems due perhaps to the lack of a pilot study. Children sometimes had difficulty dealing with the question and answer format, and the children's questionnaire contained questions worded inappropriately for younger children.

Findings

Families valued the NSPCC's intervention. All but one said that they were very happy to have worked with the NSPCC and made no criticisms. The exception was a teenager who had argued with her practitioner on the day of the interview; even she, however, was generally positive about the work with the NSPCC.

Most families were referred to the NSPCC by social services or the courts. All but two felt that they had no choice about the referral except one self-referral and one which had been negotiated with a local authority practitioner. Six families were being assessed and nine were involved in treatment. Two had been investigated by the NSPCC.

Parents involved in investigations reported feeling shocked or dazed, feeling 'left out' but were too distressed to make decisions. One mother said:

Well, I was in no fit state, you know, nobody didn't say to me, look, are you alright? I was not taken aside and told this is what has happened, this is what we want to do, it was sort of buzzing all around me, you know, you're not allowed to talk to them ... I wasn't allowed to say anything to the children, it was awful.

Parents involved in assessment tended to accept the situation and hope it would have a positive outcome (ie keeping their children). They had very little say in whether they would be referred or how the referral would proceed. None of the clients involved in investigation or assessment had a say about where meetings would be held, who the practitioner would be or how the work would be done. These issues were determined by practitioners with little consultation.

Practitioners had a much clearer view of the referral process than clients. Children especially were unclear about how and why referrals were made.

Purpose and objectives of the work

Parents and practitioners generally held similar views on the purposes of the work but there were subtle but significant differences in terms of the level of participation, especially in relation to comprehensive assessments.

Practitioners tended to see assessments in neutral terms, but parents saw them in terms of outcomes. One practitioner saw the objectives as

Assessment on mum and A to look at family relationships.

Mother, however, saw them as

Probably to make me realise where I went wrong as a mother.

and the child as

...to find the best place for me and in the long run to get me home – everybody has now realised that was a mistake.

Parents in other cases saw assessment objectives as

to help me get the children home.

or

to help me deal with my problems.

Sometimes assessment flowed into treatment, but the extent to which clients appreciated the difference between the two was often unclear, nor was it clear how they were involved in the decision about the change. They often saw their whole involvement as a helping process, rather than being divided into discrete tasks.

Written agreements

In four cases there was no written agreement. One family had a written agreement with Social Services with NSPCC participation. Five had written agreements initiated by the NSPCC. The agreements ranged from comprehensive documents setting out objectives, roles, and responsibilities to lists of dates and times of meetings. Written agreements were much more important for workers than for clients. Several parents and most children did not remember their existence and few remembered their contents.

Neither the evaluator's nor the parents' view of the level of client participation seemed to relate to the existence of a written agreement. Even some of the practitioners felt that the process by which the agreement was formulated was more important than its format. For clients, being informed of what was happening and of the practitioners' intentions, were more important than written agreements.

Nevertheless, agreements had uses beyond the immediate casework situation, being administratively useful for practitioners providing a framework for case reviews and clarifying professional roles.

In only one case was the written agreement central to the work. The practitioner put the agreement on a flip-chart during every session, and it was used as an agenda. Written agreements were usually formulated when work started. When the focus changed, for example, from assessment to treatment, agreements did not reflect other than in the case in which the 'dynamic' approach to the agreement was taken.

Access to information

All the clients were offered access to some information in their records. Assessment reports and review reports were available to all parents. Some children had seen their records, three were unaware that records had been kept. All the children felt satisfied with the access they were offered. The parents who saw their files were satisfied with the recording. Most of those who had not seen their files wanted to, but did not argue very stongly. One said that she had not considered seeing her file.

Clients did not contribute actively to the recording process, although in one case recording was shared on a regular basis with the parents and who were appreciative. Mr B said that

everything they wrote we saw

Mr and Mrs B have seen all the records about their family although they have not requested to see the videos. So as far as they were aware they saw everything on their file, and felt that the records were fair and accurate.

One parent, Mrs P felt concerned about recording

I don't really agree with records being kept. They haven't raised it and I haven't raised it. I suppose the records are to help the workers.

Access to information was an important element for parents in the development of participatory practice. However, no literature was available to clients about their rights, and in practice access was given at the worker's discretion.

Attendance at meetings

All the parents had attended some child protection conferences and review meetings but none had attended the entire initial conference. Three children had attended conferences but most had attended some decision-making meetings. Parents' and children's attitudes differed regarding attendance, most parents feeling that attendance at meetings was important and that they should have been at more decision-making meetings. Everyone felt that attending only part of the meeting was demeaning. Some experienced meetings as positive, while others felt that their attendance made no difference to the decisions taken.

Although parents favoured attending meetings, most expressed some anxiety about them and complained about how they were conducted. Parents disliked big meetings with people who they did not know in attendance and felt much more comfortable with small groups and families. Several objected strongly to police attendance. Some expressed anxiety about children attending meetings, feeling it was their responsibility to make decisions about their children.

A typical comment from a parent about child protection conferences was

I didn't like the way everyone sat there – half of them don't know you. They tell you to go away while they discuss you and then say to you come back and whether you agree or not we'll make decisions about your life.

Attendance at decision-making meetings was seen as one of the most important aspects of participation. Interestingly, many parents saw differences between policies which were in operation when they were first involved with the child protection system and current policies, those involved for more than one year noticing a shift towards full attendance and more open working.

Most children did not want to go to meetings, feeling threatened by their size. Some felt they were heard even though they did not attend. A 15 year-old girl said

I felt that I influenced the meetings and that my choices were always

respected ... they were making the decision but I was telling them what to do.

Another child felt meetings were too painful

I'm stuck in the middle, torn between my foster parents and my own mother.

Children felt much happier about the more informal casework review meeting where they knew everybody.

Stage in the work

There was a relationship between the stage of work and how clients regarded participation. Families with whom work was complete tended to feel more positive, feeling that they had influenced the work more, perhaps because the further on in the work they were, the more they had engaged with the practitioners. This relates to the degree of participation in different stages of work. Parents involved in investigations feeling that they were told what to do and had no say. Some families undergoing assessment had some choice about the process, but often not about undergoing assessment per se.

In treatment cases, more real choice was experienced, although clients still felt pressurised. In three of these cases, the children felt more powerful than their parents, who felt left out of the decision-making process.

Worker's theoretical stance

The practitioners described their theoretical stance variously as systemic, eclectic, feminist, or having no label. None used an explicitly psycho-dynamic or task-centred approach. All felt their theoretical stance was an important influence on their approach to client participation and that the theories they embraced had directed them towards greater participation.

This finding is interesting in relation to Marsh's assertion (1983) that task-centred approaches are most conducive to participation. Written agreements were used within different theoretical approaches, raising the question of how participation differs in different theoretical frameworks.

Practitioners sometimes adapted their theoretical stance to incorporate client participation, implying that the professional environment which encourages participation and their own beliefs may have influenced their theoretical approach, rather than theory influencing practice.

Of the theoretical stances mentioned, only the feminist approach explicitly addresses clients' power as an issue (Dominelli and McLeod, 1989). However, the only piece of work in this study which adopted an explicity feminist approach used a pre-set agreement which could not be altered. Work with a feminist orientation was therefore no more participative than other methods.

There seemed to be an interplay between practitioners' theoretical stance and their personal ideologies which determined how they involved clients in decision making (see Rees, 1991). In some teams a strong team ethos influenced workers to operate a team 'formula' for developing and monitoring written agreements. Policies such as NSPCC and area child protection committee guidelines on client participation were seen as a less direct influence but probably served to set the parameter of team and individual approaches.

Discussion

Parents and children were remarkably uniform in their praise of NSPCC workers and their approach to client participation. Although not a representative sample of NSPCC clients, these families are probably fairly representative of 'satisfied customers'.

Despite the view of parents, children, practitioners and evaluators that there was a high degree of participation in all these cases, on examination some interesting issues appear which challenge this consensus.

Parents and children said that the most important aspects of the casework process were that it achieved what they wanted (for example, to have their children home, to improve marital relationships), they were kept informed about their case, they could attend decision making meetings and that the practitioners were honest, open, trustworthy, and approachable.

These issues related mainly to the personal attributes within the practitioner/client relationship. The more technical aspects, ie accessing files and developing written agreements were less important.

Perhaps written agreements lacked importance for these clients because there was no conflict with the practitioners and therefore no need to resort to them. Nevertheless, clients' responses to how the work developed indicated that the written nature of the agreement would probably not have been important even in conflict. This implies that, although written agreements are seen as important by practitioners, there is no clear relationship between them and client participation. A similar point applies to shared recording and access to information.

This view was not extended to attendance at decision-making meetings. No matter how 'open' a practitioner may be deliberate exclusion of parents (and to a certain extent, children) is experienced as demeaning and frustrating, perhaps because meetings are a public symbol of decision-making, whereas written agreements and records are more private and easily ignored.

However, one difficulty about this conclusion lies in the inevitable imbalance in the power relationship between practitioners and clients. Generally, this expectation is confirmed during the investigative and initial assessment stages of the work.

When they became NSPCC clients, expectations of participation were extremely low, so any offer of participation might well engender feelings of gratitude. Gratitude can combine with the fear that unless they comply their children will be removed or they will suffer other consequences. Gratitude combined with fear create a powerful incentive for clients to comply with practitioners' decisions. This incentive may be beneficial to the protection of children; for example, parents may stop abusive behaviour through fear, until they can stop for more positive reasons. Nevertheless, it means that clients often feel powerless at this stage of the work.

Every case involving a written agreement was based on a formula employed by the team or worker. The practitioner decided whether there should be a written agreement, its format and when it was signed. Clients sometimes had a say in the content but this was not universal; the working of three of the five agreements was determined solely by the practitioner. Whatever degree of participation was practised, the agenda was always set by the latter.

This indicates a complex relationship between empowerment – the process by which clients gain power, and participation – the 'technical' aspects such as provision of access and use of written agreements. Practitioners can relate empowerment and participation in several ways:

Participation as a right

This 'human rights' view asserts that participation is a right for all clients irrespective of the therapeutic process.

Participation as empowerment training

Since intervention is designed to empower parents and children to take control of their lives, only by offering them the opportunity to do so within the social work relationship can this be achieved out-

side it. Written agreements and attendance at meetings are prereq-
uisites for the therapeutic process of empowerment.

Participation depends on empowerment

Here clients are seen to need to be empowered through a therapeutic process before they can participate fully. Participation without
this process is tokenistic at best and dangerous at worst.

Empowerment and participation

These are secondary issues and protection is paramount since the
primary role of practitioners is to protect children. Empowering
clients risks the misuse of power so it should only be given when risk
is minimalised. Only after children are fully protected can clients be
offered the right of participation in decision-making. These are
'ideal types' but they show the range of opinions which exist in the
social work profession. It is important to be clear about the relationship between empowerment and participation and not to confuse
them, otherwise mixed messages will be given to clients. Perhaps
some groups of clients, especially children, need to be empowered in
order to participate effectively. Going through the motions of participation without empowering them to use it effectively could be
self-defeating, as illustrated by many of the children's responses to
questions about whether they would like to attend meetings.

Investigation highlights the dilemma for practitioners regarding
participation. Current methods of investigation result in parents
and children feeling powerless and unable to influence events.
Keeping within the law, ensuring the safety of children and working
participatively presents a major challenge to practitioners involved
in investigations.

Practitioners can respond either by acknowledging clients' lack
of power and providing information about their rights and the process of the investigation or developing ways of investigating in
which children and non-abusive parents can retain some degree of
participation.

Clients involved in assessment felt they had little choice about
whether to be assessed. They could be given more say in how the
assessment is carried out. Parents and children stated that they felt
more powerful as the assessment progressed – a consequence of a
high standard of work, which enabled them to move from suspicion
and hostility towards acceptance of, and involvement in, the process.
In the present sample, the recommendations had mainly coincided
with the parents' wishes. It would be interesting to contrast their

views with those of clients who disagreed with their recommendations.

The casework relationship may be one in which the differences in power between practitioners and clients is perpetuated by allowing clients to feel that they have some say in the process, whereas in reality they do not have real power (Rojek and Collins, 1986).

My PG-Diss

Conclusions

Parents and children reported a high degree of satisfaction with the NSPCC. Parents were more concerned than children with participation. Many children did not want to attend meetings, nor did they want written agreements or have access to their records. Practitioners' commitment to participation related to personal beliefs and supervision rather than agency or area child protection committee policy.

The use of written agreements, access to information and shared recording was patchy. Clients were seldom given choices about venue, practitioner, type of interview, or informed of their rights. No written material was given about access to information. The degree of participation changed with the stage of work; investigation being the least, and treatment the most participative. In treatment cases clients generally felt in control of the process.

Written material should be produced for parents and children regarding:

- access to information
- agreements
- complaints
- attendance at meetings.

There was some confusion about the relationship between empowerment, participation and practice. These should be explicitly addressed by training and supervision. Standards of empowerment and participation should be developed, and access to information and shared recording be more actively pursued.

Parents and children should be more involved in decision-making meetings.

More effective ways should be developed to question children on their ideas about participation, for example, a questionnaire for younger children or by more imaginative techniques such as play or computer games.

Generally the use of practitioners as evaluators was successful and should be extended.

References

Aldgate, J. (Ed) (1990) *Using Written Agreements with Children and Families*. London: Family Rights Group.

Arnstein, S. R. (1969) 'A ladder of participation', *Journal of American Institute of Planners*.

Barford, R. and Wattam (1992) 'Children's participation in decision making', *Practice*, 2, pp. 93–102.

Bedford, A. (1986) 'An alternative view' in Brown, T. and Waters, J. (Eds) *Parental Participation in Case Conferences*. Baspcan, pp. 30–34.

Beresford, P. and Croft, S. (1992) *Citizen Involvement: A Practical Guide for Change*. Basingstoke: Macmillan.

Braye, S. and Preston-Shoot, M. (1992) 'Honourable intentions: participation and written agreements in welfare legislation', *Journal of Social Work and Family Law*. 6, pp. 511–528.

Corden, C. and Preston-Shoot, M. (1987) *Contracts in Social Work*. Aldershot: Gower.

Croft, S. and Beresford, P. (1990) *From Paternalism to Participation involving People in Social Services*. York: Joseph Rowntree Foundation.

Dale, P., Davies, M., Morrison, T. and Waters, J. (1986) *Dangerous Families*. London: Tavistock.

Department of Health (1991) *Working Together under the Children Act (1989)*. London: HMSO.

Dominelli, L. and McLeod, E. (1989) *Feminist Social Work*. Basingstoke: Macmillan.

Family Rights Group and NSPCC (1992) *Child Protection Procedures: What They Mean for Your Family*. London: NSPCC and Family Rights Group.

Home Office (1992) *Memorandum of Good Practice on Video Recorded Interviews with Child Witnesses for Criminal Proceedings*. London: HMSO.

Lewis, A. (1992) 'An overview of research into participation in child protection work', in Thoburn, J. (Ed) *Participation in Practice Involving Families in Child Protection*. Norwich: UEA.

McGloin, D. and Turnbull, A. (1986) *Parent Participation in Child Abuse Review Conferences A Research Report*. London Borough of Greenwich.

Magura, S. and Moses, B. S. (1984) 'Clients as evaluators in child protection services', *Child Welfare*, 63, pp. 99–112.

Maluccio, A. (1979) *Learning from Clients: Interpersonal Helping as Viewed by Clients and Social Workers*. New York: Free Press.

Marsh, P. (1983) Researching practice and practising research in child care social work in Fisher, M. (ed), *Speaking of Clients*. Sheffield University, Joint Unit for Social Services Research.

Marsh, P. and Fisher, M. (1992) *Good Intentions: Developing Partnerships in Social Services*. York: Joseph Rowntree Foundation.

Mayer, J. E. and Timms, N. (1970) *The Client Speaks: Working Class Impressions of Casework*. London: Routledge and Kegan Paul.

Morrison, I., Blakely, C., Butler, A., Fallon, S. and Leith, A. (1990) *Children and Parental Participation in Case Conferences*. London: NSPCC.

Ovretviet, J. (1986) *Improving Social Work Records and Practice*. Birmingham: BASW.

Pearson, S., Treseder, J. and Yelloly, M. (1988) *Social Work and the Legacy of Freud: Psychoanalysis and its Uses*. London: Macmillan.

Phillimore, P. (1981) *Families Speaking: a Study of Fifty-one Families' Views of Social Work*. London: Family Service Units.

Rees, S. (1991) *Achieving Power: Practice and Policy in Social Welfare*. Sydney: Allen & Unwin.

Reid, W. J. and Epstein, L. (1977) *Task-Centred Practice*. New York: Columbia University Press.

Rojek, C., Peacock, G. and Collins, S. (1988) *Social Work and Received Ideas*. London: Routledge.

Sainsbury, E. (1987) 'Client studies: their contribution and limitations in influencing social work practice', *British Journal of Social Work*, 13, pp. 635–644.

Sainsbury, E., Nixon, S. and Phillips, D. (1982) *Social Work in Focus: Clients' and Social Workers' Perceptions in Long Term Social Work*. London: Routledge and Kegan Paul.

Shemmings, D. (1991) *Client Access to Records: Participation in Social Work*. Gomer Avebury.

Shemmings, D. and Thoburn, J. (1990) *Parental Participation in Child Protection Conferences*.

Thoburn, J. (Ed) (1991) *Participation in Practice Involving Families in Child Protection*. Norwich: UEA.

Thoburn, J., Lewis, A. and Shemmings, D. (1991) *Family Involvement in Child Protection Conferences*. Norwich: University of East Anglia, Social Work Development Unit.

Westcott, H. (1995) *Perceptions of Child Protection Casework: Views from Children, Parents and Practitioners*. Harlow: Longman.

Note

While the issues and challenges identified in this paper remain relevant to child protection practice and policy, since the research reported on here was conducted, some areas of NSPCC practice have developed and changed.

10 Perceptions of child protection casework:
views from children, parents, and practitioners

Helen Westcott

I used to think I wish the whole subject would be forgotten really 'cos it's all happened ... and we're trying to get on with a new life now, and she used to have to come in here and discuss it all with us again, obviously because that's what the NSPCC do (Sexually abused young woman).

This chapter will describe a small study which comprised a number of interviews with childen and parents receiving casework services from the NSPCC, as well as interviews with the responsible NSPCC child protection officers (CPO). The objective of the study was to obtain perspectives from all the participants involved in the casework process; as such, the study was not conceptualised as an evaluation, although it did recognise the possibility of highlighting issues for practice. From the outset the importance of speaking with children and reporting their views was noted, with the additional benefit of being able to compare and contrast their perspectives with adults involved (parents and CPOs).

Greater detail of the study design is provided below, however a few preliminary comments are necessary here. Firstly, the interviews and the casework they discuss took place before October 1991 when the Children Act 1989 was implemented. The Act, and its emphasis on partnership with parents and on listening to children, has already had a profound effect on the delivery of child protection services. Many of the issues discussed here will have 'moved on', then, since the Act came into effect. Secondly, the NSPCC's own organisation and role in child protection services has changed rapidly in the early 1990s following an internal review. The workload and services offered by teams featured here may have a different profile.

Finally, some key terms need to be defined as they are used in this chapter. *Casework* will be used to denote any service provided by the NSPCC in any particular case. The term *family* is used to describe any parent–child relationship where a mother or father (and/or parent substitute) is sharing accommodation with their child. Hence the term may include both parents, single parents, cohabitees or relatives living together regardless of their sexual preference. *Child* refers to any individual receiving NSPCC services who is under the age of 18 years. Two teenagers who had recently received NSPCC services were in fact older at the time of their research interview, and are referred to as 'young women' thoughout. Lastly *service user* is used here in preference to terms like 'client' or 'customer'. It denotes adults and children who have received (willingly or unwillingly) any kind of service from the NSPCC.

Previous studies of service user and social worker feedback

To date, a considerable number of studies have investigated service user perceptions (Maluccio, 1979; Mayer and Timms, 1970; Phillimore, 1981; Rees, 1978; Sainsbury, 1975; Sainsbury, Nixon and Phillips, 1982). Typically, the families interviewed have been selected from Family Service Units (e.g. Phillimore, 1981; Sainsbury, 1975), or Family Welfare Associations (e.g. Mayer and Timms, 1970), and often they have experienced a number of problems within or outside of the home.

More recently, studies have specifically focussed on the views of families involved with child protection agencies (Brown, 1986; Magura, 1982; Magura and Moses, 1984; Pharis and Levin, 1991), and have sought the views of children and adolescents themselves on occasion (Bush, Gordon and Le Bailly, 1977; Jones, 1978).

Parent feedback

Magura (1982) interviewed 34 American parents of childen who were considered to be 'at risk' due to severe and multiple problems within the family. The families had been randomly assigned to either an intensive services project or to a control group which received regular agency services. More project parents saw their situation as 'much better', while more control parents saw their situation as only 'somewhat better' or 'remaining the same'. The parents most frequently cited their change in situation to be an improvement in self-confidence and capacity to cope (with their feelings, parenthoood and life stresses). They expressed the view that individualised counselling provided by the caseworker had made the greatest contribution to the perceived improvements. Magura (1982) argues that the caseworker–service user relationship may be the key factor associated with succesful outcomes for parents in this study. Parents found the following caseworker characteristics to be helpful: empathy, genuineness, and unconditional positive regard. Accessibility of caseworker was also important.

Dissatisfaction with caseworkers in the project group (which was rare) was centred upon unwanted advice or help, or lack of skill. Only one client in the project group specifically criticised the worker as unconcerned with her needs and feelings; Magura reports that the worker was viewed as 'being concerned only with needs and feelings of her children' (p. 530). In the control group, dissatisfaction was centred most upon the perceived inaccessibility of the key-worker.

In a second study, Magura and Moses (1984) conducted 250 interviews with American families from three child protection agencies. Approximately 70% of clients expressed at least mild overall satisfaction with the services or help they had received, although 'substantial remaining problems were reported in most areas' (p. 109). Service deficits were most apparent in economically related areas 'in which the responsibility of protective agencies is unclear' (p. 109). Sixty per cent of clients reported at least one 'important criticism' of the agency.

Pharis and Levin (1991) interviewed 30 American mothers of young children selected for an intensive intervention project. Casework factors selected as important by the mothers tended to be relatively abstract and pertained to the therapeutic aspects of the programme. Specific, concrete services were rated as less important. The single most highly ranked aspect of the programme was the relationship with a 'person to talk to who really cared'.

Brown (1986) interviewed 23 parents in South West England about their experiences of child protection procedures and social workers. All were families in which actual physical child abuse (e.g. bruises, fractures) had been established. First impressions of their contact with a social worker remained clear for the parents; many felt reasonably positive, although few felt that the social worker had explained things clearly. Negative impressions were created by a lack of openness, and by an over-authoritarian approach.

Brown found a major lack of clarity between parents and social workers about the focus and intention of visits and argues that this uncertainty created much anxiety for parents. Social work visits were seen to comprise largely chatting or talking, which was valued by the parents as a sign of friendliness and encouragement to relax. However, only eight parents positively welcomed their social workers' visits.

The majority of parents felt their social worker understood their problems, at least to a certain extent. Parents who felt they had a good relationship with their social worker mentioned trust, openness and honesty, friendliness, confidence in their worker, sincerity, and respect for them as an individual (being treated as an adult or as equal). Parents who felt they had a poor relationship with their worker mentioned a lack of trust, friendliness, credibility and openness, insensitivity, condescending attitude, and being treated like children or inferior beings. There were marked preferences among parents for either female (11/23) or male (7/23) social workers. Also, it was considered important that the social worker had children of his/her own and should be an older, experienced person.

Child feedback

Two early studies have sought the opinions of children in care, although their relevance to the present research is limited. Bush et al. (1977) surveyed children in foster care in Illinois. The strongest 'theme' found in the children's responses related to the importance attached by the children of receiving love, care, and understanding from foster parents.

Jones (1978) obtained information from children involved in intermediate treatment activity groups in Britain. He also interviewed their parents and caseworkers. Jones' findings suggested that children perceived social workers much more positively than either their parents or caseworkers anticipated. The parents' perceptions were also positive, especially if the caseworker had attended the activity group with the adolescent.

However, one of the most pertinent study to date is that conducted in Britain by Barford (Barford and Wattam, 1991). In his study, Barford interviewed eleven children from four different families about their experiences. He found that the social worker's initial contact was often surrounded in uncertainty, with some children wanting to speak, but feeling they were unable to, and others finding themselves expected to talk. The initial intervention was experienced as sympathetic by several children, but as confusing, upsetting or excluding by others.

Many children felt that social workers would help them, although there was considerable uncertainty as to how that might be. The social worker was seen by some as giving 'deep, meticulous help', or alternatively by others as being 'ineffective, indifferent or superficial'. For example, one boy (aged 13) was critical that his social worker did not help more with material concerns.

Barford reports that the following aspects of the social workers' approach were appreciated by the children: humour, directness, relaxation, spending time and the ability to show they cared. Generally, gender of social worker was not seen as significant by the children, except when combined with issues concerning race of worker.

Finally, decisions about case closure again appear to have been somewhat 'mysterious' for the children. Most children felt that ending of visiting corresponded to an improvement in family circumstances, though the actual breaking off of contact was met with mixed feelings (e.g. sadness) for some children.

Caseworker feedback in client studies

Some researchers have included interviews with social workers or caseworkers (e.g. Maluccio, 1979; Sainsbury et al., 1982), although these studies were not conducted wholly within child protection agencies.

Maluccio (1979) conducted a small number of in-depth interviews with a randomly selected sample of American women and their social workers soon after their involvement with the Family Service Bureau ceased. Most were white, middle-class women seeking help for personal or inter-personal problems. In brief, workers agreed with the women that the main problem solving activity in which they had engaged was talking, though workers were found to value this intervention more. Generally, Maluccio found that workers' interviews focussed more on the *content* of the casework, whereas the women spent more time discussing the casework *process*. They were also reluctant to discuss their own feelings about the casework undertaken, describing instead the women's reactions and methods of engagement or maintenance in casework.

Maluccio comments that there was frequently a discrepancy between service users' and workers' overall perspective, and that typically the workers had a more pessimistic outlook. Workers felt that activities undertaken were the most important feature influencing the success of the casework, with user qualities of secondary importance. However, for the women, the worker qualities were judged to be of primary importance. Maluccio notes a variety of discrepancies between the workers and women covering most aspects of the casework process. Further, much of the service user and worker activity during casework was directed towards coping with these discrepancies. Maluccio concluded that a substantial proportion of service user and worker dissatisfaction comes from 'involuntary' service users, that is, those who have been pressured to go to the agency by someone else. In effect, such users never assume the role of *client*, and perceive the service as irrelevant to their needs.

Sainsbury et al. (1982) interviewed service users and workers from British social services, probation and voluntary agencies during the course of a year. They found that social workers substantially underestimated families' friendliness towards them, but also, in a few cases, underestimated the strength of negative feelings towards them. Service users tended to become more adversely critical as the year progressed, whereas workers became less so; generally, workers were more critical of their performance than service users.

Service users and workers across all agencies ranked 'encouragement' as the most helpful element of casework, although a higher percentage of service users than workers rated it so. Social workers (compared with the service users) over-estimated the relative helpfulness of insightful work and the use of authority and advice giving, whilst under-estimating the helpfulness of material and financial help and negotiations with other services, as perceived by service users.

These two studies provide a useful context for the present study, although their lack of verbatim feedback from the social workers themselves is disappointing. It would appear that the current research might provide some pointers concerning workers' views of their role in the child protection field.

Study method

As noted above, the current study comprised interviews with children, parents and NSPCC Child Protection Officers. It utilised a qualitative approach, and was *not* intended to be a large scale survey of a random sample of service users.

Selection of families

Three NSPCC Child Protection Teams in England were initially approached about participation in the project. Due to unforeseen difficulties, one team withdrew from the project before any families had been approached; a replacement team was therefore recruited.

Teams selected families they thought likely to participate. No constraints were put upon the selection of families regarding the type of work undertaken at NSPCC, reason for referral or age of children. It was left open to individual CPOs whether to include 'open' or 'closed' cases. For open cases, a research interview could be construed as destructive to the casework currently being undertaken. For closed cases, it could be considered inappropriate to reapproach families whose contact with the NSPCC had effectively ceased. In fact, a number of both open and closed cases were included.

Initially, teams chose 10–12 families to approach about the project, with a view to obtaining consent to participate from four families per team. Response rates from two of the teams exceeded expectations, with five families in *Team One* responding, and six families from *Team Two* agreeing to take part. Unfortunately, a nil response was obtained by Team Three, despite additional efforts to recruit more families. In view of the considerable delays already encountered, it was decided to proceed with just two teams. For all families, participation was voluntary.

Approaching the families about participation

Introductory letters explaining the purpose of the study were available in two formats, so that workers could choose which format they felt to be most appropriate for the families selected. Introductory letters were sent out from teams (thus preserving confidentiality), and families returned a consent slip to the author at London. An acknowledgement letter was then sent to families which explained what arrangements would be made to visit the families.

Participating family and CPO details

It should be stated at the outset that some information about families and CPOs is not available here. For CPOs this includes details of their age, and career history. For the families, information, pertaining to parental age and prior involvement with NSPCC and/or social services is omitted. Details are also unavailable about the length of time families had been involved with the NSPCC, and the stage of intervention reached (beyond case open or closed). Whilst this information might have provided a useful context, the views expressed by CPOs, children and parents have value in their own right.

Five families in *Team One* agreed to participate. These families were referred to NSPCC because of intra- and extra-familial sexual abuse, physical abuse, neglect and emotional abuse. Three families consisted of single mothers and their children, and in two families both parents/cohabitees were living at home. The children in these families (two boys and three girls) were aged one to fifteen years at time of initial contact with the NSPCC and aged six to twenty years at interview. Two families were currently in contact with the NSPCC (i.e. their cases were still 'open'). Interviews were conducted with all mothers, one father and one female cohabitee. The families who participated in the project were the responsibility of one female CPO and two male CPOs.

Six families from *Team Two* volunteered to take part in the project. Two had been in contact with NSPCC as a result of intra-familial sexual abuse, three for physical and emotional abuse and one mother had self-referred because of her post-natal depression. Both parents/cohabitees were at home in five families, and in the other, a single mother was living with her children. At the time of initial contact with the NSPCC, the children (four girls and one boy) were aged two to sixteen years; they were aged five to nineteen years at research interview. Four families were still in regular contact with the NSPCC (their cases were open). Interviews were conducted with all mothers and two fathers.

The participating families were the responsibility of three female CPOs and NSPCC family care staff. One female Family Care Worker was interviewed in addition to the CPOs. One CPO interview was conducted by telephone.

Initial (face-to-face) contact with families

For *Team One*, the CPO responsible for each family accompanied the author on an initial visit and left after introducing her to them. At this meeting, date and time of the actual interview was agreed. This approach was discontinued for *Team Two*, since instead of being reassuring (as intended), these visits made both the families and author uncomfortable. The families seemed uncertain as to the purpose of the initial visits, and the author felt less indepedent as well as awkward. Hence, for *Team Two* only one visit to each family was made.

Conducting the family interviews

After introductions, consent forms were discussed before the parents signed them. All parents signed consent for themselves and for their children, with the exception of two young women who signed for themselves without parental consent. Where the child was judged to be of an appropriate age, they were asked if they would like to sign their own consent form, having ensured that *all* children had had their rights as interviewees explained and had been given the opportunity to not take part.

Each parent and child was asked whether he/she would consent

to the interview being tape-recorded; this was agreed for all interviewees. The tape recorder was, in fact, very popular with the
younger children, and playing with it, for example, by recording
them singing songs, helped to facilitate interviews.
All interviews were conducted at the family home. For *Team
One*, most children were interviewed in the presence of their mother
and/or father. This resulted from a number of factors, including
approaches initiated by children in front of parents, and one young
woman choosing to speak with her mother present. For *Team Two*
most children were seen on their own except where they elected to
have parents present.
On completion of questions, the parent or child was asked if they
wanted to make any other comments. The author made sure they
knew how to contact her if they wanted to ask any questions or clarify any point at a later date. The shortest interview with parents and
the two young women was thirty minutes, the longest one hour.
Interviews with children lasted approximately five to twenty minutes.

Conducting the CPO interviews

Before starting the interviews the child protection officers were
reminded that their rights were equivalent to the family interviewees: that is, they could withdraw at any time, refuse to answer any
question and so on. They were also asked to consent to the interview
being tape-recorded. CPO interviews lasted from 25 to 45 minutes.

Interview schedules

The interview questions were developed by the author from an
amalgamation of published protocols (e.g. Brown, 1986; Phillimore,
1981; Sainsbury, 1975) and other personally devised questions. The
protocols provided by Maluccio (1979) and Barford (this volume)
were particularly helpful. Typically, the initial question prompted a
free narrative which covered many of the issues to be raised by later
questions. Interview schedules for all participants followed roughly
the same pattern, with questions covering the 'beginning, middle
and end' of casework. For children particularly, questions were
asked in a format judged suitable to their age and understanding.
Interviewees were also encouraged to give any additional information (not covered by questions) they wanted. Some examples are
given below:

> *What did you do the first time your social worker visited?* (child).
> *What went on in the initial session?* (parent/CPO).

What was your social worker like? (child/parent).
What was the child/parent like? (CPO).

What led to the end of you seeing the social worker? (child).
How did you happen to stop going? (parent).
How was the case closed and why? (CPO).

A number of more specific prompt questions were used to pursue issues raised by these broader questions. Questions to parents and CPOs sometimes requested more specific information. The final questions asked interviewees to sum up their experiences with the NSPCC, and whether they felt casework had had any impact.

Follow-up to interview

The audio tapes were transcribed, and subjected to qualitative content analysis by the author. The drafting included time for CPOs to read and comment upon the initial report. It was felt important that at least this group of interviewees had the opportunity to make an input into the final version, and their support in this respect was helpful.

Following their interviews, all families were sent a letter thanking them for their co-operation. Some families requested feedback from the research as offered, which was subsequently sent on completion of the report.

Participants' perspectives on casework[1]

Before participants' views are presented, a few comments are necessary. Participants' views have been extracted and are presented here in relation to specific issues; thus, it is difficult to obtain the overall 'feel' (e.g. positive or negative) for any one interview, since each has been broken down into relevant segments. Further, the views of CPO, parent and child involved in any one case are unavailable for direct comparison, in order to preserve confidentiality for all involved.

Co-ordinating the wealth of material resulting from interviews was difficult for a number of reasons. First, trying to relate the different viewpoints often seemed impossible, as it appeared that

[1] In the subsequent discussion, where quotations appear, use of '...' between words indicates that text has been omitted. For example, 'I didn't mind going ... well, I were a bit excited.'

clients and CPOs could not be discussing the same process. Secondly, the apparent contradictions inherent in any one individual's narrative made it difficult to comprehend their perspective on a number of occasions.

Expectations, CPO roles and reactions to intervention

The majority of children and parents in this study found it difficult to recall their initial contact with the NSPCC, and to remember if they had any expectations about what would happen. Many spoke of feeling like a 'timebomb' had exploded, with everything 'happening so fast'.

> *I didn't have an instant reaction because from (child) telling me what happened to actually phoning up and getting help it never occurred to me, I was still in shock ...* (Mother).

> *To have that great burden on you for all them years and then to finally tell some person ... it was a great relief and you didn't know what was going to happen ... There was a lot of involvement off everybody at once, I mean all at once everyone seemed to know something I'd kept for years, basically it confused me a lot ... to be honest I weren't even sure what I wanted* (Young woman aged 20 years).

A couple of parents were quite clear about what they expected of the CPO. For example

> *(CPO) were there to say what the problem was with (child), right ... (CPO) was there to help (child)* (Mother).

> *All I had to do was pick up the phone and they'd tell me what to do and ... get (CPO) out to us* (Father).

By way of a contrast, most CPOs were clear about what they expected from the parents and children. For example,

> *We expected that they would co-operate with us, that they would attend their appointments and that when they came to the Centre they would work quite hard* (Female CPO).

In some cases, it seemed that families' uncertainty about the *role* of social workers prevented them from holding any expectations about the CPO and what they could achieve. However, the CPOs and family care staff themselves felt their roles to be well defined within the casework process.

> *I think it helped for me to reassure (Mother) ... again in the role of the official expert to reassure them that they had done the right thing* (Male CPO).

My role is one of protection foremost and to try and determine the risk factor, once I determined the risk factor ... Then it became more of a child welfare, a repairing job as far as the children were concerned and a supporting guidance to mum ... so I see myself as a formulator of work plan, if you like, within the child protection procedures (Female CPO).

Two other important issues emerged from CPOs in relation to their perceived role in casework; first, their fear of creating dependency in parents, and secondly, their difficulty in balancing the 'care and control' of parents within child protection procedures designed to promote the rights of the child. For example,

After you've been going (x) years ... you have to try and get a balance between sufficient input to protect the children versus trying to take over the family (Female CPO).

Two mothers particularly graphically recalled their reaction to intervention, which consisted of fury and feeling 'ripped apart'. Following from her experiences, one mother made the comment that:

I think the NSPCC is so used to dealing with child abuse cases that they forget that nine times out of ten for most people its the first time, they've never been through it before and for most people that is a very scary, frightening situation.

This seems a pertinent observation for professionals making contact with families for the first time.

Children's reactions to invervention varied considerably, although most were positive.

I suppose I was glad it was out in the open to be honest, I suppose I was glad to know that it would stop. (Young woman, aged 19)

I enjoyed doing it, I enjoyed going there 'cos it gave me a chance to say what my feelings were like. (Girl, aged 11)

I didn't mind going ... well, I were a bit excited. (Girl, aged 6)

Surprised, shocked, I didn't understand what was going on. (Girl, aged 12)

For themselves, CPOs tended to describe their initial reactions to intervention in terms of it being an appropriate or suitable case for the NSPCC to 'take on'. (It was not clear exactly which criteria CPOs used to assess this suitability, however.) Generally, CPOs described parents' reactions as either positive, accepting and co-operative or as denying and hostile. Co-operation generally was seen by the CPOs as the parents admitting the problem existed, whilst non co-operation occurred if the parents denied the problem's existence, or its magnitude. Children typically were judged to react well to the family care (FC) intervention.

Perceptions of the NSPCC, individual CPOs and families

Comments from parents relating to the NSPCC's image were predominantly negative, and frequently referred to the NSPCC taking children away. One mother reported having this same initial fear, but went on to say that this image of the Society, in fact, prevented people from finding out more about the NSPCC's work:

> *Yeah it's just the image that they give, you know like when you hear anything about the NSPCC they've either taken a child away haven't they or they've whatever, I mean people don't actually realise what they actually do do, what there is around ... but I really thought I was going to lose (child) you know ... At first it was a shame thing to ... but it isn't like that any more, it isn't the way that people think it is, it isn't that bad* (Mother).

This image – of taking children away – existed regardless of whether the parent had actually experienced their child's 'removal' or not. It was not always clear whether the parents' image was one specifically of the NSPCC, or whether it was a more general image of a social work agency.

CPOs also referred to this image of the NSPCC. One described her admiration for a couple who had approached the Society for help in the light of its existence. Discussing this issue, one CPO made the following remark about the power dynamics involved in removing a child from the home.

> *At the back of their mind they have a worry that we'll receive (child) into care and that they'll have no say in the matter, they find it hard to understand that it's their own decision whether (child) goes into care or not, it's not really ours, it's their decision to look after (child) properly or (child) comes into care* (Female CPO).

By way of a contrast, one mother felt the NSPCC did not do enough to check the welfare of her child. Other complaints about the image of the NSPCC centred upon help (especially of a practical nature) which parents did not feel they had received.

Children were much more vague about the Society's image. In fact, it seemed irrelevant to and/or unconsidered by them. In one case, the child had disclosed her abuse following a visit to her school by an NSPCC speaker. Only one young woman explicitly referred to the NSPCC's image: she felt that repeated family discussions about the abuse (which she found difficult) were inevitable *'because that's what the NSPCC do'*.

Comments by two other childen may be related to the perceived image, although not explicitly so. One young girl thought she saw her CPO *'because I was naughty sometimes'*, and another revealed that she told her school friends the CPO *'was just a friend'*. She didn't really want them to know that someone from the NSPCC (or, at least, a social worker) was visiting.

The parents in this study raised many different issues relating to the characteristics of their worker which they had either appreciated or found problematic. Positive attributes included being easy to talk to, a good listener, friendliness towards the parent and genuine interest in the parent's problems – *'it was as though somebody out there cared'*. Several parents stressed the CPO's sense of humour which helped to provide a 'balance' in difficult times:

> *With child abuse it's very heavy, but when things were getting too heavy or too much (CPO) was very lighthearted about it, (CPO) also helped us keep a sense of humour about a lot of things and put it into more of a perspective ... (CPO) helped to keep a balance on it all* (Mother).

Parents who expressed a negative view of their CPO complained of a lack of most of these positive attributes. In addition, they described a lack of trust, a 'hard attitude' and a propensity to 'interfere':

> *But they want to pry into our lives now, which I don't think is right, they're there to help (child) and they want to pry into our lives* (Mother).

One father felt the CPO had acted unprofessionally in breaching confidentiality:

> *(CPO) left the garden here one day ... and went up a couple of doors and actually called one of the children .... out of their friend's garden, now I don't think that was very professional ... OK, like (CPO) does stick to this (CPO) won't tell anybody about us and whatever ... but that was telling the street.*

The issues of age, sex and experience of CPO came up frequently, although not always negatively. One young mother had appreciated the fact that her CPO was the same age as herself, and felt it enabled them to be more open and 'share a laugh'. Another mother felt it was good that a male CPO was allocated to the case as her daughter 'needed to trust a man'. For others, though, these factors were seen as causing problems in the CPO–parent relationship, for example if the CPO did not have children.

One young woman went into great detail about how these issues (age, sex and experience of CPO) had affected her.

> *The thing I did like about the group was that (group leader) was there,*
> *and he was the only male, and they'd (group leaders) both been abused*
> *and that made it a lot easier ... To talk to a male who'd been abused as*
> *well as being just a male was excellent. It's easier talking to someone*
> *else who's been abused than someone else who hasn't because they don't*
> *know what you're going through. It's like trying to enter someone else's*
> *career when you don't know what you're doing* (Young woman, aged
> 20 years).

One male worker in this study also brought up the gender issue with
respect to his clients, particularly in child sexual abuse cases. He
indicated feeling uncertain about the effect his gender would have
on a teenage girl victim, and commented that, with hindsight, he
would have involved a female worker much earlier in a separate case
where sexual abuse had occurred.

The importance of life *experience* over and above training was
stressed by some parents (*'it's like me as a bachelor trying to give mari-*
tal information' – Father), connected to a feeling that as parents, they
were disempowered by professionals 'who thought they knew better'
than the parents themselves.

Children's perceptions of the CPO often mirrored those of their
parents. With one exception, all children spoken to described their
CPO in a positive manner, typically as being 'kind' and 'caring'. An
11 year-old boy was the only child interviewed to express some dislike for his CPO:

> *There's something about (CPO) I don't like ... just tries to be funny*
> *with me but I don't like it.* (Boy, aged 11 years).

The boy's apparent dislike of humour (although use of the term
'funny' may mean it was not viewed as humour, but as superficial) is
in contrast to the value put on humour by other children and parents in this study.

Workers' perceptions of families tended to represent an assessment of their strengths or weaknesses (as seen by the CPO) and how
this defined or shaped the activities to be undertaken as casework.
For example, several children were described as 'needy' or 'damaged', whilst parents were frequently seen as 'immature' and 'vulnerable' themselves.

> *(Mother)'s very immature herself, and therefore puts an awful lot onto*
> *(child) and the very nature of the fact that she's not happy in herself*
> *causes the risk to (child)* (Female CPO).

Honesty and motivation to 'work hard' alongside the workers
seemed to be qualities of clients most respected by the CPOs. Where

they felt parents had been genuinely motivated to participate in casework, CPOs were quick to express their appreciation.

And then (child)'s mother told us that she was very glad indeed to have been stopped, that she'd been escalating in tension and stress ... and she was glad she'd been caught and I believed her at the time and I still do. She then accepted a co-operative input and they were very, very co-operative the entire time (Female CPO).

Perceptions of children seemed to be virtually always positive, with most CPOs and family care staff expressing their concerns for the children's welfare within the home. Children were almost always thought to have responded well to the casework, and no CPO described any child in a negative manner.

All the images and attributes so far discussed combined to shape the relationships that developed between CPOs, parents and children. Surprisingly, most parents did not explicitly discuss their relationship with the CPO, presumably leaving this to be inferred from their other comments. Those parents who did refer to their relationship after questioning stressed how positive the interaction had been:

Yes, it's good. I still feel I can go and talk to (CPO) ... they've got to know me so well (Mother).

If I didn't get on with them I wouldn't have listened to them would I ... that was important to me ... I trusted (CPO) and it was important to me that I had that trust (Mother).

Parents feeling this way expressed the belief that not only did the CPO understand their position, but also that they understood the CPO's objectives. This mutual understanding seemed lacking for parents feeling predominantly negative:

(CPO) didn't understand the problems, (CPO) didn't understand what we had gone through ... the only ones who would understand that are ourselves because we've gone through it (Father).

For parents, therefore, understanding reflected an acceptance by the CPO of what the family situation was. For CPOs, however, understanding by the parents would be evidenced by their co-operation with the CPO's view of the situation. In general, most CPOs and family care staff felt that parents and children found it difficult to understand their objectives, especially at the time of intervention, although understanding could improve with hindsight.

They had an idea of this and an idea of that, but I don't think they could

always see at the time why we were going down particular paths, why
we were focussing on particular issues, though I think in retrospect they
might do, but at the time no (Female CPO).

CPOs also tended to distinguish between parents' ability to understand at an abstract level, and their ability to put that understanding
into practice:

> *I think they understood because they could see that [child]'s life was*
> *actually improving while (child) was here and they understood to the*
> *extent that they carried through the easiest bits but ... when things kept*
> *piling up they reacted at times in their same old way.* (Female FC
> worker).

Older children were judged to have a limited understanding of what
was happening in most cases, but generally the issue was not raised
in respect of younger children. For one child (aged eight) the family
care worker felt:

> *(Child) understands in so far as if [child]'s behaviour is really bad ...*
> *(child) understands that life's better when [child] sees us but equally it's*
> *difficult to gauge whether (child) realises why we stop* (Female family
> care worker).

Dissatisfied parents specifically described poor communications
between themselves and the CPO, stressing a lack of feedback about
what was happening in general, and particularly with respect to their
children's sessions with the CPO. They felt the CPO to be inacces-
sible, and mentioned having to 'ask about everything', instead of
being 'told'. From the CPO's point of view, it was often difficult to
provide help immediately it was required as parents, children and
workers reached different stages in the casework process at different
times.

Parents were more forthcoming about describing the CPO's relationship with their children. Even if their own relationship with the
CPO was strained, they generally described their children's as quite
positive. Only one father revealed any reservations, about the CPO
'policing' his child.

Several parents felt that good CPO–child relations were to be
expected and represented the 'job' of the CPO.

Children did not describe in any detail their relationship with
their CPO, although most liked the workers with whom they had
had contact. When questioned specifically, most agreed that they
could talk to their CPO, and would discuss a problem with him or
her.

I liked (CPO) … (CPO) helped me. I couldn't talk to anybody else about my feelings and I'd just open up to (CPO) (Girl, aged 11).

Generally, CPOs felt that relationships are secondary to the aims which they are pursuing with families. Some CPOs thought they had good or difficult relationships with clients (particularly parents) but in general this was not a key issue for them in casework. Certainly, relationships did not carry the same significance for CPOs that they did for clients. For example,

I'm a bit reluctant really to talk in terms of relationship. I don't think it's about a relationship, I think it's about me as a professional working with them, I think how good we get on is irrelevant really, to how we instigate change and get them to look at their own lives. Their response is inconsistent – we're certainly not working towards a good relationship – what we're working towards is them acknowledging their problem and doing something about it (Female CPO).

The nature of casework

Pinpointing exactly what occurred during casework turned out to be difficult. From the parents' perspective, the typical first response to the open-ended question 'What do you do with your social worker?' was 'nothing much'. After questioning, activities described included chatting to the CPO, working on marital relationship, play sessions with children, day trips for families and afternoon sessions spent at the family care centres. There was no apparent relationship between the stage of casework reached by the families, and the types of activities undertaken.

A couple of parents specifically mentioned benefits from learning new child management techniques from their CPOs. Other mothers welcomed the provision of information from the CPOs relating to the abuse situation, and also the personal counselling and support they received:

They gave something that I never realised before – that I was more capable of helping [child] than I realised, um, I also discovered that I was stronger than I ever believed (Mother).

The ability to talk to the CPO about problems, and the feeling that the CPOs were there when the parents needed them appeared to be seen as one of the most helpful aspects of casework. Several parents commented that the CPO was 'just a phone call away' if they needed them.

In general, CPOs referred to the same types of activities when talking about what constitutes casework. Specifically, they referred to teaching new child management techniques, marital counselling and play sessions with the children. It was noticeable, however, that the CPOs described these activities in much more abstract terms, and emphasised their role (versus that of the parents) in the casework process. CPOs also tended to overlook the process of gaining 'access' into families as part of casework. The activity of 'identifying' the family's problems (rather than simply stating what the problems were) was not included in their descriptions of casework.

> *Essentially it was about helping and advising [Mother] with problems in her relationships ... she just could not manage her life, totally disorganised, insecure and needed a lot of practical advice and a lot of support* (Male CPO).

> *And for [child] it was giving [child] some time to express how [child] felt about living where [child] did* (Female CPO).

The provision of material and/or practical support seemed to be rated very positively by parents, and was frequently referred to by them. This practical support ranged from arranging accommodation, providing clothes, toys and accessories, to providing holidays, child minding facilities and negotiating with other agencies on the client's behalf (e.g. over payment of bills). Its provision did not appear to conflict with the value placed on 'relationships' from the parents' perspectives. The perceived lack of support over such practical issues was a major source of discontent for several parents. Some children also referred to material help that the CPO had provided. For example, an eight year-old girl said:

> *The first time ... I got lots of clothes from the NSPCC ... I got a great big teddy, I brought it home. They said I could keep it.*

Many CPOs referred to the practical help they had given to clients, and it was apparent in other cases that, in retrospect, they thought they could have offered more.

> *I think she always saw help as a practical matter not 'jaw jaw' help and I think that for some considerable time I thought the kind of help I should be offering was 'jaw jaw' and she thought the kind of help she should be getting was things or material matters – although she never asked for anything material – I include things like removing her troublesome son (in material)* (Male CPO).

From their comments, it was not always clear whether CPOs realised just how valuable practical aid was judged to be by clients.

The young children in this study unanimously stated that they 'played with toys' when they saw the CPO, but beyond that most did not elaborate on the activities that had been undertaken. Some children had been taken on trips and 'given a little treat', and some referred to clothes and toys they had received. One girl remembered:

We were video camera'd ... my brother, me, my mum ... we was talking as why my mum kicked (boyfriend) out (Girl, aged 8 years).

Older children mentioned talking with the CPO, and recalled how it had helped them.

What I did at school, um, what like I do in the day and uh (CPO)'d ask me questions about me mum. What I don't and what I do like about her and I could say (Girl, aged 11 years).

(CPO)'s been talking about what happened, explaining it all to me in sort of great detail ... sees if things are going well, asks if mum and dad are having any late arguments or anything like that, mum still holding her strongness and everything, just mainly that (Girl, aged 12 years).

(CPO) pointed out like different things and made us realise like how we felt, and um then it got more serious, and what we'd like to do if we could do anything about it (Young woman, aged 20 years).

When asked specifically what they had liked or disliked, young children simply said they liked playing with toys, and didn't dislike anything. Older children were more discerning, and were able to elucidate some specific aspects they had found helpful or not. One young woman described a meeting with her CPO she had enjoyed:

I arranged to meet (CPO). (CPO) took me for a meal and we sat and discussed things ... I can remember we went out. I think I was really nervous at the time ... That was really nice, to get out somewhere on neutral ground and have a chat, and do it not like across a table was really nice (Young woman, aged 19 years).

This same girl disliked 'painful' family discussions regarding her abuse, and reported finding the police investigative interview very difficult. Another young woman disliked certain aspects of her group meetings, although overall she thought they were 'brilliant'. For her, difficulties arose over the amount of time devoted to one individual in the group, and the abrupt ending of group meetings.

Very few parents or children spontaneously mentioned either the Child Protection Register or case conferences. Even when questioned, most parents had little to say. Mostly, for those who did talk about it, registers and case conferences were regarded as negative, and 'coming off' the register was a source of relief:

We had a case conference and they discharged it and took them off the register so that wasn't so bad ... I am relieved they're off 'cos I didn't feel they were at risk ... I felt as if they were blaming me. Now they've come off that's the relief you know 'cos I don't feel as I'm getting the blame for it any more (Mother).

One father felt the register was a means of guarding the agency's own interest:

> *Personally, I don't see the difference if they're on the at risk register or not … All the time they're on the register the NSPCC are safe … it just means the NSPCC have clean hands* (Father).

Other mothers voiced their feelings of exclusion from the registration and case conference process:

> *They just say there's a case conference coming up and we'll let you know the outcome of it. I haven't been invited to one other than when (child) first went in. They just tell me say whether they've come off or not come off and a little bit of what was actually said, not a full run down* (Mother).

> *We can go to this one [case conference], but the first one we didn't which I think is wrong. If they're talking about the family we've got a right to be there. We could only go at the end when everything's said and done* (Mother).

CPOs referred to the register and case conferences as a matter of course, and tended to simply describe reasons for registration:

> *The children's names were put on the register because at the beginning it wasn't known whether (boyfriend) would stay away … so it was felt they needed to be on the register* (Female CPO).

> *It was felt at the case conference that a supervision order should be requested on (child) before the dad went back* (Female CPO).

Some CPOs appeared to appreciate some of their clients' feelings regarding the child protection procedures. However, it is questionable whether there was a general recognition of how excluding these procedures can be from the parents' perspective.

Mothers and children

Some of the most striking feedback in this study came from mothers, specifically in relation to their role as the primary caretaker for children whom they viewed as difficult, and also as partners of perpetrators of abuse. These women spoke of the tension they had experienced during the casework process and of the isolation they often felt. They viewed the CPO's role as antagonistic, feeling that the CPO was 'for' the child and either disinterested or hostile towards themselves. This conflict may have arisen from confusion about the CPO's role; only one mother seemed able to appreciate and accept the situation.

*'cos like there's the child's side isn't there and there's my side, so there's
a social worker for me and a keyworker for my children, even though I
work with the keyworker for my children ... 'cos I won't know about
(child)'s work with [CPO], only what [CPO]'s told me ... that was a
point of trust between [child] and [CPO], what (child) and [CPO]
done* (Mother).

Another mother expressed the opposite view:

*That's [CPO]'s and [child]'s time but not ours but we would like to
know what's happening ... if we don't know how can we help?*
(Mother).

Others felt even more strongly that their needs and views were
directly opposed to those of their chidren:

*(CPO) seemed ever so much for [child], I suppose [child] was the
favourite, anything [child] wanted [child] could have ... but if I'd got
what I considered a genuine complaint against [child], [CPO]
wouldn't listen to it* (Mother).

This situation led to mothers feeling isolated, and that their requests
for help were ignored.

*I suppose [CPO] came in weekly but [CPO] wasn't there for me,
[CPO] was there for [child] which I can understand but I also needed
somebody too, and there was nobody there for me ... when I got a problem if I phoned up I got it flung back in my face ... and [CPO] just
doesn't seem ... to care* (Mother).

*At that time I felt I was isolated, I felt cut out, um, I knew it was good
for [child] to go to group meetings but when [child] came back from the
meetings [child] was so hyped up that I felt at a loss to be able to help
[child] ... I agreed wholeheartedly with what they were trying to do but
it was at that time that a lot of my family didn't agree with what I was
doing and I felt isolated* (Mother).

One CPO explicitly acknowledged this problem, commenting that
the relationship between the mother and herself had 'deteriorated to
zero' after the child's disclosure of sexual abuse. She explained that
before this disclosure she had been viewed as the mother's 'ally', but
subsequently had had to become the child's 'ally'.

For some mothers the problem seemed to be that they felt the
CPO did not know the 'real child' whom they had to live with, so to
a certain degree the CPO's involvement was seen as inappropriate

and/or limited:

> *(Child) comes back and rubs it in our face, Oh [CPO] lets me do this, and [CPO] lets me do that* (Mother).

> *[Child] could do no wrong in [CPO]'s eyes, but [CPO] didn't have to live with [child], live with [child]'s moods ...* (Mother).

> *Well they say 'there's no way we don't think [child]'s bad enough' but they don't see [child] they don't live with [child]* (Mother).

In part, CPOs did appreciate the difficulties parents were facing, and would refer, for example, to children's disturbed or aggressive behaviour stemming from their abuse. One CPO described a mother's expectations of her child as 'over the top', and commented that one mother *says 'they manipulate her by using her'*. This discrepancy could again arise from a lack of clarity about the CPO's role.

Three mothers talked about the difficulties they faced after their daughters had been sexually abused. One woman felt she had been made to feel guilty by the CPO:

> *After the abuse came to light, we'd spend an hour sitting and talking and all [CPO] was virtually saying to me 'well it's your fault, you're a rotten mother, admit that he did it' ... and I can't admit something I haven't seen, something I'm not party to or anything. I mean the hours I've spent in the kitchen with [CPO] and I was crying because I wouldn't do what [CPO] wanted me to. I mean, alright, I have now accepted the situation, he abused my daughter, but it's something you can't have forced upon you. You've got to come to terms to it in your own time* (Mother).

Another woman felt, in hindsight, that she had not received the help she still needed:

> *It's just time that will heal me, won't it? [CPO] said that I was shouldering all the stress and everything ... I felt that it was me, that I was like the victim ... I think maybe if they'd done a follow-up visit or something a few months after ... At the time when (CPO) thought I was alright I was alright ... it wasn't until it got to the court case I was really under stress with what was coming ... that was the worst time* (Mother).

The third woman spoke of her feelings at being used as a go-between for professionals working with the perpetrator (her husband), and also her sense of injustice at her continued involvement in casework after the perpetrator's involvement had ceased:

> *If they couldn't get through to (husband) they went through me to get to (husband), if you know what I mean. If he didn't tow the line it was*

harder on me. They leaned on me to get to him ... which I could under-
stand in a way, but at the time it didn't help none.

And,

It's all a very dramatic experience from start to finish because though
I've caused no wrong, it all boils down, in actual fact, that the innocent
party is involved a lot longer than what the guilty party is ... I resent
that to a certain degree. That's an intrusion on my life, perhaps that's
being a bit selfish and I know it's being for the good of the children ...
but now [husband] has finished his probation period I'm still involved
with the NSPCC (Mother).

Ending casework and moving on

Most parents whose involvement with the NSPCC had effectively
ceased expressed pleasure that this was so. Many talked of a mutual
agreement with the CPO to stop contact, although several stated that
they 'still had the number' if they needed help at a later date. For
most parents in this position, closure was seen as affirmation of their
improvement.

[CPO] felt that I'd improved and I didn't need it but how did I feel?
It was sort of mutual (Mother).

They said we can't teach you no more ... I mean I didn't come out of
the office and that was it, I mean I have got a phone number ...
[CPO]'s still there for me (Mother).

One mother expressed some dismay at closure:

I was a bit worried when they said there was nothing else they could do.
It was like (CPO) was going, but (CPO) did say they'd always be there
... I think I could have done with something but I don't know what
(Mother).

Children did not generally comment upon their feelings regarding
closure – but two girls did expressed some regret:

I would have liked to carry on ... just to see them (Girl, aged 8 years).

So we don't go there no more ... sad, 'cos I want to go play with all my
favourite toys (Girl, aged 5 years).

Positive images of closure were generally reported by the CPOs.

We felt that we were ready to release them from the family care support
system and I felt that the marital therapy had come to the point where
they could at least have a break on it although they were free to come
back. So all those ... had come together and we made a joint decision

at family care review (Female CPO).

After the children's names were taken off the register ... the review decided we had made sufficient progress ... and we would close the case. I have a feeling it was a con-joint agreement between the parents and ourselves (Female CPO).

Again, as with parents, there was the feeling by professionals that parents could always return for further help, even after 'official' closure. Parents whose contact with the Society was ongoing generally expressed the wish to cease contact. They stressed the desire to 'move on' with their lives:

Perhaps things could have done a little quicker, it must be about (x) years now, I'd like it to have finished sooner, like to have moved on with my life (Mother).

These sentiments were echoed in the comments of one young woman:

I used to think, God, I wish the whole subject would be forgotten really, 'cos it's all happened, and it's all over with, and we're trying to get on with a new life now, and (CPO) used to have to come in here and discuss it all with us again (Young woman, aged 19 years).

And were also recognised by several CPOs:

Child has in the last few months become ... she wants it all to be over now and I think that's fair enough (Female CPO).

It's difficult to get a balance, because you don't want to keep harping on about it because people have to get on with their lives and continue to repair the damage, and harping on what's happened isn't always helpful, and yet, you've got to make sure they're reminded time to time so they don't lapse into a sort of apathy about it all (Female CPO).

Casework: final comments

At the end of the interviews, participants were asked to summarise their experience of casework, and/or their experience with the NSPCC. This tended to 'polarise' parents into two groups: those who were predominantly positive ($n=7$; usually their 'cases' were now closed) and those who were predominantly negative ($n=4$; usually their 'cases' were still open).

Good, very good, excellent. No problems at all (Father).

Waste of time because it hasn't changed, it's been (x) years now (Mother).

Children found it more difficult to summarise their opinion of the NSPCC, and almost all were positive about their experiences. Young children simply commented that they had liked it, or 'it were great', but one young woman expressed in more detail how she had benefited.

> *For the first time it felt like I could become my own person instead of having to hide something and they made me feel good about it ... I feel for myself that they were excellent* (Young woman, aged 20 years).

CPOs were noticeably less positive about casework, in terms of both their own input and the families' ability (or motivation) to sustain progress.

> *There was change ... for better at the time, I can't say it would have continued* (Female FC worker).

> *I wasn't sure whether the change of attitude the mother had towards [child] would stay in place ... I wasn't sure whether [child] would be scapegoated again sometime in the future* (Female CPO).

This section has endeavoured to draw together different participants' perceptions of the casework process. Substantial differences have emerged in some areas, which tend to indicate that the relative importance of different aspects of casework varies between parents, CPOs, and children.

Overview and discussion

Methodological issues in the current study

Throughout, this study has attempted to address and overcome some of the weaknesses noted in previous studies of service users (Sainsbury, 1987). For example, it has included the perspectives of all participants in the casework process, not just users, and not just parents (see Marsh, 1983; Robinson, 1983). Inevitably, however, it has its own shortcomings which should be noted here.

First, and perhaps most obviously, this study comprised a relatively small number of interviews with white, non disabled chidren, parents and child protection officers. This partly reflects the historical development of the NSPCC and its failure, to date, to fully provide services to families from minority ethnic communities, as well as to families with disabled children. However, these are major deficits and should be examined in any future research.

Secondly, in order to preserve confidentiality, and also to expedite the project, selection of families was at the discretion of CPOs and family care staff. This compromises the generalisability of the findings somewhat, as the cases selected cannot be assumed representative of all NSPCC cases. However, as illustrated by their comments, the families selected were not chosen on the basis of them holding particularly positive views of the NSPCC, or of individual CPOs. Further, for a qualitative study of perceptions, the requirement of representativeness is not as pertinent as it might be in other types of research (Bertaux, 1981). The comments that different participants have made are valuable and represent more than just the views of idiosyncratic individuals (see Phillimore, 1981).

Thirdly, it was anticipated that each family would have been assigned to a different CPO, thus ensuring a large number of worker perspectives in the research. This did not occur for several reasons; some CPOs had no response from any families they contacted about participation, whilst for others, every family approached agreed to participate. Thus, some CPOs were interviewed on more than one occasion, and their experience of the initial research interview may have influenced their comments upon later cases. Also, this resulted in a smaller number of CPOs being interviewed overall, although a CPO perspective was obtained for every family seen. The role of family care staff in the project should also have been clarified so that interviews with workers were more systematically included in the research.

Fourthly, despite obtaining the views of a number of children and young people upon the casework process, it is perhaps a disappointment that more were not available. A greater amount of feedback from more children may also have presented a rather different view of casework, expecially in cases where parents were interviewed but not children. (It should be noted that these cases were both 'positive' and 'negative' in terms of the parents' overall perspective on casework.) In a number of cases, the children involved were very young, and so unable to contribute. The real value of comments by younger children, for example that they liked seeing the CPO because they played with toys, is also unclear. Excluding these cases might be inappropriate, however, as some of the NSPCC's work is conducted with such families. The children in this study, as well as falling at the predominantly younger (less than eight) or older (eighteen plus) age range, also comprised largely females. More input from children in the mid-age range, and from boys and young men would have been desirable.

A fifth comment concerns the advantages and disadvantages of interviewing families in either open or closed cases. In hindsight, it has been valuable to obtain the perspectives from both categories, since participants raised a number of issues intrinsic to the different statuses. However, a number of other issues stemming from this 'open/closed' factor have become apparent throughout the study. Farrar (1985) reported that clients were reluctant to criticise their caseworker, and it was certainly noticeable that I had to specifically prompt families in many cases (especially closed) on a number of occasions to elicit any sort of negative comment (however mild or unequivocal). There was a quite clear difference between the overall attitudes of parents in either open or closed cases as shown below:

6 open cases   – 4 negative
– 2 positive

5 closed cases – 5 positive

In contrast, virtually all the children and young women's feedback was positive, irrespective of whether their case was open or closed.

It is possible that the passage of time obscures the intensity of any negative feelings the parents experienced in cases which were closed at interview, whereas for open cases, these feelings were still very real or otherwise clearly remembered. Robinson (1983) and Wallace and Rees (1984) have discussed the problems associated with retrospective methodology in client studies, and argue that service users' needs and expectations (and therefore perspectives) will vary in relation to the stage of casework that has been reached. It is also possible that CPO behaviours which are distressing to parents are inevitable given the CPOs' directive to act 'in the best interests of children' and thus, take action not seen by parents to be in their own 'best interests' – an issue that is discussed below, and relates to the CPO's role in relation to the family.

Following Maluccio's (1979) distinction between 'voluntary' and 'involuntary' service users, it may be worth noting that the four 'negative' parents were all involuntarily involved with the NSPCC. Some of the 'positive' parents were also involuntary, however, so as a factor this did not, on its own, predict the parent's overall perspective.

Robinson (1983) argues that the solution is to examine social work 'face-to-face' rather than retrospectively, and presumably this would be possible through observation of CPO–family contacts (either directly or indirectly through videotape). The difficulty here is whether the research interviews (which could be many in a long-term case) would interfere with or otherwise adversely affect the casework process. Also, when this issue was discussed with CPOs in the current study, several felt that the researcher would be in danger of being scapegoated and/or manipulated should the family be unhappy with any aspect of casework – a viewpoint which would be interesting to discuss with families. A totally satisfactory resolution to the problem seems unlikely.

Another interesting issue that arose in relation to the open–closed status of cases was that pertaining to confidentiality. As interviewer, I repeatedly felt that, in those cases where the parents were predominantly dissatisfied with their CPO (all of which were open cases), there was an unspoken desire for their views to be fed back to the CPO – despite my assurances that the contents of each interview were confidential (cf Wallace and Rees, 1984).

One final methodological issue pertains to the role of the interviewer. Wallace and Rees (1984) state that ideally the interviewer/researcher should be independent of the service-providing agency, so that she/he is not in a position of power in the eyes of the family. Where this is not possible, then the researcher should emphasise his or her 'distance' from the service providers. In the current study, this task was made easier since not only could the researcher stress her lack of social-work qualifications, but also was known to live and work some distance from both participating teams. It is still possible, though, that association with the NSPCC may have made it difficult for some clients to be openly critical (Farrar, 1985; Wallace and Rees, 1984); from my experience as interviewer, however, I am not convinced this was the case (refer to critical comments made by parents). The effect of other interviewer characteristics upon client/CPO response should also not be disregarded. That is, clients may have been influenced in responding by interviewer, age, gender and race.

Current findings: comparison to existing literature

Generally, there appears to be a good deal of consistency between the present findings and those reported in previous research: thus families involved with the NSPCC share at least some of the same experiences as families involved in casework with other agencies.

In addition, however, the current study has provided information relating to areas or issues not discussed previously, especially in relation to feedback from children and CPOs. Thus, the study can contribute knowledge from *participants* involved in child protection services. For ease of presentation here, the findings will be discussed within the same structure as that given previously.

Expectations, CPO roles and reactions to intervention

The confusion experienced by parents and children in this study has been widely reported elsewhere (Barford, this volume; Brown, 1986;

Phillimore, 1981). The lack of clarity over the purpose of CPO visits, and the role of the CPO, as judged by parents has also been discussed in previous studies (Brown, 1986; Phillimore, 1981).

Goldstein (1983) suggests this confusion arises since social workers are 'so different' from other professionals which families have encountered. Certainly, this uncertainty from the families' viewpoint seems worthy of greater consideration, for example, in its effect on their motivation to participate in casework. Other issues raised by this study in relation to expectations have not been widely discussed in service user studies (cf Phillimore, 1981), generally reflecting the lack of worker feedback. CPOs in this study contrasted with children and parents in that they had, in most cases, quite clear expectations of both their own role, and of the families' role, in casework.

Perceptions of the NSPCC, individual CPOs and families

As the first formal documentation of service user feedback in the NSPCC, there is a lack of relevant existing information with which to compare the current research. It is also important to note that reflections on image may pertain to the Society's role as a child protection social work agency, rather than as the 'NSPCC' per se. Barford reports that the children in his study expressed similar fears of being removed from their homes by social workers.

In general, the perceptions of CPOs given by children and parents here mirror those of social workers elicited in previous studies. Families prefer their worker to show humour, empathy, friendliness and care, and dislike insincerity, inaccessibility and unfriendliness (Barford; Brown 1986; Magura, 1982; Pharis and Levin, 1991). In general, parents appear to desire *partnership* with their worker (Marsh, 1983) as opposed to less equal power relationships. The age, gender and life experiences of CPOs in this study were important for many clients, in agreement with other studies (Brown, 1986; cf Barford). The desire to feel 'understood' has also been noted by a previous author (Lishman, 1988).

From the CPOs' perspective, the preference for open and responsive clients was also reported by Maluccio (1979). In general, however, the existing literature has failed to address the workers' perspective in any detail, and the discrepancy between parents' and CPOs' valuation of the worker–user relationship noted here has also not been addressed. This latter issue particularly would seem worth further exploration, and may directly impinge on the success or otherwise of casework. The preference for workers who have themselves been abused, as expressed by one young woman in this study, is also of interest.

The nature of casework

The recognition that talking represents the key feature of casework has previously been noted in studies of both service user feedback (e.g. Brown, 1986) and of caseworker feedback (e.g. Maluccio, 1979). Many authors have commented upon the importance for clients of talking to someone who really cared (Magura, 1982; Pharis and Levin, 1991; Phillimore, 1981), and this perspective was described by several mothers in the current study. The question as to whether social workers or CPOs overestimate the importance of talking compared to clients reported by previous authors (Maluccio, 1979; Sainsbury et al., 1982) has not been examined here, although the comments of one CPO would suggest this might be the case at least occasionally.

The perceived value of practical support and/or material assistance has proved rather inconsistent in the existing literature, with some studies stressing the importance of such aid as perceived by clients (e.g. Barford; Magura, 1982; Phillimore, 1981), and others commenting that therapeutic counselling was seen as more important (e.g. Pharis and Levin, 1991). For children and parents in this study, practical support seemed to be very important, supporting the former position. Magura and Moses (1984) argue that confusion concerning the perceived role of social workers is at its most acute in relation to the provision of financial or practical aid, with knock-on effects likely on expectations and client satisfaction or dissatisfaction. It did appear here that CPOs perhaps underestimated the perceived value of practical aid, as noted previously by Sainsbury et al. (1982).

The children's perspectives outlined here are in broad agreement with those obtained by Barford, but further research on the child's viewpoint is desirable. In particular, it may be that children's experience of other types of activities in casework, e.g. groupwork, should be sought. One young woman in this study, for example, held quite definite views on the value and difficulties involved in the groupwork she had experienced.

The child protection register and case conferences

The parents and children in this study displayed the same lack of knowledge regarding the register and case conferences that has been previously noted (e.g. Brown, 1986; Smith, 1990). Parents' concerns about 'being on the register' have also been shared by parents in an earlier study (Phillimore, 1981). Their feelings of exclusion from case conferences, when either invited to attend only the final part, or not invited to attend at all, have also been reported elsewhere (e.g. Thoburn, Lewis and Shemmings, 1991). Given these findings, and in the light of the Children Act, this whole area has recently been given much greater practice and policy attention (e.g. Marsh and Fisher, 1992; Smith, 1990; Thoburn et al., 1991).

Mothers and children

Attention is increasingly focussing upon the difficulties facing mothers of sexually abused children (e.g. Hooper, 1992), and some support is available in earlier studies. Magura (1982) reported the case of one mother who felt her needs were sacrificed for the needs of her child, and Malekoff (1991) comments upon the isolation experienced by parents whose children are participaing in groupwork. Stewart (1985) hints at the 'real child' phenomenon reported in the current study:

> The parent who is under pressure trying to manage a difficult child is pleased when we focus on this, and relieved if we get to see the child's difficult behaviour they are complaining about. (p. 24)

The isolation experienced by mothers who feel their needs are unmet during casework reflects again the confusion regarding the CPO's role – is the CPO 'for' the child or the mother? In this respect more work is needed to show how CPOs 'bridge' this mother/child 'divide', and to explore further the specific problems encountered by mothers of child sexual abuse victims (see Hooper, 1992). In addition, it might be worth considering to what extent the mother–child relationship, as perceived by the mother, is the 'gatekeeper' to the success (or otherwise) of casework.

Ending casework and moving on

The children in Barford's study shared the same 'mystery concerning closure' as expressed by some of the children in the current research. It is interesting to note that the experience of closure was perceived as predominantly negative by children, whilst predominantly positive by parents and CPOs (cf Phillimore, 1981). The desire to 'move on' expressed by parents who had already been involved in casework for some considerable time may merit further attention in terms of its relationship to the success or otherwise of the intervention. The CPOs' pessimism concerning parents' ability to sustain improvement after closure has been noted by Maluccio (1979). Such pessimism may reflect the fundamental differences that exist between workers and parents regarding casework, and which are discussed later in more detail.

Outstanding issues

Having discussed the methodology and findings of the current
study, several fundamental issues remain outstanding, although
hinted at in previous discussions. In reality, these issues are all inter-
linked, although they will be discussed separately here.

CPO–parent differences in perspective

Many differences have become apparent in the way in which parents, CPOs and, to the lesser degree, children view casework. These
differences have come to seem somewhat irredeemable, and may
undermine the success of casework in a number of cases. Whether
these differences arise as a result of factors such as ethnicity, sex or
socio-economic status of participants (Wallace and Rees, 1984), or
from different interests and investments in the casework process
(Appleton and Minchom, 1991), their consequent effect on the interaction appears predominantly negative and unhelpful (Maluccio,
1979). Not everyone would agree, however, and some would instead
see such differences as healthy (Appleton and Minchom, 1991).
Indeed, Marsh (1983) argues that the very value of 'client' studies
lies in documenting the different perspectives that are obtained.
     The current study suggests that parent–CPO differences are
almost inevitable unless all participants agree from the outset on
what the explicit aims, objectives and focus of the casework will be.
This seems unlikely in certain cases, given the power dynamics
involved (and intrinsic inequity in power between participants) and
the likely 'involuntary' status of many 'service users' with whom the
NSPCC works (see Maluccio, 1979). In their study of family involvement in child protection conferences, Thoburn et al. (1991) differentiate between 'worst scenario', 'best scenario' and 'middle
scenario' cases, with regard to the degree to which full parental participation will be 'possible'. Thoburn et al. comment that:

> A worker striving very hard to achieve parental involvement
> may not succeed if the abuse is of a persistent and deliberate
> nature, if parents deny responsibility for the abuse, if parents and
> social workers disagree about the degree of damage and ways of
> helping, if parents reject social work involvement ... and if the
> alleged abuse is of a sexual nature and is denied. (p. 5)

Until agreement is reached, it seems likely that differences in perspective will continue, as workers focus on the content of casework,
and parents on the process (Maluccio, 1979).

The effect of casework on the CPO

Only two CPOs voluntarily referred to the way in which the family (or the case) had affected them, the majority discussing instead service user reactions to casework and their management of those reactions. This phenomenon was also noted by Maluccio (1979) in his study. Phillimore (1981) commented that many of the clients in his study viewed their relationship with the social worker as much more one sided than it actually was, and Maluccio (1979) concludes that workers' helping efforts are contingent upon families' personal impact upon themselves.

This issue of the worker–family relationship, and the effect of the family on the worker, has been examined by Goddard and Tucci (1991) who argue that the social worker–family relationship has always been considered the primary *uni-directional* medium of social casework (i.e. practice focusses only on what the worker can do for the worker, and not vice versa). Goddard and Tucci argue that the consequences of this include increased risk for the child, and questions about the competence of social workers (rather than the feasibility of the task) when they are unable to form 'constructive, helping' relationships with all families.

Another consequence of the historical assumptions regarding the social worker–family relationship is the romanticised portrayal of the families as motivated (i.e. voluntary) help seekers. Further, the historical position also fails to consider the problems inherent in the worker–family relationship where the 'true' service user is a child who may be too young or too frightened to discuss what is happening. If Goddard and Tucci's (1991) arguments are accepted, then it is possible to see why the differences in perspective discussed above arise, and why it is that reappraisal of the social worker–family relationship is necessary to facilitate success in the casework process. Implementation of the Children Act legislation has provided the impetus for the beginnings of such a reappraisal to be undertaken.

The value of children's and parents' feedback

What *is* the role of 'client' studies – especially one which makes no claims about evaluating the services provided? Are they useful, valuable sources of information about practice (Marsh, 1983) or disproportionately powerful voices of minority opinion (Shaw, 1975)?

This final question comprises possibly the most fundamental issue, and one still in need of attention. Shaw (1975) has provided a fierce critique of 'client' studies, focussing on sampling problems, and the difficulties in 'generalising out' from those service users who

have been included. Shaw argues that in order for service user opinion to be valuable the views expressed must be relatively permanent,
and must be given after consideration of the possible alternative
ways of dealing with the problem. Further, Shaw discusses problems
in deriving policy recommendations from service user opinion –
'studies' of the present should not dictate services for the future.

Shaw represents a rather extreme position, and it is debatable as
to whether service user studies are indeed as influential as he sup-
poses them to be. However, the issues he raises are still in need of
proper debate – almost 20 years after he stated them.

Concluding remarks

This discussion may have given the appearance of being all negative,
yet a glance back shows this not to be the case. Delivering a summary positive or negative verdict on the families' or CPO's
experience would be superficial and would only obscure issues.
There were many favourable comments from families, but also some
less favourable.

This research illustrated the complexity of the casework process,
and has also highlighted the necessity of considering all participants' perspectives. Children appeared to be very happy with the
casework and their CPO, but reactions from parents were more
mixed, and in several areas their views contrasted with those of
CPOs. Discussion has suggested that attempts to resolve these differences, especially for involuntary service users, may improve the
quality of casework services offered, and also their success.

This study has highlighted the value of obtaining children's
views, and older children especially had much to say about their
CPO and casework. A subsequent study has examined sexually
abused children's and young people's views of investigative interviews (Westcott, 1993), and has built upon the experiences gained in
conducting the present research. Separating children's perspectives
from those of their parents would seem a pre-requisite for further
research, and it may be of value to study the degree to which parents
act as gatekeepers for casework undertaken 'in the best interest' of
the child. Certainly, this study supports the Children Act's objectives of listening to children, and giving credence to their views.

References

Appleton, P. L. and Minchom, P. E. (1991) 'Models of parent partnership and child
development centres', *Child: Care, Health and Development*, 17, pp. 27–38.
Barford, R. and Wattam, C. (1991) 'Children's participation in decision-making',

Practice, 5(2), pp. 93–102.

Bertaux, D. (1981) 'From the life-history approach to the transformation of sociological practice', in Bertaux, D. (Ed) *Biography and Society: The Life History Approach In The Social Sciences*, Beverley Hills: CA Sage.

Brown, C. (1986) *Child Abuse Parents Speaking: Parents' Impressions of Social Workers and the Social Work Process*, Bristol: School for Advanced Urban Studies, University of Bristol.

Bush, M., Gordon, A. C. and Le Bailly, R. (1977) 'Evaluating child welfare services: a contribution from the clients', *Social Service Review*, 15(3), pp. 491–501.

Farrar, J. (1985) 'Joint evaluation by worker, supervisor and client', *FSU Quarterly*, 36, pp. 33–37.

Goddard, C. and Tucci, J. (1991) 'Child protection and the need for the reappraisal of the social worker–client relationship', *Australian Social Work*, 44(2), pp. 3–10.

Goldstein, H. (1983) 'Starting where the client is', *Social Casework*, 64(5), pp. 267–275.

Hooper, C. A. (1992) *Mothers Surviving Child Sexual Abuse*, London: Routledge.

Jones, R. (1978) 'Intermediate treatment and adolescents' perceptions of social workers', *British Journal of Social Work*, 8(4), pp. 425–438.

Lishman, J. (1988) 'Social work interviews: how effective are they?' *Research, Policy and Planning*, 5(2), pp. 1–5.

Magura, S. (1982) 'Clients' view outcomes of child protective services', *Social Casework*, 63,(9), pp. 522–531.

Magura, S. and Moses, B. S. (1984) 'Clients as evaluators in child protective services', *Child Welfare*, 63(2), pp. 99–112.

Malekoff, A. (1991) '?D2?"What's goin' on in there?!?!"': Alliance formation with parents whose children are in group treatment', *Social Work With Groups*, 14(1), pp. 75–85.

Maluccio, A. (1979) *Learning From Clients: Interpersonal Helping as Viewed by Clients and Social Workers*, New York: The Free Press.

Marsh, P. (1983) 'Researching practice and practising research in child care social work', in Fisher, M. (Ed) *Speaking of Clients*, Sheffield: University of Sheffield, Joint Unit for Social Services Research.

Marsh, P. and Fisher, M. (1992) *Good Intentions: Developing Partnership in Social Services*, York: Joseph Rowntree Foundation.

Mayor, J. E. and Timms, N. (1970) *The Client Speaks: Working Class Impressions of Casework*, London: Routledge & Kegan Paul.

Pharis, M. E. and Levin, V. S. (1991) 'A person to talk to who really cared: high-risk mothers evaluations of services in an intensive intervention research program', *Child Welfare*, 70(3), pp. 307–320.

Phillimore, P. (1981) *Families Speaking: A Study of Fifty-one Families' Views of Social Work*, London: Family Service Units.

Rees, S. (1978) *Social Work Face to Face*, London: Edward Arnold.

Rees, S. and Wallace, A. (1982) *Verdicts on Social Work*, London: Edward Arnold.

Robinson, T. ((1983) 'Lessons from elsewhere: the case for enriching the client studies tradition', in Fisher, M. (Ed) *Speaking of Clients*, Sheffield: University of Sheffield, Joint Unit for Social Services Research.

Sainsbury, E. (1987) 'Client studies: their contribution and limitations in influencing social work practice', *British Journal of Social Work*, 17, pp. 635–644.

Sainsbury, E. (1975) *Social Work With Families*, London: Routledge & Kegan Paul.

Sainsbury, E., Nixon, S. and Phillips, D. (1982) *Social Work in Focus: Clients' and Social Workers' Perceptions in Long-Term Social Work*. London: Routledge & Kegan Paul.

Shaw, I. (1975) 'Consumer opinion and social policy: a research review', *Journal of Social Policy*, 5, pp. 19–32.

Smith, N. (1990) *Learning from Parents*, Penrith, Cumbria: Cumbria County Council Child Protection Unit.

Stewart, B. (1985) 'Never mind the child – what about me', *Child Abuse Review*, 1, pp. 23–25.

Thoburn, J., Lewis, A. and Shennings, D. (1991) *Family Involvement in Child Protection Conferences*, Norwich: University of East Anglia, Social Work Development Unit.

Wallace, A. and Rees, S. (1984) 'The priority of client evaluations', in Lishman, J. (Ed.) *Evaluation*, Aberdeen: University of Aberdeen, Department of Social Work.

Westcott, H. L. (1993) 'Sexually abused children's and young people's perspectives on investigative interviews', Manuscript submitted for publication.

11 Involving and empowering children and young people:
overcoming the barriers
Phil Treseder

In 1979 the United Nations celebrated International Year of the Child. As part of those celebrations the UK Organising Committee, in conjunction with the British Youth Council, held a children's parliament for under 17 year-olds at the then Greater London Council headquarters. The event was very high profile with the then recently elected prime minister Margaret Thatcher opening the Parliament. The conference involved some 200 young people between the ages of 14 and 17 selected from across the UK from voluntary organisations and local education authorities. The conference was very well organised, and the British Youth Council made sure that young people were fully involved in the planning of the event.

However, the deliberations did not produce the results some may have expected. The parliament threw out a resolution on the lowering of the voting age to 16 and threw out a resolution proposing abolition of corporal punishment by parents.

Fifteen years after the United Nations International Year of the Child, there is still no permanent structure to allow children and young people to be part of the debate on children's rights issues. There is no contribution from children and young people at a national level into any of the children's organisations or any supported forum for children and young people under the age of 16.

On a few occasions, at conferences, when I have pointed out the need for a contribution from children and young people I have met with the response of 'we tried that once by having a children and young people's parliament in 1979 and it didn't work, they came out with all the wrong answers'. It is interesting that nobody has really looked at why they perceive it as not having worked, and that we write off the contribution of children and young people to the national debate on the basis that they did not come up with what we felt were the appropriate answers the first time they were offered the opportunity.

As luck would have it I am in a position to evaluate the event because, as an angry 16 year-old who had just left an awful school with no qualifications to work in British Leyland, I was there. It was I who proposed the resolution on lowering the voting age to 16 only to see it lost after a young woman related a one-off story of a 17 year-old being murdered after he left care and returned home to a violent stepfather after ignoring the advice of a social worker. The problem was quite simple. Although the event was very well organised and very enjoyable for those involved – it had brought together some two hundred children and young people from across the UK who had never met each other before – they had little or no previous experience or background in discussing fairly complex social issues. The result being that various emotive arguments won the day. The result should be no surprise to anybody, the same result would occur if we selected 200 adults at random and brought them together to discuss law and order issues. Public opinion would no doubt be reflected and so they would most likely demand the restoration of public flogging and the death penalty, possibly including the two ten year olds convicted for the murder of James Bulger.

Fifteen years later we have seen the UN Convention on the Rights of the Child with Article 12 on participation central to its underlying principles and the Children Act of 1989 which recognises the right of children and young people to give their views on decisions affecting them though in very limited circumstances. There has also been a growing recognition by voluntary organisations of the need to consult children and young people. Yet, when we attend any conference on issues related to children and young people, the most important voice and contribution remains missing, the voice of children and young people themselves. The contribution of children and young people is very often missing from the grass roots debate and, with the exception of the National Association of Young People in Care, is always missing from the national debate. In cases where there is a contribution to the debate by children and young people it is ad hoc and one-off and therefore does not reflect an informed debate from them which may be pursued as an ongoing campaign for change.

The challenge for policy-makers and professionals is to make participation a reality for all children and young people so that, in the future, they are empowered to make a contribution to decisions that affect them as individuals and as a group at both local and national levels. The principles for involving groups of children and young people are often the same as involving adults in a process.

As Youth Development worker with the Children's Rights Development Unit, an independent charity set up to promote the UN Convention of the Rights of the Child, I have specific responsibility for promotion of Article 12 of the Convention on participation of children and young people. Article 12 states,

> Parties shall assure to the child who is capable of forming his or her own views the right to express those views freely in all matters affecting the child, the views of the child being given due weight in accordance with age and maturity of the child.

> For this purpose, the child shall in particular be provided the opportunity to be heard in any judicial and administrative proceedings affecting the child, either directly or through a representative or an appropriate body, in a manner consistent with the procedural rules of national law.

The reasons for this lack of participation by children and young people remains one of the great unanswered questions of our age. Why is it that everybody seems to agree that it is a great idea, but so little of it actually goes on?

For me, one particular cartoon I recall seeing in an education pack some years ago summed up the main reason – fear. The cartoon showed a youth club with some young people dressed in stereotypical criminal/gangster outfits who were gathered around a table looking at plans and a map with a bank marked on it. The youth worker is standing nearby and addresses them by saying, 'yes I know I said you should start to work towards self determination but I'm not sure that planning to liberate three million pounds from the Nat West is the best way of achieving that'.

As an individual working in a field of the empowerment of children and young people over many years, I feel more and more that professionals are generally very sympathetic to the need to empower them, not only for the reason of the right of the child but also recognising the benefits to be gained from the process for children, young people, workers and organisations. Empowerment of children and young people is still very much on the agenda of professionals yet it seems that guidance is needed on what empowerment means in practice as well as strategies for making it effective.

This chapter will examine what are the barriers to empowerment and how we may overcome them. It will look at the need for workers and organisations to examine their own intentions before embarking on the road of progress to empowering children and young people as individuals or as a group.

This chapter raises questions which can be addressed to all workers and organisations in contact with children and young people in a range of settings, for example, teachers in schools, community workers supporting local projects, local authorities looking to involve children and young people in local decision-making through local forums or national voluntary organisations looking to involve children and young people in decision-making at a national level. It would not be possible to describe all the situations in which children are involved so the information contained covers in a broad sense the involvement of individual and groups of children and young people in decision-making. Information on more detailed examples may be found in *Participation of Children and Young People in Social Work – a Resource Pack*, by David Hodgson, National Children's Bureau 1994. Individual examples in this chapter of individuals participating will include children's and young people's involvement in review meetings or school expulsion hearings. Examples of group involvement would include involving children and young people in determining to local authority care policies or school councils.

Although the questions raised in this chapter are directed more towards group involvement, the issues raised are just as important to the involvement of individuals. It is important to bear in mind that the empowerment of children and young people in groups will lead to them having greater confidence and ability to deal with situations that may later confront them as an individual.

Definitions of terms

For the purpose of this chapter there is a need to clarify some of the terms used, in particular the terms *involvement, tokenism, consultation, participation, empowerment,* and *control.* Words are often used interchangeably, and therefore we need to be sure that we are all talking the same language.

Throughout the chapter the word *adults* appears in quotation marks to clarify 'adults' in this context as meaning non-users of a project or service and therefore with the power and control as workers, managers or some other role. *'Involvement'* is an overall term to describe the activities of children and young people in decision making at any level. The levels of involvement begin with tokenism and end with control.

'*Tokenism*' is involving children and young people in a decision-making process as a one-off without any follow-up or involving them in an ongoing process without support. Examples of tokenism include a local authority requesting the views of children and young people in a school on a planning issue without giving full information on budgets and options and failing to convey the results to them and being open to challenge on the final decision. Children and young people often describe school councils as tokenistic for these and other reasons. An example of a tokenistic on-going process would be inviting a few children or young people to sit on a committee of professional 'adults' without any means of support.

'*Consultation*' is a process which has been thought through in terms of *why* we are doing it, *how* we will consult, and the *commitment* to taking on board the views expressed by children and young people and presenting that information back to the group. Consultation can also be an on-going process, such as a local authority consulting with a permanently established council of children and young people, or an organisation having a separate committee of children and young people to access their views. The key to successful on-going consultation is an established group of children and young people who have gelled and who have a background in discussing common issues together.

Definitions of the word '*empowerment*' and '*participation*' are often interchangeable. I prefer to use the word empowerment as it is more assertive and explicitly brings in the power relationship. The most useful means of using the terms is to consider 'participation' as a process and 'empowerment' as an outcome. The following are some definitions offered for participation or empowerment and are mostly taken from a youth work context:

> *Empowering is enabling young people to understand and act on the personal, social and political issues which affect their lives, the lives of others and the community of which they are part* (Youth Work Statement for Wales).

> *By participating we mean a process by which young people can find a voice, an influence, a decision-making role in matters which affect them. It is the means by which they share power, take responsibility, and come to organise things for themselves* [Youth Clubs, UK).

> *Participation is involvement and responsible power-sharing by all those with a key interest in the service offered. Participation in the youth service is sharing responsibility with as many young members or users as*

possible at all levels; the aim should be to encourage them to initiate and carry through activities and projects and to give them an effective voice in decisions about aims, expenditure and programmes.

An excellent example of empowerment in a national voluntary organisation is the National Members Group (NMG) of Youth Clubs UK (YCUK). The group of 16 young people aged between 14 and 23 are elected from regions at their yearly conference which is open to any young person from a youth club in membership. The NMG elects its own officers and meets as a group six weekends a year. Members of NMG serve on the management council of YCUK and all of its standing committees where constitutionally a third of all places on committees are reserved for young people. There is a member of staff who is responsible to the group and for participation development throughout the organisation. NMG has a budget of approximately £60,000, including staff and resources which amounts to 4% of the overall budget of YCUK.

'*Control*' is when we reach a point where an organisation or project is run and managed by chidren and young people, for children and young people, without any adult involvement or with 'adults' acting in only an advisory capacity. Examples of control at a national level are Voices from Care Cymru and Who Cares Scotland. These are organisations for children and young people, managed and controlled by children and young people who employ staff, apply for funding, manage the staff and finances and carry out the functions of trustees.

Another example of control is local children's and youth councils where local issues of concern are discussed and action taken. One such council is in the West Everton area of Liverpool for eight to fifteen year-olds which lobbies politicians for improvements to children's amenities and organises recreational activities.

Why empower children and young people

The arguments for the need for rights for children and young people particularly in relation to decision making are laid out by Lansdown in her chapter of this book. When looking at the issue of involvement in decision-making, we must begin by looking at it from that rights perspective, and constantly challenge those who do not involve children and young people to justify themselves if they do not. However, it is also valuable to examine other reasons why the empowerment of children and young people may be of benefit to workers, organisations and children and young people.

Tam Tansey from Youth Clubs UK offers seven arguments for empowerment.

A voice and an influence

Empowerment opportunities offer children and young people a level of influence and an element of choice about the kind of provision offered by a service. Empowerment will help children and young people to be clear about, and understand, their own wants and needs.

To stay in touch

It forces whatever services you are providing to meet the changing needs which arise from the everyday interests and problems defined by children and young people.

Developmental needs

The developmental needs of children and young people, particularly the need for responsibility, respect and recognition, and for new experiences, can be met in empowerment activities.

Social and political education

Empowerment provides opportunities to acquire the skills of debate, communication, negotiation and individual/group decision making. It contains within itself the first steps of the political process.

Creators not consumers

Through empowerment, children and young people are encouraged to be active creators rather than passive consumers. It follows therefore that the service must be adapted to a childen's rights service acting as an agent of social change rather than one of social control.

Participation in the wider society

By beginning at a unit level, we offer a sensible starting point for encouragement of empowerment in a wider society.

Democracy

The promotion and practice of the management of a unit or project, open and accountable to its users encourages democratic procedures and respect for the principles and ideals of democratic life.

David Hodgson points out the need for five conditions to be met for empowerment to succeed. These conditions, which apply to adults as well as children and young people, are:

- access to those with power
- being provided with relevant information
- genuine choice between distinctive options
- a trusted and independent person to provide support and, where necessary, act as a representative
- a means of redress for appeal or complaint.

Hodgson moves on to highlight the fact that taking advantage of the above conditions is determined also by other factors such as motivation, capacity to comprehend, and ability to communicate.

Whatever context in which we may work with children and young people, if asked about our aims, we are likely to come out with similar answers. Social education, education for citizenship, empowerment of the individual, motivation, moving towards independence, and so on. In reality, we very often fail to achieve our aims and in so doing we fail children and young people at the same time.

If we look at a social work context, there is considerable evidence to show that young people leaving care are very often inadequately prepared for independence and as a result unable to cope, and so many become homeless. This is hardly surprising when children and young people in care have little or no experience of handling money and budgeting for themselves. Very often workers fail to provide the kind of learning experiences of life that formal education fails to cover. Involving children and young people in the decision-making processes can provide the learning experience that many children and young people do not receive. If they were involved in planning something as simple as the menu for a week along with information on the constraints of the budget and nutritional factors, lessons would be quickly learnt on the need to buy cheaper fresh food rather than take away food. Often their needs are only considered in care plans when the young person is within a few months of leaving care rather than building on the process from the start.

> *When you leave care, you are worse off because you don't know how to pay your bills; always in debt, you never have any food in the cupboard and you just sit back and leave it all to go on around you. And you wish that one day you will do this or that and it's just a big dream because you are left there and nobody calls to see if you are managing OK and before long the flat is taken away, you become homeless and social services just say it's your own fault* (18 year-old, London).

The benefits can be shown in a very basic example of a trip to a zoo.

If a teacher, residential worker or any other 'adult' organised the trip for a group of children and young people, they will experience a good day out (subject, of course, to the worker consulting the group about where they wished to go beforehand). However, the learning experience will be nil, except possibly some learning about the animals themselves. Alternatively, if the children and young people decide the venue, plan and execute the trip the learning experience for that group could be all of the following and more: they will have had the opportunity to learn communication skills through telephoning and writing for information and quotes; negotiating skills through haggling over transport prices and group discounts; budgeting through the need to work out overall costs of transport, entry fee and the number of places available; skills such as working as a team; problem-solving; and producing publicity. There will also be benefits in terms of experiencing responsibility and gaining self confidence.

Of course, as with every outing there is the possibility of it all going horribly wrong. There is the true story of an outing which after a successful day out to the zoo, ended in disaster for one worker when she realised, on the return journey, that there was a baby penguin on the back seat of the bus. The bus had to return to the zoo, the worker had to apologise to the management, undertake considerable grovelling to prevent the police being called and, of course, the bus company sent a supplementary bill for the extra hours. An extreme example maybe, and possibly a bit of a disaster, but in reality the learning experience continues. Dealing with conflict, particularly within the group, breach of trust and the implications of it and breach of contract and the financial implications are all important experiences. If we examine an alternative scenario of the venue being closed for refurbishment, then a whole bus full of people would have learnt one of life's great lessons – always phone first to check if a place is open.

Needless to say, the trip could have been organised more easily by a worker. It would have taken less time than supporting a group to undertake the task and potentially this is one of the main reasons given as to why we fail to involve children and young people in decision-making. However, if we do take the time and effort, the learning experience and benefits can be considerable. For children and young people the benefits of being involved in higher levels of decision-making can be immense. The knock-on effect of group empowerment is providing the individual with the motivation, capacity to comprehend, and the ability to communicate their own wishes and needs to ensure their own self-empowerment.

Benefits and gains

An important factor in any relationship between an individual child, young person or group is whether or not the relationship is forced or is voluntary. Local authority care is an example of a service where the users are not usually there initially out of choice.

I recently spoke to two young people who were upset because half their school had been burned down in an arson attack. It was an odd experience for me as I wondered back to my experience of school where arson attempts were a regular occurrence and sincerely welcomed. It made me wonder what circumstances result in students feeling such a sense of ownership of a school that they are upset over an attempt to burn it down – a totally alien concept for me at that age. I don't know the whole answer but I am certain it partly lies in the feeling of frustration I felt over the curriculum being irrelevant; the fact that I had no say in the system and that the teaching staff controlled the school through fear and regular violence. In contrast, the young people whose school was burnt down felt their own school treated them as individual adults, encouraged outside interests and encouraged good and positive relationships between students and staff. The philosophies of the schools were in marked contrast and the attitudes of the students reflected that contrast.

Rules are a fact of life for children, young people and 'adults', yet whether or not we abide by them depends not only on the threat of punishment if we ignore them but also on our perception of whether they are legitimate. Factors in determining their legitimacy will include feelings of ownership. Yet it is rare that we involve children and young people in drawing up rules or codes of conduct. We make up and enforce rules, some of which are even outside our control but we often fail to mention that fact or offer explanations as to why they may be needed.

As professionals, we often force children and young people into situations about which they are unhappy and we fail to listen to their needs and views. Often, if we override their wishes for reasons we judge to be in their best interests, then we fail to give an explanation for the decision. A very common complaint from children and young people in care, about review meetings, is their feeling that the decisions have been taken before the review meeting itself and their presence is pure tokenism. The end result is a decision that the individual involved feels no ownership over and therefore no feeling of responsibility in attempting to make the outcome of the decision a success. An individual who feels forced into a particular foster placement can quite easily, through negative behaviour, force the placement to break down. An individual forced to change schools can do the same.

Staff always have meetings to discuss where you are going next but they never involve you. You should have the right to know what they are thinking of doing with you (16 year-old, London).

They held a meeting and pretended to involve me by calling me in at the end and saying, 'We think it would be best for you to go to a secure unit. What do you think?' but I wasn't prepared, so I didn't really say much. But it was a farce anyway, because they had a social service minibus parked outside with a driver waiting for me to be taken there (18 year-old, South Wales).

Involving children and young peope in decision-making is not only about recognising the rights of children and young people, it is about developing co-operation and working relationships which will be of benefit to the individual and workers. A means of examining the benefits is to play a game of gains and losses. Taking examples of potential decisions in your own particular settings where you could involve children and young people, plot the potential gains and losses on the graph illustrated below.

Gains and losses graph

	'ADULTS'	CHILDREN AND YOUNG PEOPLE
GAINS	• improved services • enhanced reputation • better access for users, etc	• influence over services • promotion of interests and concerns • improved individual prospects and skills, etc
LOSSES	• time and resources • difficult, challenging meetings • power • control over decision-making, etc	• loss of leisure time • boring meetings • potential conflict, etc

The involvement of children and young people is also of benefit to organisations and projects aiming to serve their needs. While there is a considerable number of youth organisations within the UK, many are so out of touch with young people that they are not in fact youth organisations, they are 'adult' organisations which allow young people to join them. As many of the youth organisations fail to involve young people, so they become further removed from their needs and resort to opening younger age sections to keep up the numbers, as they fail to adapt to the changing needs of their original target age range.

In many areas, the statutory youth service is heading down the same path, more and more we see the average age of those attending youth clubs dropping and the opening of what is commonly termed junior youth clubs. Money spent on proper consultation with young people to ascertain their needs, and on the empowerment of young people in determining the local authority youth policy and youth service spending, would be very small in comparison with the benefits, as is the amount spent by Youth Clubs UK on the National Members Group.

A contribution to the debate at a national level from children and young people could also be achieved through other avenues. Whilst empowerment of children and young people is firmly on the agenda of some of the large child welfare organisations, few have made any real attempt at involving children and young people at a national level. The annual expenditure of the NSPCC last financial year was £39 million of which 75 per cent is spent on services to children approximately £29 million. Using the Youth Clubs UK model for empowering children and young people in a national organisation, the cost of a support worker, conference/meeting costs and administration would be approximately £60,000 or 0.001% of the overall budget of NSPCC. The benefit of the investment at a national level would mean developing more child centred services and making a real impact on the services for children at a project level. It could be argued that it would pay for itself just through better targeting of fund-raising strategies directed towards children and young people out of the approximate budget of £2.8 million for raising revenue costs.

Often small-scale projects make similar mistakes which, although may not be a waste of considerably large sums of money, could be a considerable proportion of the project budget, not to mention considerable hard work. One such case was a rural community centre who contacted their youth officer for advice on involving young people in the community centre.

The group of mainly quite elderly users were genuinely concerned about the lack of local provision in the area, which they felt was contributing to increased levels of crime and late night disturbances in the area. As a result, they raised through various activities the sum of £500 to spend on facilities to attract the young peope into the centre. The group took the decision to spend the money raised on sewing machines and other similar craft materials, working on the basis that it would attract the young women to the centre, and the young men would soon follow as a result. Good intentions, hard work and £500 gone to waste.

Issues that must be addressed

Many attempts at empowering children and young people end in failure and frustration for organisations, workers and children and young people. The most common cause is a failure to think through the process or consider basic issues. The following questions need therefore to be addressed and answered truthfully before we start to look towards the development of policies which empower an individual child or young person or a group. The following list of questions should not be seen as in any way an order of priority.

Why do we want empowerment?

Is it simply a matter of whether you believe in the empowerment of children and young people and, just as importantly, whether your colleagues believe in the idea or whether there are other reasons at work? Reasons may include: orders from above that must be obeyed, your funders have listed it in the criteria, young people in the organisation are making an issue of it, or your organisation adopted the UN Convention on the Rights of the Child, and you need to be seen to be doing something. At the end of the day, everybody involved or affected needs to be committed to the rights of children and young people, or recognise that the benefits will outweigh any extra resources and time that will be needed to allow the process to be successful. Embarking down the road towards empowerment is likely to end in failure and frustration for yourself and the children and young people involved, if those around you are not supportive and block your good intentions. If the eventual outcome of your discussions is that you do not wish to involve children and young people or that the necessary support is not available, then it may well be better to accept that situation rather than frustrating children and young people or resorting to tokenism. However, you should at least have the decency to be honest and state your position, and justify it to the children and other agencies with whom young people are in contact.

Why have we not done it before?

It may be helpful to examine and question why you have not involved children and young people before now. It will provide a useful exercise in identifying the barriers that exist and need overcoming, particularly in relation to attitudes of other 'adults'.

There are likely to be all kinds of barriers to the successful involvement of children and young people. Barriers will exist for organisations, projects and workers as well as for children and young people. Barriers for organisations, projects and workers will include attitudes, such as: users are too emotional to be able to take the responsibility of making difficult decisions; the cost of involving new people in terms of expenses and staff time; the fear of being seen to fail in the task; fear of losing control and power.

Barriers for children and young people will include financial limitations; lack of training to counter a feeling of not having the skills and confidence; the formal culture and structure; not being able to attend due to lack of transport and or inappropriate times of meetings; not having adequate support either from the organisation or being in minority to the group; and not having access to phones and modern technology to access further involvement.

What are we aiming to achieve?

Again, everybody involved or affected in the organisation will need to be clear about what level of involvement in decision-making you are trying to achieve. Consultation is an important step but hopefully is not seen as an end in itself, but consultation can mean different things to different people and could mean either a one-off consultation with a particular group of individuals or regular consultations with an established group. Empowerment is a longer-term process that involves shared decision-making with children and young people, and will have time and resource implications for the whole organisation. Control, where possible, should be the ultimate goal where the children and young people run a project or organisation with the role of 'adults' being one of support for the children and young people involved. Whatever level you are aiming for the whole organisation needs to be involved in setting the overall aim, and all need to be clear on definitions and terms used.

What will the children and young people get out of it?

All too often the answer is 'not a lot'. For children and young people to sustain an interest, they need to be getting something out of being involved. Part of that may well be the new skills and knowledge they will gain as a result of involvement, and this will be recognised as important. But just the same as for 'adults' wishing to get involved, many children and young people are looking to use their valuable spare time towards something that will be interesting, **fun** and add to the general social life. Working on the basis that children and young people will wish to get involved because it will look good on their CV, it will keep them out of mischief, it will give them something worthwhile to do, 'they should never have done away with national service', is quite simply not good enough. You must also think clearly and honestly about whether or not you will end up in a position of being tokenistic. Spend some time looking at developing your own definitions of empowerment, then examine the barriers and policies needed to overcome them.

For individual children and young people, the answer is obviously more clear-cut, the individual may have an influence on their whole future life.

Are we being honest with children and young people?

It is important from the outset that full information and honest discussion take place with the children and young people on several crucial issues. Are you being up front about what they can expect from the experience? Are you clear about what can and can't be changed, who will be setting the agenda, who is on their side and who in the organisation is opposed to any form of empowerment or change, and how far as individuals the children and young people may be able to become involved? Are you also prepared to give full information to those we involve and lay out all the different options?

In the case of individuals, full information and possible options are essential for informed choices to be made. Consideration would also need to be given to discussing honestly the possible different agendas that may exist particularly between 'adults' and children and young people. An issue raised by some children and young people is the problems of losing control over disclosures of abuse which may be made to professionals.

What are your expectations?

Very often 'adults' tend to expect more from the involvement of children and young people than they would from involving any other user group in their work. The most common example I find is speculation over whether or not the group involved are 'representative' or just an elite group. Groups of children and young people will be no different from any other user group, they represent a sample of people who are interested in the particular issue and wish to be involved. The same problems of 'perfect representation' exist in terms of representation in trade unions, professional associations or political parties. We also need to be careful about how much time and commitment we expect from children and young people, and to recognise that the level of commitment may vary greatly between individuals. It is important to recognise that children and young people are a particularly fluid group and therefore there will be peaks and troughs, and the support and training will need to be an on-going process. Considerataion will also need to be given to the fact that the conclusions a group of children and young people reach on an issue may not be what you were expecting or indeed hoping for.

Are we prepared for the resource implications?

Empowerment is an on-going process that will require commitment in terms of staff time and resources. If the process is to be successful, then consideration will need to be given to extra costs such as the expenses of children and young people attending meetings and other related conferences. Training may be needed for real empowerment to be achieved, preferably residential to enable the group to gel, and with the added bonus of being a good carrot in relation to what the children and young people will get out of the experience. Staff time will also need to be committed for a successful outcome in terms of training time, on-going communication with the group, time given towards preparation for meetings (most of which will likely be evening or weekends), undertaking the general administration for the group or, alternatively, providing the resources such as access to phones and word-processors to enable the children and young people to able to undertake those tasks themselves. Appointing independent advocates for children and young people will again, have resource implications.

Are we prepared to give up some power?

This is probably the central question we need to address. Are we prepared to give up some power and control and place it in the hands of those we are involving in the decision-making process? This may not be as daunting as it at first sounds: children and young people given the full information can make informed choices for themselves. An example that could be used is publicity for a project. If the project aims to serve children and young people, then it would make sense for children and young people to design and write the content of the publicity as only they can tell you if it will attract other children and young people. Provided that full information and any other restricting factors are given on the budget then the publicity produced will be accessible to its target audience, and the children and young people involved will feel a sense of real involvement through the responsibility and a sense of achivment. Take the controversial example of a leaflet on safe sex, where the children and young people involved wish to use the sexual language that would be

used at street level. Arguments against it may be put for consideration, such as the dangers of not reaching the target audience because
those in authority are offended by such a leaflet. However, given the
information, it should still be left to the children and young people
to consider that argument and reach a decision based on an
informed choice.

Information is power. Children and young people will need the
relevant information in order to be able to exercise genuine choice
between distinctive options. Access to those who have the power,
and who are making the decisions, is another important requirement.

Are we prepared to involve children and young people from the start?

If a new project is being established, then children and young people
should be involved from the start. Normal practice tends to be to initiate a project-steering group, apply for funding, appoint a worker
whose function then includes involving children and young people
in the project. The practice outlined can lead to several problems. A
steering group meeting for a period of time is likely to impose a particular culture and method of working in which it may be difficult
to accommodate children and young people at a later stage. The
funding application may fail to take into account the needs of children and young people, such as training resources and adequate
expenses. Without input from children and young people, there is a
danger of appointing a worker who is inappropriate to the needs of
the target group of children and young people. Residential workers
are in constant contact with children and young people, so why are
the young people not involved in appointing them? The same would
apply if we were to look at setting up new policies or procedures
which have a direct impact on our methods of work with children
and young people, i.e. why not involve the children and young
people in drawing up the policies and procedures if they are to be on
the receiving end at a later date.

Do we recognise this is a long-term commitment?

Involving children and young people is a long-term commitment,
which needs to permeate all areas and levels of a project or organisation. Involving children and young people is not something an
organisation can do for a one-off or set period of time before revert-
ing to the more routine practice. It will need on-going resources and
support. Many years ago a colleague who worked as a participation
project worker covering youth clubs told me about how he called
into a youth club involved in the project only to be told he had the

wrong night, 'it's five-a-side football tonight, participation happens on a Tuesday night'.

Are we prepared to take some criticism?

Do not expect the children and young people you involve to be automatically grateful for the 'wonderful opportunity' you have offered them. The methods of involvement and structure of the organisation, and possibly other factors, may justifiably come under criticism from children and young people. Obviously, you will need to consider those issues and respond in an appropriate manner, including outlining reasons and entering into a debate on those issues which for whatever reason you feel cannot be changed. The means of redress via an appeal or complaint would be another requirement.

Are we prepared to institutionalise the change?

In the long term we need to be careful that we do not set up a process that can be dropped once involving children and young people goes out of fashion. It is therefore necessary to be committed in the long term to incorporating the involvement of children and young people into the constitution, if one exists, and institutionalising the full involvement of children and young people into the project or organisation.

Reasons why children and young people may wish to be involved

The reasons children and young people may wish to be involved will vary between individuals and different situations. Broadly speaking, they can be divided into several categories: first there are personal development reasons which would cover acquiring skills, experience for possible employment in the long term, a wish to experience greater responsibility, wishing to undertake a new challenge, pursuing a worthwhile activity working through an experience or just wishing to extend a social life. Secondly, there may be a wish to do voluntary work in order to see services better targeted, to prevent others suffering the same experience, or to satisfy feeling a need to offer something in return to a project. A third consideration pertinent to child protection is that empowerment has a therapeutic significance. There are some good examples of survivor groups particularly for sexually abused girls and young women which, although run by social services department staff, are autonomous and confidential forums.

The most important points to bear in mind are that, whatever needs are being met through that involvement, the nature of the relationship is voluntary and therefore, if the involvement is boring or tokenistic, then that involvement will not be sustained.

Overcoming barriers

The barriers that prevent us from successfully involving children and young people can be split into five categories:

- access
- attitudes
- custom and practice
- information
- resources.

To overcome the barriers, we need to consider our practice very carefully and apply it to individual children and to groups when involving children and young people.

Access

It may seem obvious, but very often the first barrier that is encountered is the time and date of the meeting. Professionals have a tendency to meet, for example on the first Tuesday of every month at 10 am – not a good time for people who have to attend school every day or for those on a YTS placement. How many times have review meetings been held during school-time, or when a young person is at work, just to facilitate the needs of professionals or carers?

Those able to attend owing to unemployment may find themselves having problems from the social security office on the basis that, if they attend too many meetings or conferences, then they are not available for work and therefore benefit may be withdrawn. Transport may also be a problem, particularly for those having to travel long distances or living in rural areas where the last bus home may have already left before the meeting was even due to start. Children and young people involved at a national level may also need expenses in advance or cash on the day.

The venue for the meeting can be a barrier. All too often, professionals arrange meetings in a venue and in seating arrangements with which they feel comfortable. It is rare for consideration to be given to holding a meeting on the territory of children and young people. If a local authority wishes to hold a consultation with children and young people, then it should be done where they feel comfortable – in a local café, bus shelter, or wherever children and young people gather, rather than in a very formal council chamber where they would be confronted by somebody with several pounds of gold and silver hanging from their neck. Outreach youth workers could be involved if any are employed in the area. Similarly, an individual involved in a review meeting should not be taken to a formal meeting room in social services; instead, the meeting should be conducted where the individual feels comfortable in the residential unit or another alternative.

The means by which a meeting or conference is conducted must also accommodate children and young people. Breaks being held more often, and cutting out the customary boring welcome speech from the local dignitary, would help the situation. With a bit of imagination, meetings and conferences do not need always to be the boring endurance test they often turn out to be. Regular breaks in meetings are good opportunities for groups to evaluate a meeting, or for an individual to consult with their advocate.

An individual child or young person must be allowed and given the chance to question the attendance of 'adults' they feel are not relevant to the meeting and be able to request individual 'adults' to leave at any point. A common complaint of children and young people in foster care is the attendance of foster parents at review meetings which makes an honest contribution from them very difficult. Children Act regulations state that children should be informed who is to be invited to attend their statutory review, and the child's views on their attendance would be obtained. However, it does not give them any power to exclude anyone, for example, a teacher. However, the provision of written factual evidence may be an acceptable compromise.

> *They put me into a foster home where the foster mother was having an affair with the lodger and the foster father was talking about killing himself all the time and would get drunk and pretend to be affectionate by trying to snog me* (18 year-old, Merseyside).

If it is a group of children and young people you wish to involve in your project or organisation alongside 'adults', then the number you invite could be a barrier. Those involved will have more confidence if they represent a group such as a children's forum or youth forum, and feel even more confident if there is a significant percentage of children and young people on the project. Access to the organisation or project will be significantly improved for those involved, if the group can be given time and space to gel preferably through a residential training event which could include assertiveness training and training on group decision-making.

Some groups of children and young people, for example, those who are disaffected, suffer racism, or who are lesbian and gay, will face further barriers to their involvement which may need even greater resources and commitment. Extra issues for children and young people with disabilities would include access to information particularly in relation to possible communication difficulties and low expectations from professionals and others about the ability of a young person to contribute significantly to decision-making. It would be impossible to cover these issues with justice in this chapter and therefore I would urge those seeking to achieve it to undertake further reading on the appropriate issue from other chapters in the book and/or elsewhere if needed.

Attitudes

It may be argued that the main barrier is the attitudes of professionals and others to children and young people. Some of the common myths we hear are 'they are irrational', 'they are unreasonable', 'they don't want to be involved', 'they are not representative', or 'they are too emotional'. There are many common excuses to go alongside the attitudes including 'they lack the knowledge and experience', 'we tried it once before and it didn't work', 'it is not their place they have to earn our respect', 'let's talk about responsibilities first'.

In reality, many children and young people do wish to be involved in decision-making that affects them, they are not too emotional, not irrational and, if given full information, including essential facts, such as budget limitations, they are not unreasonable. Nobody is representative. Children and young people, in the same way as the rest of the population, only represent a group of people who have an interest in a partiular issue.

On the issue of attitudes, something must be said on the issue of individual attitudes of professionals. During consultations for the Children's Rights Development Unit it was clear that many experiences of care were determined by the relationship with the social worker. Young people who truant from school on an occasional basis stated that when they played truant would depend mostly on the teacher they had rather than on the subject itself.

I do not have the answer to the question of why children and young people are able to relate to some professionals and not others, but I suspect some of it lies in the attitudes shown towards an individual child or young person. It would make for an interesting piece of research.

Probably the pet hate of children and young people who have been involved in any kind of committee or project is to be patronised by 'adults'. Professionals need to be vigilant in what they say and express and need to be prepared to be challenged.

Custom and practice

The whole culture of an organisation may be a barrier if it conducts meetings and other activities in a very formal manner. A rigid constitution, or rules that people are keen to work to, may also present problems. It may be possible to change the culture of the organisation by challenging the need to arrive at all decisions through a formal meeting or following a rigid constitution. If you are a group meeting on a regular basis, it may help to hold some ice-breakers, for example, at the start of the meeting ask everybody to tell the group the best and worst thing that has happened to them since they last met. It breaks the ice in terms of everybody speaking right at the start of the session, and may illustrate to the children and young people involved that the professionals sitting around the room in their formal dress are, in fact, from the same human race as they are.

Information

One major disadvantage children and young people face in groups in the power relationship with 'adults' is that information is power Children and young people very rarely have access to their own direct information networks. Information on NAYPIC conferences, *Who Cares* magazine will usually need to find its way past a professional before it reaches the child and young people. How many times have we filed the information in the bin on the basis that we did not feel they would be interested or we did not wish for any extra work to come our way. We cannot empower children and young people if we do not provide the information on the complaints procedure or details of the local NAYPIC group.

'Adults' in a group situation know all the acronyms of the organisations, names of the people who work in them, and all the jargon and social policy speak that goes with the profession. The 'adults' involved very often know each other through other meetings or on a social basis. Children and young people are then introduced to the group, and we expect them to fit comfortably into the group and be empowered individuals.

The process can, however, be aided for children and young people through various methods. The essential requirement is to allow time and space for them to discuss the issues in a pre-meeting possibly with a support person if those involved feel it is appropriate. The pre-meeting will allow the individual or group to discuss the items on the agenda in a 'safe' environment, clarify the issues and explore some possible solutions to put to the later meeting. The pre-meeting will also have an opportunity to read the papers and clarify acronyms and the role of other organisations thereby allowing the later meeting not be be interrupted so much by questions or clarification. It may also prevent some of the group feeling disempowered by not having to ask for clarification. A pre-meeting can also be a useful time to give some background information on the other individuals attending the meeting, who they are, what is their role, the 'politics' of each, and who is happy about children and young people joining the group, and who was not – all the kinds of information the rest ot the group will have anyway. Input into conferences from children and young people will have far more impact if resources are made available to give them time and space to discuss the issues and develop ideas or presentation. A group evaluation meeting at the end is also of considerable benefit in terms of evaluating the extra information needed, if any, and possible changes to the structure of the main meeting. Where there is a constant group of children and young people attending, the need for pre- and post-meetings tends to decline.

In cases of individuals, such as those attending review meetings where a decision taken can be a matter that could change the course of a young person's life, the need to brief the individual involved fully cannot be over-emphasised. Time should be spent beforehand briefing the individual on why the meeting is being held, on the potential options that will be explored, who will be in the meeting, their role and their rights such as independent advocacy and appeal, and how they would like to have their view put across and by whom.

It can be difficult to make professionals break their bad habits of using jargon and therefore it may be worth compiling an alphabetical list of the common acronyms and jargon as a resource for children and young people to use during meetings. The chair of any meeting will also need to summarise clearly the discussions held and to explain in clear terms any decisions taken and why.

There are always some small but important issues that professionals need to remember when involving children and young people. Sending correspondence to carers rather than to the individual is one issue. Another is sending out a notice for a meeting weeks in advance when many children and young people do not carry diaries.

Resources

Lack of resources is often a cause of frustration for organisations wishing to accommodate the involvement of children and young people successfully. The first issue to consider when involving groups of children and young people in consultations, conferences or meetings is whether there is the money to pay for their contribution – a contribution which is of equal value to that of 'adults' but which is very rarely considered so in terms of the going rate. If resources are not available for the contribution they make, that should be made clear, along with the reasons why not.

Involvement in a group will require financial resources for several children and young people to be involved rather than a tokenistic one or two. The financial resources should include travel expenses and subsistence and, in cases of attending overnight conferences and meetings, also incidental expenses. Expenses should always be available in cash on the day or in advance if needed. Expenses should also be available for individuals to become further invovled between meetings if they wish to.

Resources will also be required in terms of staff-time in cases both of empowering individuals and groups of children and young people. Time will be needed for organising and attending pre-meetings, time which may well need to be outside the usual hours of 9am to 5pm. Time may also be needed for communication between meetings and for occasional training. Training and support for staff through supervision may also be required.

Towards developing a policy for organistions

An essential starting point for creating the opportunities for children and young people to participate in an organisation is to develop and formalise a policy.

Any policy must be developed in relation to the 12 questions raised earlier in the chapter. The overall aim or statement should arise out of discussions with professionals at all levels within the organisation, to enable them to feel ownership, and with the children and young people, without whose contribution the policy will have no credibility. An agreed initial statement of aims must not be seen as a substitute for action, but should create a framework for development and a timetable for action.

The content of the policy should include the aims and perceived benefits, how the policy links to other documents and builds upon them, for example, the organisation's equal opportunities policy, and its policy for the implementation of the UN Convention on the Rights of the Child. The policy would also need to address specific objectives for developing the empowerment of groups and individual children and young people for identifying the barriers and how they will be overcome, for identifying the staff and financial resources required, for meeting training requirements, for explaining the methods to be used for monitoring and evaluation, and for the role of the person responsible for co-ordinating the policy.

The role of the co-ordinator could include information co-ordination, being a contact and reference point for children and young people in the organisation, identifying and planning training for children and young people and others, providing reports on progress, and giving the administrative support that will be needed.

Children have the knowledge and experience

Children and young people do not lack knowledge and experience. They have the essential knowledge and experience to contribute to the debate. Only an individual child or young person can tell you why they ran away from care or played truant from school. Only a group of young people can tell you what care provision would meet their needs in a particular area. The lack of knowledge and experience lies with professionals who fail to draw out, listen, and act upon the knowledge and experience of children and young people. The practice and policy of organisations and professionals is the richer for involving children and young people through an empowering process.

12 Child advocacy – getting the child's voice heard

Nicky Scutt

Children and young people have a right to participate in decisions affecting them. The decision-making process is enhanced by this process. Ironically, one result of the Children Act is that more parents are attending child protection case conferences, but there has not been a marked increase in children being involved. If children and young people are to participate, they are likely to need support and advice. This chapter describes a project which empowered children and young people who had been abused by recruiting independent advocates to help prepare them for the case conference and support them through it.

In March 1993, West Devon Area Child Protection Committee commissioned the running of a six-month Child Advocacy Project. The aim of the project was to enable each child aged ten years and upward, referred to a child protection case conference, to be offered an independent advocate. The advocate's brief was to prepare the child or young person prior to the conference to enable them to decide in what manner they wished to participate. A variety of methods of participation was offered. The pilot commenced on 4 May 1993 and was completed on 29 October 1993. On completion of the project, 22 children had participated.

The Youth Enquiry Service is a Plymouth-based charity which recruits and trains volunteers in order to support young people.

They advise young people on a range of issues such as homelessness and drug abuse. Although it is a fairly new service, it has become well established and is well used.

Following the implementation of the Children Act in 1991, much time and effort was spent by stragetic bodies facilitating parental attendance at case conferences. From both a training and policy perspective, the emphasis was on parental participation with very little consideration of issues relating to young people being given. Devon County Council's policy for child participation was written in broad terms, allowing for considerable scope for interpretation and usage at the local level. There appeared to be little opportunity for social workers to discuss the issues, to share concerns or influence the policy-makers. An implementation gap developed with individuals at the grassroots being given scope to pursue their own direction, with little attempt by those at the top to control the operating core to ensure that they acted in accordance with the authority's objectives. At this time, the guidance on children and young people attending case conferences was contained within a section on parental participation in Devon's *Multi-Disciplinary Handbook*. Insufficient time and consideration had been given to the issue of child participation at a policy level and subsequently at the grassroots.

In West Devon, the NSPCC is contracted by Devon Social Services to chair all child protection conferences, excluding those with a legal component. The NSPCC chairpersons raised concerns about the small numbers of young people attending case conferences and the limited extent to which the young person's views were being heard at conferences. Two doubts were expressed: first, whether it was appropriate for the social worker to prepare the child for conference when they had other family members to consider, and secondly whether they had sufficient time to achieve this task effectively.

Doubts were also expressed about the appropriateness of the tasks of inviting and preparing young people to participate being the primary responsibility of the local authority social worker, due both to an acknowledgement of time constraints on the workers, and to the potential dichotomy in the social work role.

A meeting between Plymouth NSPCC, Social Services Child Protection Officer (West Devon) and the Youth Enquiry Service (YES) was set up to share concerns and to consider a way forward. The outcome of this collaborative approach was an agreement to develop an independent child advocacy service which would be piloted in the West Devon Social Services Districts over a six-month period. This was subsequently reduced to three Districts, mainly to make the monitoring and evaluation process more manageable.

These District Teams were chosen to participate as they had the highest number of children on the Child Protection Register in the age range 10 years and upwards.

The aim of the project was to provide each child with an independent advocate. The brief of that advocate was to prepare each child for their case conference in a manner that allowed them to decide how they wished to participate.

The independence of the advocate was considered to be a key factor in enabling children and young people to participate. They were offered a variety of methods:

- children attending with their advocates

- the advocates attending on their behalf

- use of audio tapes

- use of video tapes

- live video link.

The Youth Enquiry Service agreed to offer, free of charge, some of their existing volunteers as advocates. The advocates finally chosen were those who had expressed an interest in undertaking this task, and who had been chosen by their line manager on the basis that they had the necessary skills, sufficient understanding and were able to work successfully in partnership with other agencies. Following selection they were trained by NSPCC child protection officers. The training covered the legal aspects of child protection, the case conference process and the advocate's role within it. As volunteers of the Youth Enquiry Service they had already received approximately 120 hours' training.

In collaboration with social services, all the volunteers were vetted and approved in accordance with social services procedures for the recruitment of volunteers.

It was agreed that, given the complexity of this project and the fact that this was uncharted territory for the Youth Enquiry Service, all advocates should be supported in their work through supervision by their line manager with an opportunity to debrief after every contact with a child or young person.

The age-range of children to be offered this service was ten years and upwards. This decision was made on the basis that children of this age-range were thought generally to be more cognitively able to benefit from such a service. However, the possibility of offering an advocate to a younger child if the social worker felt that he/she had sufficient understanding to make use of the conference process was not ruled out. This was felt particularly to apply to younger siblings.

Child advocacy

235

Furthermore, it was agreed that each sibling should, wherever possible, be offered their own advocate. However, it was recognised that, for large families, this may be difficult to achieve, and that time constraints would be a major factor in achieving this.

The system of referral

The Youth Enquiry Service operate an 'open door' policy, and therefore do not usually accept referrals. However, in order to operate this system, it was necessary to make an exception. The process of establishing this pilot took ten months. Considering the complexities of the subject and the moral and ethical dilemmas encountered, this was not surprisng.

In developing a referral procedure, we aimed to design a system that was simple and unobtrusive. The model finally agreed on is completely inter-agency, and dependent to a large degree on people's ability to work together in an atmosphere of trust. It is the role of the social worker to introduce the scheme to the parents and children, and the NSPCC to refer the children to the Youth Enquiry Service, and on the Youth Enquiry Service to visit the parents and children to elicit their permission to act as the child's advocate. Some concern was expressed by the Youth Enquiry Service, since this method of operation was contradictory to their established approach. However, it was important that this service should be seen by both the parents and the children as independent from the outset, and there was concern that requiring the social workers to elicit this agreement may compromise that independence. With some trepidation it was agreed that this system would be operated, and subsequently evaluated, as part of this pilot.

Moral and ethical dilemmas

The Youth Enquiry Service operate a total confidentiality policy. This is fundamental to their work and, as such, they felt unable to compromise this. Devon Social Services and the NSPCC are charged with the duties and obligations of protecting children from harm and are therefore obliged statutorily to act on any information where harm is alleged. These conflicting policies had to be reconciled for this project to become operational.

The starting point taken was a corporate desire to empower children in the case conference process. This was defined as giving children the necessary information and support to enable them to participate meaningfully in this process. It was therefore agreed that, for this to be successful, it was necessary to invest trust in the young people, and to allow them to make decisions concerning any disclosures they might wish to make. The Youth Enquiry Service recognised the potential for young people to make disclosures and had had some previous experience of this. They also recognised that young people have the right to be protected and on this basis had always counselled the young people to approach the relevant authority to make their disclosures. Their experience has been that, once the young person has received the necessary information about Social Services and NSPCC, they have invariably referred themselves very shortly afterwards.

The final agreement was that the young person's confidentiality would be preserved unless they disclosed anything which was life-threatening either to themselves or to another child or young person. This policy is a departure from Devon Social Services' and NSPCC's normal operational stance and served to challenge social workers' wishes to protect, and their concern to follow procedures (many of which have been written as a result of various enquiries into child deaths). However, we believed that this policy would assist not only the empowerment process for the children and young people but that it would also avoid the likelihood of the advocates being joined into the inter-agency process as quasi-professionals. In other words, independence would be maintained.

Further dilemmas were considered; what could be the response to parents who refused permission for this service when the child wanted it? No conclusions were reached other than that each situation would be judged on its merits. Priority was given to ensuring that the initial approach to the parents was as effective as possible.

Would this service undermine the role of the social worker/care manager? It was felt that it would not, provided the advocate kept to their brief, and provided both parties communicated effectively with each other prior, during and after the conference. In any event, it was felt that the pilot would provide an opportunity to monitor this relationship. The results of the evaluation would determine the nature of this relationship.

How the project worked

On completion of the project, 22 children had participated. Within the three pilot districts, there had been 23 meetings, 20 of which were initial case conferences and three were reviews (See Table 12.1).

Table 12.1.

District	Initial	Initial legal	Review	Review legal	Total
Devonport	5	2	0	1	8
Budshead	4	1	2		7
St Budeaux	2		0		2
Efford	4		0		4
Ham/Trelawney		1	0		1
Estover	0	1	0		1
	15	5	2	1	23

It was decided that the young people should be informally interviewed by someone independent of the project. An interview guide was developed, designed to probe the young people's views about being invited to participate, their role in, and experiences of, the conference process, their evaluation of the advocacy service, their understanding of the purpose, function and authority of the child protection process, and their role and rights in that setting.

The majority of young people interviewed received independent advocacy, hence their views about participation are dependent largely on their experiences of that service. They were all in favour of child participation, valuing the opportunity of deciding on their preferred method of involvement. For some, this meant attending with an advocate, whilst others did not attend but were represented by advocates.

The views of the children and young people

Young people offered the following reasons for why the child protection case conference was being held:

To see what everybody thought of what was going to be happening ... to make sure I would be safe.

To think about what help was needed in the future and get everything sorted out.

Trying to see what could be done to help.

To see how I'm getting along ... to get me to do normal 15 year-old things ... to try and protect children ...

Because they thought my parents were beating me up.

To talk about what was happening between Mum and X.

The variety of responses reflect both the different circumstances of each case as well as individual children's knowledge, understanding and perception of what had occurred and why. Children reported being uncertain about the authority and purpose of the conference and what would take place at such a meeting prior to contact with the advocates, and felt these issues were much clearer following discussions with the advocates.

The Child Protection Register remained a nebulous thing. The majority felt the Register was of little or no relevance to their daily lives, whist one young person thought, right until the end of his meeting, that registration meant he 'would be taken away from his carers'.

For the majority of young people, the importance of the meeting was to operate as a forum for sharing information, challenging inaccuracies and deciding how they could be helped, the issue of the Register playing a much less significant role.

Young people felt preparation was important, helping them to decide how to participate. The majority saw the advocates as their sole source of preparation. They received support from their advocates twice prior to the conference, for about one hour on each occasion.

The young people found the following issues helpful to discuss:

- details about the meeting

- who would be there, what might be said, what would be decided and what this might mean for them

- the role of the chairperson

- what they wanted to say to the meeting and how this could be achieved, some prepared written statements for the meeting

- discussion about feelings, both about what has happened as well as about attending the meeting

- practical matters such as a description of the venue, knowing there was a choice about where to sit, and who to sit next to in the meeting

- the formal and informal 'rules' about the meeting, when to speak, who to speak to, whether they could talk to their advocate, knowing it is acceptable to sit and listen and not speak, whether they could leave and return later.

Lessons to be learnt from the project concerning the preparatory stages include: the importance of offering young people audience alone without parents/carers present at the meeting. The needs of younger children and children with learning difficulties require careful consideration, in particular, more preparatory time, and in some circumstances the need for specialist advice.

Forms of participation

The main forms of participation offered were to attend with an advocate, or be represented at the meeting by an advocate. There were no discussions about other forms of participation, for example audio or visual tapes, one-way mirrors, drawings, and so on. The majority felt, even if this had been offered, they would have declined it. One young person who did not attend thought a two-way mirror with a telephone link would have been helpful so that he could see and hear the meeting and, if necessary, communicate with his advocate or vice versa, but not be seen or heard by the meeting.

The following reasons were given for not wanting to go:

I was afraid I would be asked something and wouldn't know the answer and anyway it may be I wouldn't want to answer.

I was embarrassed about hearing what people might say about me ...

Talking with my advocate helped me decide not to go as he was going for me and I didn't want to go. It took the pressure off and I didn't feel I needed to go.

Young people had clearly thought about why they did not want to attend. However, these comments raise the question of whether they were given a broad enough range of choices about other forms of participation. Additionally, some were concerned about being made to speak, whereas this research highlights that those who did attend did not feel pressurised to do so. All those involved in the child protection conferences need to be sensitive to this concern of young people, in particular the chairpersons and advocates, whilst young people need to be informed that it is perfectly acceptable to attend and not be heard if this is what they wish.

Those who wanted to attend gave the following reasons – to see, to be seen, 'to hear' and in some cases 'to be heard'.

Better than staying at home while they are all talking about me ... I wanted to listen to what they said.

I didn't want to go but even more I didn't want them talking about me behind my back ... I wanted to be able to challenge anything I thought was wrong.

They wanted me to be let in on what was going on and they told me I could say anything I wanted to so I thought I should go.

I wanted to go to tell people what I thought and why.

If I wasn't there and we hadn't discussed it my advocate wouldn't have been able to say anything because she couldn't have said what I thought.

If I thought something was wrong I could say so. If I'm not there my advocate can't say because she can't assume what I think.

Young people were very clear about why they wanted to be at the meeting, offering a variety of reasons in support of this. A theme throughout was that the decision to attend was made much easier knowing the advocate would be present to support them and speak up for them if it became too difficult to do so themselves. However, no one felt that advocates took over or said too much or spoke without having their permission. Young people felt very much in control of how they used the advocates.

They all felt it was right to give them the opportunity to attend the meeting even if they themselves chose an alternative form of participation. They all felt it had been their decision about how to participate, in consultation with their advocates. None felt pressurised into going or not going either by professionals, family members or advocates.

The case conference

Although there was evidence that those who attended had a better understanding of the processes and functions of the meeting, both those who attended and those who were represented felt their contributions had been important from a personal perspective as well as from the meeting's viewpoint.

They got to hear my views insted of just what the grown-ups think about me and what they think I want.

They heard both sides [young person and parents] with me being there.

Attenders commented on being nervous initially, in particular about talking in front of a group of adults, and some did feel upset by what they heard. However, this did not appear to detract from their desire to be present. The project suggests that the quality of information shared at the meeting was more accurate owing to children participating. Young people felt the plans were both more acceptable, and more appropriately targeted their protection needs, because of their involvement in drawing them together. The findings indicate that child participation does not adversely affect the decision-making concerning the child protection register.

None of the young people felt jargon had been used inappropriately. However, discussions highlighted that many young people did not understand terminology such as 'minutes of the meeting'. Professionals must remain diligent in challenging jargon and cautious about making assumptions about the words they use.

Young people were generally happy with the behaviour of the professionals and family members in the meeting although they did suggest the following:

- professionals should ensure they arrive on time

- the meeting should start on time

- the meeting should be restricted to those who work with young people and their families on a regular basis

- social work reports should be given to young people in advance of the meeting

- a less formal atmosphere with comfortable chairs, tea and biscuits was preferable to sitting around a table

- time should be set aside for breaks during lengthy meetings

- chairpersons should offer young people a choice of where to sit as they felt their position in relation to other attenders was an important factor

- young people would like copies of the minutes of the meeting, but stressed these should not be sent direct to them, as they wanted the opportunity to discuss the contents with an independent adult

- the importance of ensuring reception staff are both aware of, and sensitive to, the needs of young people attending meetings, and the need for user-friendly waiting areas.

Advocates

Young people valued the fact that the advocates were there for them alone. The separateness of the advocates from the formal support systems and from direct knowledge of the family networks and relationships was an important factor in furthering the empowerment of the young people in their chosen method of participation. A number of young people stressed the importance to them of the confidential service offered by advocates which, in their eyes, differentiated advocates from the agencies.

Young people's comments about the advocates' role included

My advocate was there to put my views across ... she only knew my story, and not Mum and Step-Dad's and therefore she was able to say what I felt and not get in-between it all. If she knew their story maybe she would get muddled up and not want to say something because it may upset them.

My special person who didn't know anything about anyone else in my family.

My advocate was there for me and not for anyone else, to bring my rights forward and to have a word in there for me ... different from my social worker because he [advocate] offers a totally confidential role. I can say what I want and it won't go any further unless I want it to.

He was there to say things for me if I wanted anyone to speak for me.

She was there to say my bit, to say what we said to her.

To be my voice in the meeting. If I don't want to go he attends on my behalf to say what I want him to say.

Advocates at the meeting and post-meeting support

Young people felt their experience of attendance was greatly enhanced by the support of their advocates. Advocates undertook a variety of tasks within each meeting ranging from support, by being there, to talking on the young person's behalf.

He spoke on my behalf about my thoughts and what I was like ... I wouldn't have been able to do that.

My advocate was the only one in the meeting who was there for me.

Having my own advocate and foster carers there helped me to stay for the whole meeting. If I'd been on my own I couldn't have coped with what my parents were saying.

He made sure I understood what was going on and sat next to me so I could nudge him if I wanted to say something or wanted him to say ...

He was great to have there ... like a best friend.

The advocate's presence at the meeting was an important part of helping young people to undertake the unfamiliar role of case conference attender. For those who did not attend, they felt advocates had put their views across and given them good feedback about what had happened. One young person was receiving on-going counselling from hers, while the remainder had a good grasp of the short-term nature of the advocate's role, all being aware that they could make contact between meetings if they want to.

Evaluation of the care manager's role

Twenty-one care managers were involved in this project and on completion of the service were asked to complete a questionnaire. Of these 52% were returned. Broadly, the questionnaire addressed two issues: first, the communication between the agencies prior to the service commencing, and secondly the care manager's view of the service in completion. Of care managers 90 per cent agreed that there had been contact between themselves and the advocates prior to the service and that they had been kept informed of the advocates' progress.

The reasons given for care managers' failure to discuss the project with the family prior to commencement were meetings being called urgently and at short notice, the care manager thinking that the children were not eligible for the project, and one discussed it with the family after the meeting had been called.

The vast majority of care managers were contacted by YES prior to the conference and were kept informed of the advocates' progress. The one factor identified that precluded this liaison was a meeting called urgently at very short notice where the Youth Enquiry Service had not been able to meet with the young person prior to the day of conference. In these situations it is important that discussion takes place between the chair, the care manager and the advocate to determine whether the child or young person's attendance would be detrimental to their well-being.

Care managers were asked a range of questions in an effort to determine their view of the service offered, whether it was complementary to their role as care manager and whether it assisted their tasks. The results are as follows:

Table 12.2. *Care managers' views of the case conference*

Care managers' views of the case conference	Yes	No	Unable to comment
Did the advocate have sufficient understanding of their role?	8 72.7%	0 0%	3 27.2%
Were the child's views brought to conference?	9 81%	2 18%	0 0%
Were the children's views represented appropriately?	10 90%	0 10%	1
Was case conference procedure enhanced?	10 90%	0	1 10%

The majority of care managers felt that the advocates had a good understanding of their role, that the child's views were brought to the conference and that they were represented appropriately. Ninety per cent felt that the case conference procedure had been enhanced as a result. The one factor identified that jeopardised the success of this project was case conferences called at short notice when the advocate had been unable to meet and prepare the young person prior to conference.

Some of the comments from the care managers on this service are as follows:

This service enabled the young person to feel supported during a stressful case conference.

It enabled decisions to be made with full knowledge of the child's wishes. The advocates' involvement was invaluable and this service should be extended to other areas of child care.

This service assisted the care manager in managing the case conference process.

It empowered the child at the meeting.

The child felt more at ease and enabled her to feel involved in the case conference process. Conference participants had a clear understanding of how the child viewed the situation.

Timing of the advocates' involvement is crucial. In this case it was impossible for the advocates to get involved until the previous day.

In summary, our findings were that the advocacy process did not hinder the care managers in undertaking their duties. Comments made by the care managers showed a high level of satisfaction with the service with 90 per cent feeling that the whole case conference process was enhanced as a result of child participation. A key focus to this success was having clear and effective lines of communication between the care manager and the advocate throughout the process.

The advocates' understanding of their role and their commitment to it also avoided any straying into care management tasks. Many of the care managers commented that the advocates, far from hindering progress, had assisted it considerably with a greater understanding being gained by all.

The chairperson's role

In setting up this project, it was felt important to elicit the case conference chairperson's views of the service as they are in a unique position being independent of the district and have a good overall view of the process. It was felt important to establish what their involvement was in finally determining whether a child should attend the conference.

Of the questionnaires 65 per cent were returned. Over 80 per cent agreed that the child's views had been presented appropriately by the chairpersons at the conferences. They also felt that their participation had enhanced the case conference process. Of chairs 68 per cent felt that they had been involved in the final decision for the child to attend. Eighty-six per cent felt that it had been in the child's best interest to attend with 13 per cent being unclear about this. No other conference attenders had objected to the child's attendance.

In summary, the project sought to obtain a reasonably objective overview of the chair's role in this process and their view of the service. Despite agreement that the chairs would still hold the final decision about a child's attendance, there were a significant number of conferences where this process did not take place. This was partly due to the care manager's lack of knowledge of this procedure which resulted in a failure to communicate a child's likely attendance with the chair prior to conference. Assumptions were made that, if the child had an advocate, their attendance was guaranteed. On the surface, it appears that this issue needs to be addressed further. However, when the results of this questionnaire are compared with the children's views, it would seem that, despite chairs being unsure whether it was in the child's best interest to attend, the young people themselves did not have these reservations.

In working with their advocates prior to conference, the children and young people were able to decide this issue for themselves, and those who felt particularly vulnerable chose to send their advocates on their behalf. As chairperson of a number of these conferences, I was reminded that, whilst we have a duty to ensure no further harm comes to the child from either their family or from this process, it is impossible to protect children from the pain of the abuse they have already suffered. Overall, the chairs felt that the child's or young person's attendance had resulted in a more balanced conference.

The service was viewed extremely positively by the chairs who all expresed a high degree of satisfaction with the commitment and professionalism of the advocates.

What makes this project different?

On completion of this pilot, 23 children had participated. All of them had participated in their case conference in one form or another. Eighty per cent either attended with their advocate or allowed the advocate to attend on their behalf. Prior to this project, only 20 per cent of children had participated in their conference for the whole Plymouth area. This is a highly significant increase and, as far as we are aware, represents the highest number of children participating in their case conferences in the country.

This was a first attempt to address social services' failure to consult young people who were subject to child protection investigations. It has given children and young people an opportunity to participate in their case conferences which the vast majority have made use of. Although some found it difficult and at times distressing, they all wanted to be involved. For some, this was the first occasion they had felt consulted, despite the child protection service being primarily concerned about them.

While this is by no means the only model of advocacy, it is a model that worked for the children and young people. Clearly they were able to have confidence in their advocate with much importance being attached to the advocate's independence. Although social workers strive to meet the child's or young person's child protection needs, they do so in the context of the child's families, and are therefore unable to offer either the level of independence necessary or the time to prepare children adequately. It was found that the whole process was taking between five and six hours per child.

Confidentiality proved to be another significant factor for the children and young people. They were able to feel safe with their advocate. This was to a large degree because they knew that only the views they wished to share would be comunicated to others. Despite the initial reservations concerning the level of confidentiality offered to the children, it has been a key factor in the empowerment process.

The evaluation identified that other professionals gained a much greater understanding of the issues for the children, thus demonstrating that this is a two-way process.

Despite their initial trepidation, advocates did not have any difficulty in eliciting agreement from the parents to operate as the children's advocate. The children were well prepared for their conferences and were able to contribute with their advocates' help. The standard of the volunteers used for this scheme was extremely high. They all possessed a high level of commitment to and a strong belief in the process. They were well trained and well supported by their own agency, and had a strong philosophical base from which to operate. This combined greatly to their abilities to advocate effectively for the children.

The independence of the advocates and the confidentiality they offered were crucial factors in enabling the children to participate. The obvious corollary to this is that this is likely to be the case for children participating in any form of meeting within the care planning process. Care therefore needs to be taken to ensure that, once given an advocate, children are supported through the process by that advocate until they are able to self-advocate.

Both the Children Act and the United Nations Convention on the Rights of the Child give statutory bodies the duty of ensuring that children's views and opinions are both heard and considered when planning for their protection. Children have a right to be heard. This project offered them a mechanism for doing this. Abused children have already suffered. Any subsequent suffering can be reduced by offering them a place in the planning arena in a manner that gives them understanding and allows them to contribute. They want to be heard and understood.

13 Improving quality through participation:
an approach to measuring children's expectations and perceptions of services
Murray Davies and John Dotchin

Promoting participation

The development of children's rights has focussed on three main areas: provision of rights, for example through education, health and standard of living; protection from sexual or economic exploitation, and from other forms of abuse; and participation which involves freedom of expression and rights to be consulted, heard and taken seriously. Whilst there is an acceptance of the rights of children to provision and protection, only recently has there been a growing awareness of children's rights to participation.

Achieving participation requires that: children have adequate information with which to form opinions; are provided with opportunities to express their views and explore options; have their views considered with respect, and are adequately informed about how their views will be considered.

This chaper outlines an approach being developed by the NSPCC to promote the participation of children in the services being provided for them. It reflects a recognition of the need to provide child-centred services, and describes a method to work with childen to identify, quantify and respond to some of the key requirements of community based services. As a result of using the approach described in this chapter, it is possible to monitor, with reliability, the extent to which services meet the requirements of the children and young people they are provided for.

The nature of perceptions of service

Children and young people need to be encouraged to participate by communicating how they feel about the services they receive since few are likely to volunteer objective comment. Professionals need to be informed about how children rate all aspects of services, but evaluation of services is difficult for everyone involved, provider and user alike. Unlike tangible products, services are much more about performances than either objects or outcomes. It is important to recognise that consumers of services make their judgements not just on what is done and what is achieved but also on the process. Gronroos (1984) distinguished *what* is done – which he called technical quality – from *how* it is done – functional quality. A simple example to differentiate these concepts relates to public transport in which technical quality is about getting from A to B whereas functional quality is centred on issues such as how well needs for comfort and courtesy are met. It seems obvious that both must be present to satisfy the consumer. It is unlikely that any of us would be satisfied if the London to Manchester train ended up in Bristol (poor technical quality) but it is not enough just to get to the right destination. The condition of the carriage, the attitude of staff, etc. are also important (functional quality). Gronroos observed that technical quality must always be present and that functional quality cannot, in the long run, make up for its absence. There are, however, service situations where *how* the service is performed has a disproportionately large influence.

The services provided by the NSPCC and Social Services Departments are certainly ones where functional quality plays a major part in determining the child's perceptions, and *how* the service is performed becomes very significant. The child may not fully understand all the reasons for many technical aspects of the service, even when they are fully explained, so the child's perceptions are likely to be heavily influenced by people's behaviour, expressions of empathy, people's appearance and the look of buildings, furniture and rooms which are used, in fact everything about the way the service is delivered.

A corollary of these considerations is that we cannot rely just on the views of professionals since despite, and in some ways because of, their knowledge and experience they are not always able to see in the same way as children and young people. All professionals need to find and use a variety of ways to gauge their clients' views and expectations and the children's services professional is no exception.

tations and the children's services professional is no exception. Satisfaction research has some considerable bearing on this area. Research to understand and measure satisfaction has focussed on the relationships between satisfaction, expectation, disconfirmation and performance. Satisfaction, and dissatisfaction, is usually assumed to be the subjective evaluation of the *surprise* inherent in a user experience (Oliver, 1981), whereas expectation is the perceived likelihood that a particular outcome will occur (Olsen & Dover, 1976) and disconfirmation is the difference between the individual's initial expectation and the actual performnce (Olshavsky & Miller, 1972). There is some evidence that expectations and performance individually affect satisfaction, and that it is also directly influenced by disconfirmation.

Although these concepts appear to have some relevance to services there are difficulties in applying them to the NSPCC which is a relatively long term service in which the child is involved in multiple interactions, sometimes with different people, over a protracted period. Satisfaction as defined above, is a relatively short-lived, transitory reaction to perceptions acting on prior expectations but the NSPCC felt the need to measure the more stable, underlying attitudes, which can be called service quality. Service quality in this sense is assumed to be established by numerous, individual satisfaction and dissatisfaction experiences.

During the 1980s extensive research was undertaken to investigate the concept of service quality, and a methodology for measuring service quality was developed (see Zeithaml, 1990). This methodology was based on the finding that consumers used basically similar criteria in evaluating the quality of a service in different organisations.

The model of service quality which is now widely acknowledged is based on the notion that service quality as perceived by a consumer depends on the magnitude and direction of the gap between expected service and perceived service. Thus a consumer may perceive a service as providing more than was expected, resulting in a judgement of high quality, or the provision may be less than expected and a consumer judgement of low quality results. Thus an understanding of consumer expectations is of paramount importance as a foundation for the development of service quality. Meeting the requirements of customers becomes a crucial gauge of quality, and commercial organisations are anxious to know and understand these requirements so that they can respond to them. For non-commercial organisations, the need to understand and anticipate requirements is at least as great since the market mechanism, the option to go elsewhere, which provides an extreme proof of quality of service, is not available.

This approach, focussing as it does on consumers' expectations, can be adapted to focus on children's expectations of the help being provided to them in response to their needs. The emphasis during the 1980s on the importance of the consumer and satisfying the consumer has been highlighted in commercial areas with many companies developing standards for their response to customers. Customers' views and expectations have been looked at and companies have responded to these. The same has not been true of children and young people to the same extent, and in the welfare field developments, despite legislation such as the Children Act, have been few. However, it is possible to use the developments in the field of service quality to promote the participation of children and young people in the design of the services provided for them, so that their needs and expectations are reflected in service provision.

Previous research studies provide little information about the criteria children use to evaluate the quality of services provided for them. Twenty years ago Meyer and Timms (1970) noted the absence of information about clients' responses to case work services, about 'their reactions to what occurred, their assessments about whether it was helpful and their views as to why it was helpful or not'. Over a decade later, similar views were being expressed about the little attention being paid to client opinion, when drawing conclusions about the nature and quality of service and when making recommendations for changes in practice and policy. Rees and Wallace (1982) for example drew attention to the relative lack of information on adolescents' perceptions of social work,

> children are among the most powerless of people. Their views are rarely sought, important decisions affecting their lives are frequently made without consulting them.

Children's expectations – beginning participation

An approach to identify children's expectations of NSPCC community services has been devised, and is described in this chapter. The approach draws on the finding from other research that consumers use some basically similar criteria in evaluating the quality of a service, even when the services themselves are different. The approach described here also found consistency in children's expectations in different settings.

The approach used was consistent with Churchill's recommendations for developing more reliable instruments for measuring attitudes and involved the following six stages (see Churchill, 1979):

• critical incident interviews

- identifying key sevice attributes
- developing the questionnaire
- administering the questionnaire
- refining the questionnaire
- application of the questionnaire.

Critical incident interviews

In this first phase of gathering information, the critical incident technique was used with a sample of children who had experienced NSPCC services. The criteria for selection were that the children had experienced abuse and that their involvement with the NSPCC had ended during the previous 12 months. The time interval from the end of the service provision was felt important in case there was any anxiety about the children's responses jeopardising the help being provided for them, or affecting whoever was helping them. The children selected were aged between eight and sixteen years and all were given a choice about whether or not they participated in the interviews. Parents, and if necessary, the local authority, were approached for their agreement and permission for children to participate. A final sample of 11 children were involved at this stage.

The children who participated were eager to share their views. They were interested in how the information would be used and positive about improving services for other children.

The critical incident approach has been applied in a number of different areas: measures of performance; measures of proficiency; training; motivation and leadership attitudes and in counselling and psychotherapy. Ostell (1987) describes the use of the critical incident technique in identifying 'specific behaviours that are particularly important (i.e. critical) to the successful performance of a job, rather than to simply identify the tasks involved'.

The technique, rather than collecting opinions, hunches and estimates, obtains a record of specific behaviours from those in the best position to make the necessary observations and evaluations; in our case, the children we are working with.

An incident in this context is any observable human activity that is sufficiently complete in itself to permit inferences and predictions to be made about the person peforming the act. To be critical, an incident must occur in a situation where the purpose or intent of the act seems fairly clear to the observer, and where the consequences are sufficiently definite to leave little doubt concerning its effects.

A basic requirement in order to develop a description of an activity is to ensure that the objectives, and the general aims of the activity are understood. Without this, it is impossible to comment on whether a person is being effective or ineffective in their task.

In this investigation, it was important for the children being helped by social workers to clarify the purpose for their involvement. What did the children see as the objective of the social work activity? The children had little difficulty in grasping what was required of them in the interviews, and easily and definitely identified the purpose of their involvement with the NSPCC.

The children went on to describe behaviour which was considered to be helpful or unhelpful to them in relation to the purpose for the involvement as they saw it. Behaviour was described as 'critical' if it made a significant contribution either positively or negatively to the general aim of the activity. Children were able to comment on the significance of behaviour and to give explanations for their judgements. Vague reports by children suggested that a particular incident was not well remembered and that some of the information may be incorrect. Such vague reports were not included.

In interviewing children, leading questions were avoided, and interviewers were encouraged to use remarks that were neutral and permissive and show that the child or young person was the expert. Samples of the statements from children are included below:

They asked if I'd have an examination and I agreed but it was very embarrassing. I didn't know that they would ask me to take off most of my clothes.

The social worker gave me a piece of paper with a number on it in case I needed to get in touch with her. I hid the number away.

I was not asked if I would like to be on my own – it's better on my own.

We got told off at school for being late. I wanted the NSPCC to explain to school we were up late waiting for Dad. They didn't do this.

When I first visited the NSPCC, I thought that the inside of the building looked like a nursery and I felt I did not fit in. I felt uncomfortable and would have preferred a room more like a lounge.

I hated notes being taken on the first interview and wondered who they were for and who was going to see them. Did the whole world know about what had happened to me?

Key service attributes

Having established key categories from the critical incident interviews, the next phase of the process was to identify the key attributes contained within each of the criteria. The judgements about the attributes to be included were made by a group of experienced child protection and child-care practitioners. The aim was to ensure that the attributes encompassed all of the relevant items identified by the children. The outcome of this process was commented on by the children involved, and led to a description of the key service categories as follows:

1. *Professional competence:* an expectation that staff would have a broad based knowledge about children, their families and the difficulties that can arise, and be trained to use and apply this knowledge.
2. *Tangibles:* expectations about the appearance of buildings and other facilities, the age appropriateness of materials used, physical attributes of practitioners, and information about services.
3. *Reliability:* an expectation that practitioners will keep promises that are made to children, and keep appointments on time.
4. *Responsiveness:* concerns the availability of the practitioner for the child during the course of the work, and whether the child is felt to be the primary client. This criterion concerns work being set up for the child at a time when the child feels the need for it.
5. *Customisation:* this relates to children's abilities to choose, about the location of work, about who is present, about the way in which help is provided, about the timing and ending of work and about the method of work.
6. *Core service:* this concerns the relationship between the practitioner and child as a process of identifying problems and working together on solutions. It is about producing improvements for the child.
7. *Courtesy:* describes the demeanour, the manner and the ways in which people are treated. Key elements are warmth, friendliness, respect and consideration.
8. *Credibility:* is about being honest and truthful in order to build up trust. Credibility is also drawn from the reputation of the organisation, of social workers in general and of social workers' experience of working with children.
9. *Security:* concerns not only physical and emotional security, but also confidentiality and ensuring that children feel at ease and comfortable and not under pressure when focussing on problems and painful matters.
10. *Access:* concerns availability and the avoidance of disappointment. It is about establishing regular patterns of contact and negotiating changes. At times it is about keeping children

informed and practitioners making themselves available to children who may otherwise be unable to reach them.

11. *Communication:* concerns the child's experiences of the worker
listening and hearing, as well as assuring and talking. It is about
clarifying the purpose of any contact. It is about giving information about other meetings concerning the child and about
future plans.

12. *Understanding the child:* this encompasses a broad empathy area.
in which the child feels the worker understands what is being
said and experienced. The process empowers children to express
their own remedies to problems, and maximises on choices, so
when a choice exists the child should be given it. Understanding the child demonstrates that the individual is valued in their
own right.

Developing the viewpoint questionnaire

The initial qualitative phase was followed by a quantitative stage
involving a larger number of children and young people. The quantitative stage involved the children and the group of practitioners
developing a questionnaire in respect of the twelve service quality
categories. The aim in developing the questionnaire was to develop
a number of statements for each category which reflected the
attributes included in each one. Alongside each statement was a five
point Likert scale recording the degree of agreement or disagreement to each statement. (1) indicated strong disagreement whilst (5)
indicated strong agreement. After consultations with teachers and
child care staff, it was judged that children over the age of seven
years would be able to evaluate statements in relation to a scale. A
five point scale was chosen because it was not expected that children
would not make the finer degrees of judgement associated with a
longer scale.

Some 49 statements were identified for inclusion in the questionnaire with an open question at the end for any areas which had
been omitted to be included. Children's views were sought about
their ability to complete the questionnaire, about the phrasing of
statements and children's abilities to respond to them, about the
number of questions and about any additional statements that were
required. The questionnaire was piloted with a group of children
and although the response was positive, it was apparent that the
questionnaire would need to be administered to children individually so that any areas of misunderstanding or difficulty could be
explained and clarified. No difficulty was reported or observed in
completing the Likert scale and from obsevation the children

appeared to be evaluating each question and not following a fixed pattern of response.

A revised version of the questionnaire was produced which was then administered to a much larger sample of children. Some of the statements included are shown below:

	DEGREE OF AGREEMENT				
	strongly disagree				strongly agree
I should be able to choose where to see my NSPCC worker.	1	2	3	4	5
I should have information about what happens to me before my first visit.	1	2	3	4	5
I should be able to talk to my worker about things that are private to me.	1	2	3	4	5
I should be able to meet with other children/young people with a problem like mine.	1	2	3	4	5

etc.

Administering the questionnaire

The revised questionnaire was completed by a sample of over seventy children. The criteria for inclusion in the larger sample was that the children had at least one interview with an NSPCC worker, whether alone, in a family or in a group, in the preceding 18 months. The children would be within the age-group 7–16 years at the point of referral.

Children were selected from the case loads of NSPCC child protection teams on a random basis, out of the total group of children who met the criteria. Children being looked after by a local authority were included subject to agreement by that authority. Children were again given the opportunity not to participate, and were only approached following initial contact and permission being granted by their parents. Of children 55 per cent were female and 45 per cent were male, only two children in the sample were not white European and these were of African-Caribbean descent. Of the children 65 per cent had been seen on a voluntary basis whilst 28 per cent were subject to care orders. Of the children 14 per cent were living in residential institutions, and 14 per cent of the others were living in foster homes whilst all the other children were living at home.

Refining the questionnaire

It was anticipated from the outset that some items which were included in the first version of the questionnaire might be eliminated later if they proved ambiguous or presented any other difficulties in use. The primacy of the child's perspective was acknowledged in this aspect as well as other stages in the development process. In practice, this meant that items would only be retained which were shown to be providing reliable information based on statistical testing of the data collected from children. The data were subjected to formal statistical (factor and reliability) analysis for these reasons. the provisional factors which emerged from this work are as follows:

- a trusting relationship with the worker based on honesty and provision of prior information

- a warm and friendly environment

- adaptability of the worker

- consideration of the child's needs and wants and feelings

- empowerment of the child

- information and explanation in suitable language and in confidence

- the worker's experience and willingness

- empathy with the worker.

These factors were different in many ways to the 'service attributes' recognised at the qualitative stage. For example the factor described above as '*A warm and friendly environment*' included items which previously had been categorised as '*tangibles*', '*courtesy*' and '*security*'. Further investigation was required. Informal methods were used in which small groups of children and, separately, groups of service professionals were asked to examine all the items. Each group was asked to discuss which items were similar and which were different and to finally arrive at consensus about which items could be placed together and how they could be named. The professionals found this process much easier than the children but both, with different amounts of encouragement, managed to complete the task.

The different groups of professionals arrived at broadly similar combinations of items and gave them similar names. These were, furthermore, broadly similar to the categories identified at the qualitative stage. The children, however, produced quite different groupings to the professionals. It was notable that items in the children's groupings coincided to a moderate extent with the factors determined in the statistical factor analysis of the data collected from children whereas the professional groupings did not coincide with the factor analysis at all.

Although these findings were not statistically testable, here was some support for the intuitively appealing assumption that children's perceptions as users and recipients of the service are influenced by different considerations than are the professionals who provide it, and hence some justification for the previously made claim that we cannot rely just on the views of professionals but need to find and use a variety of ways to 'measure' children's views and expectations.

This stage of the work enabled the elimination of several items reducing the questionnaire to 22 items. The expression of these items was also changed in a consultative process among professionals with substantial experience of work with children and in tests with a small further sample of children. It was felt that the remaining items would provide useful if not complete information about the child's viewpoint and thus support child participation. The much smaller number of items than had been used in the early stages would simplify the data gathering process for the child. It was recognised, however, that the questionnaire would need to be subjected to further testing and refinement to be able to confirm the factor structure to identify the underlying influences on children's perceptions of service.

The 22 items are listed below:

● for the NSPCC worker to be good at helping children/young people sort out their problems

● for the NSPCC worker to be warm and friendly

● for the NSPCC worker to be on my side

● for the NSPCC worker to be honest with me

● for the NSPCC worker to be someone I can trust

● to be sure the NSPCC worker won't tell other people without talking to me first

● to understand what the NSPCC worker is saying to me

● to be able to talk to the NSPCC worker about things I don't understand

● to be able to tell the NSPCC worker that I do not agree

● for the NSPCC worker to tell me what they think should happen

● to be able to tell the NSPCC worker what I want to happen

- to be able to spend time alone with the NSPCC worker for the NSPCC worker to understand how I feel
- to be asked about what I want or need
- to be given information about the NSPCC before the first visit
- for the NSPCC worker to tell me about meetings that are important to me
- that the NSPCC rooms feel friendly
- to be able to meet other children/young people with a problem like mine
- to be given the choice about what I do or talk about
- to be able to say when I want to stop seeing the NSPCC worker
- for the NSPCC worker to try and fit in with the other things I need to do
- to know when I am going to see the NSPCC worker.

Monitoring participation

The questionnaire, which was named Viewpoint, represents 22 statements of conspicuous significance to childen. Clearly, the aim of practitioners is to act in the ways which satisfy each of these. To this end, practice can be monitored by sensing children's perceptions of the services provided for them with the aid of Viewpoint. In the extended format, children are asked to give two responses to each of the statements: importance and the extent to which the service provided met or exceeded the child's expectations.

	Not at all important	Very important to me	Much worse than I expected	Very much better than I expected	
For the NSPCC worker to be warm and friendly.	1 2 3 4		1 2 3 4 5		
To be sure the NSPCC worker won't tell other people without talking to me first. etc	1 2 3 4		1 2 3 4 5		

Viewpoint can be used in different settings, and can provide information about individual children's experiences, and about the performance of a team, and the extent to which childen's opinions are to be valued. Any individual or team shortcomings need to be addressed and modified. The questionnaire also provides another, immediate means for children to express concerns which might otherwise remain hidden.

For example, one practitioner was surprised when a child she was working with was negative about the statement that 'For the NSPCC worker to be someone I can trust'. When this particular point was pursued further, it emerged that the child was concerned about informtion about her being shared with others. She had not been prepared for this. She was able to discuss this further with her practitioner, who recognised how the situation had occurred, and a closer relationship with the child developed subsequently.

The combination of information from several cases has also proved very powerful. Simple charts can be drawn which graphically highlight the areas of concern for groups of children. This information can then be used by professionals working in teams to help them understand the child's viewpoint and with that firmly in mind to devise means of addressing children's and young people's needs.

Figure 13.1 shows schematically the form that charts can take. For each of the 22 items making up the questionnaire, importance is referenced vertically, and perceptions of service is referenced horizontally.

Items which are of high importance but which are perceived by children to be worse than their expectations fall into the top left quadrant and are appropriately labelled as top priority in the diagram. Ideally, no items occur to the left of the diagonal line connecting low importance and low perceptions to the opposite corner but in practice, of course, they often do. When they do, they must be recognised as opportunities for improvement. In these practical situations, the chart can act as a diagnostic tool for the condition of service.

The three charts which follow represent the pooled viewpoint of a fictitious, but typical, sample of children. The pattern of dots produced by plotting the averages of the responses to each of the items in the questionnaire is divided into quadrants using median lines.

The first chart (Figure 13.2) shows immediately that items 4, 14, 15, 17, 19 and 21 are more important than average and at the same time children's perceptions of them relative to their expectations are lower than average. The objective of this analysis is to make possible participation of children and young people, albeit indirectly, in the service improvement process. It allows professionals to perceive their work from the child's viewpoint, encourages them to reflect on the meaning of the child's perceptions and to take action accordingly.

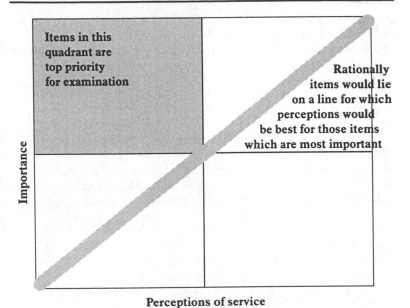

Figure 13.1

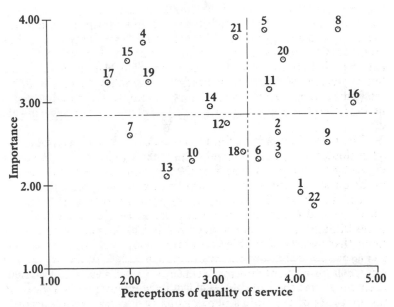

Figure 13.2

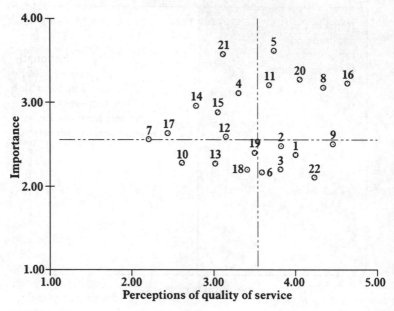

Figure 13.3

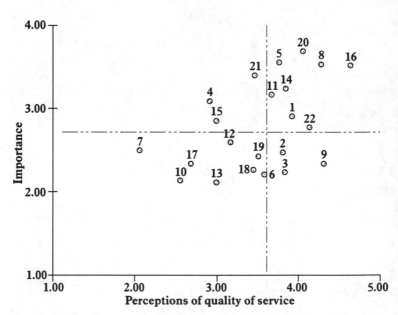

Figure 13.4

Accumulating results over time can also be useful, perhaps to shed light on children's changing perceptions of the overall service as changes and improvements are made. The next two charts represent data collected at two later periods of time. A gradual improvement of perception is detectable. In Figure 13.3, the number of items in the priority quadrant is reduced by one but perhaps more importantly the items are moving in the direction of improvement. The trend is maintained in Figure 13.4 so that only three items remain in the priority quadrant.

Improving quality through participation

By opening up services to comment by children and young people, and by being responsive to these comments, the quality of the service, its responsiveness to the expectations of users, improves. This does require an openness on the part of the organisation, to listen to the views of users, and a willingness to change and respond to the information that is provided. The process is a dynamic, not a fixed one, and approaches and methods of work need to change, as users and their needs and expectations change. If information from service users, in this example children, is gathered consistently and regularly, a reliable database can be established for an organisation to respond to. For example, the key requirements of a service are known, and performance can be measured against these, through regular monitoring. It is also important to regularly re-evaluate expectations of users. Are these the same? Have they changed in any way? In this way, expectations can be regularly updated, and active and effective participation in services maintained.

References

Churchill, G. A, (1979) 'A paradigm for developing better measures of marketing constructs', *Journal of Marketing Research*, **16**, pp. 64–73.
Gronroos, C. (1984) *Strategic Management and Marketing in the Service Sector*, Chartwell-Bratt, Bromley.
Meyer, J. and Timms, N. (1970) *The Client Speaks*, Routledge and Kegan Paul.
Oliver, R. (1981) 'Measurement and evaluation of satisfaction processes in retail settings', *Journal of Retailing*, **57**(3) Autumn.
Olsen, J. C. and Dover, P. (1976) 'Effects of expectation creation and disconfirmation on belief elements of cognitive structure', in *Proceedings of Association of Consumer Research 6th Annual Conference Advances in Consumer Research*.

Oshavsky, R. and Miller, J. A. (1972) 'Consumer expectations, product performance and perceived product quality', *Journal of Marketing Research*, 9 Feb. pp. 19–21.
Ostell, A. (1987) 'Recruitment selection and placement', in Molander, C. (Ed.) *Personnel Mangement*, Chartwell-Bratt.
Rees, S. and Wallace, A. (1982) *Verdicts on Social Work*, Arnold.
Zeithaml, V. A., Parasuraman, A. and Berry, L. L. (1990) *Delivering Service Quality: Balancing Customer Perceptions and Expectations*, New York: Free Press.

14 Forging the circle:
the relationship between children, policy, research and practice in children's rights

Christopher Cloke

The report paints a positive picture of the UK's record on the care of children. It shows how the UK's policy, law and practice meet the provision of the Convention. It shows the safeguards that exist, and that we are constantly seeking to improve, to ensure children's rights to special consideration and protection are met. The report also shows the measures we have in this country for the voice of the child to be heard. The UN Convention's principles are closely allied to those of the Children Act, which meets in whole or in part the provision of 13 of the 40 main Articles of the Convention. (John Bowis, Parliamentary Secretary, Department of Health, on launching the UK government's report to the UN Committee on the Rights of the Child: Department of Health, 1994a).

It would be good to be able to report that in the UK the obligations of ratification were being taken seriously, that there was an open commitment to giving a high priority to the best interests of children throughout the political agenda ... While the decision to ratify is of course welcome, from the perspective of children the lack as yet of any serious attempt at implementation must be deplored ... There has been no attempt to place Government policy as it affects children (and most of it does) within the context of the Convention. (UK Agenda for Children, Children's Rights Development Unit: CRDU, 1994).

How can there be such a discrepancy of view between a Government minister's fine words and the opinions of non-governmental organisations on how the Government in the United Kingdom is implementing the Convention on the Rights of the Child? There appears to be a significant gap between practice, research, and policy on children's rights, with on the one hand Government stating that children's rights are a priority and that there is a great respect for children and on the other hand practitioners and non-governmental organisations reporting a quite contrary view. And what about children and young people themselves – who has asked them about their experiences? With some notable and highly laudable exceptions, some of which are documented elsewhere in this book, in the main children have not been asked their views or involved in decisions which affect their lives. Certainly the Government is not actively involving children and nor are most service providers. And this is all despite ratification and adoption of the Convention by a wide range of agencies.

This chapter addresses why there should be such a gap between practice, research, policy and children's own experiences and will suggest some ways in which the gulf can be reduced. If children's rights are to be placed at the centre of the political agenda and words translated into action there is a need for a major commitment to be made to reconciling these differences. That is no easy task but it is necessary for the well-being not only of children and young people but also for society as a whole. We all have a vested interest in bridging the gap but this requires creative thinking, planning over periods of time which are longer than those to which most politicians are accustomed, and resources. Above all, it requires changes in attitudes and the development of skills in communicating with, and listening to, children and young people and taking what they say seriously. Such changes are challenging and it must be questioned how many politicians and practitioners who are well established in their patterns of working and thinking are really willingly prepared to make the necessary changes. Such changes require a fundamental questioning of action and thought and they are not easily achieved.

In the 1990s, the notion of children's rights can no longer be considered new. In 1959 the United Nations adopted the *Declaration on the Rights of the Child*. While this was a significant step forward in advancing the rights of children it was to be a further 30 years before the United Nations was to adopt the Convention on the Rights of the Child. Moreover, it was nearly two years before the UK Government ratified the Convention after it had come into force on 2 September

1990. Why have there been such delays? A number of reasons may be offered but close to the top of any list of explanations must be the gap or discrepancy which exists between policy, principle, and practice.

The stated commitments of governments and politicians to children's rights should be queried. Prime ministers and leaders from many nations attended the World Summit on Children at the United Nations in New York in 1990 and in the declaration adopted at the close of the summit made a firm commitment to meeting the needs of children and respecting their rights. The declaration stated that 'the well-being of children requires political action at the highest level. We are determined to take that action. We ourselves make a solemn commitment to give high priority to the rights of children.' In reality however, actual progress has been slow. Similarly, progress in implementing the Convention on the Rights of the Child has been patchy.

In the United Kingdom, the Government has finally issued its first report to the United Nations Committee on the Rights of the Child (Department of Health, 1994a). The process by which this report was produced is interesting as it would appear that the Government was not prepared to make this piece of work a high priority nor did it devote a significant amount of resources to the task. In producing the report the Government did not consult with either children and young people or non-governmental organisations – thereby contravening at least the spirit if not the letter of the provisions of the Convention itself. Only at the eleventh hour, just before the Report was due to be submitted, did the UK Government seek to consult with voluntary organisations. Not surprisingly, those organisations were reluctant to participate in such a cosmetic exercise.

The Government's performance was in marked contrast to that undertaken by the Children's Rights Development Unit, (CRDU), which produced an alternative report (CRDU, 1994). The CRDU, an independent organisation set up to promote and monitor the implementation of the Convention, carried out a substantial initiative which analysed the state of children's rights in the United Kingdom. Grouping articles around fourteen broad themes, the Convention was dissected and a commentary provided on an article-by-article basis on how the Convention was being implemented and what needed to be done in order to fulfil the pledge which the Government had made in ratifying the convention. Again unlike the Government, the CRDU undertook an extensive consultation exercise and involved children and young people, and also statutory and voluntary organisations.

The report published by the Government was seen by many as a bland and complacent document. Predictably it claimed a good record on children's rights but much of this claim was based on what had been achieved through the Children Act 1989. Children's rights, however, should extend far more widely than simply to that area of child care law and provision. Moreover, as an 'advanced democracy' the UK Government should be at the forefront of recognising and respecting children's rights. While children's rights should be well advanced in the UK, that is not the case. Not unsurprisingly, the CRDU's report highlighted deficiencies in the Government's record and pointed to areas where progress is needed.

Why is there a policy vacuum?

If the concept of children's rights is not new and Government has stated a commitment to implementing the Convention, why has there been such little progress? Why is there a gap between policy and practice and, indeed why does there appear to be a policy vacuum? A number of reasons can be put forward and these need to be addressed if children's rights are to become a reality.

It has to be faced that the notion of children's rights – like all forms of human rights – is complex. Policy makers and politicians are not used to thinking about the rights of children and young people. In the main children are not seen as having any power or influence, they do not have a vote, and they do not pay taxes. Their dependency status means that they are a drain on the public exchequer and if their needs were to be recognised and fully met that could mean additional expenditure. Children's rights are thus a difficult concept for politicians and it is easiest for them to ignore them.

If children and young people lack influence and as a result are ignored, politicians are mindful that it is their parents and adults who do have power. Thus, when it comes to addressing adults' and parents' or children's rights, it will be the former which are given priority. Until fairly recently children were seen as possessions by their parents – indeed, some would still view children in this way. There is certainly a widespread view that adults, rather than children know best. Linked to this is also the notion that the state knows best. There can be a conflict between adults' and children's rights and rather than seeking to reconcile that conflict or deciding whose need really is greatest, the politician's response is usually to opt for the least troublesome course of action and to uphold the rights and interests of the adults.

As already suggested, understanding children and young people – particularly young children – will take skill, time, and patience.

Many politicians – like other adults – are not renowned for having these attributes in abundance. Children will not always be able to express themselves clearly and in adult terms. This may be particularly the case when children have been hurt or traumatised. They may not even want to express how they are feeling or what they are wanting. They may not know how they feel or what they want. Adults may need to interpret what they are saying and how they are acting. Perhaps surprisingly, because we were all children once, this is not easy.

Conversely, adults may not be understood by children and young people. If they want to be understood by children, adults need to express themselves simply and clearly and to use concepts which are familiar to their listeners. In other words adults need to get down to the child's level and in many instances that may mean quite literally getting down on your hands and knees and devoting time to responding to the child in a supportive way.

It is, of course, also difficult for professionals to do this for a variety of similar reasons. This is not how professionals are taught to behave. Professionals are taught to relate to adults and indeed they will often seek to put a barrier between themselves and the client. Some professions have long histories which cultivate a mystique. This is perhaps most vividly seen in the legal profession which is almost totally adult oriented. While a number of reforms have been introduced, and these are to be welcomed, until comparatively recently the courts have made no concessions towards children. Barristers still use complex language sometimes designed to trick the witness, they may intimidate the child by wearing wigs and gowns, and the child may have to appear in the seemingly threatening environment of the Victorian court room. Is it any wonder that children go to pieces and are unable to give evidence and as a result it is not possible to successfully prosecute alleged abusers?

This indicates the need for adults – policy makers and professionals – to look at how they communicate with children and young people. It also highlights the need to adapt our institutions in order to meet children's needs. Institutions are slow to change and the drive to do so rarely comes from a wish to be responsive to the needs and rights of children. To be child centred would require a radical shift in how we organise our institutions. To be child friendly and to be an institution would almost seem to be a contradiction in terms. Our major institutions and organisations are almost without exception adult oriented and fail to recognise that children have needs of their own. If it is difficult for adults to penetrate these institutions how much more so is it for children. The way in which complaints systems operate, for example, is that they are responsive to articulate, middle-class, English speaking, white adults. With some exceptions, notably children accommodated by the local authority, no attempt is made to be accessible to children and young people.

In policy terms, children's rights and needs have been placed in the pigeon hole which is labelled 'health and social welfare'. This compartmentalisation has had a number of consequences for the promotion of children's rights within the political process. First, children's rights tend to be construed only in terms of health and social services and it is left to the Department of Health at national level and to the social services departments at local government level to take the lead. This has meant that vast areas of children's and young people's lives – housing, income support, leisure and recreation, education, employment, the law, environmental services, and so on – do not receive a rights perspective or receive priority attention. It was, for example, the Department of Health which co-ordinated the Government's report to the United Nations on how the UK was implementing the Convention.

In making children's rights the responsibility of the Department of Health, it is left to a second tier department of state to champion the cause of children. At a time when Government clearly has the 'defence of the realm' and 'the creation of a sound economy' as its priorities, it is no wonder that the needs of children are not seen as a key area of Government activity.

Moreover, the positioning of children's services in this way means that even within that department they are facing competition for resources. The Department of Health and the local social services departments are already large spenders of resources and nationally, and often locally, there is not a willingness to find new areas of activity in which to invest. One social services department, for example, estimated that it would need an additional £2.5–£4.5 million to fully and effectively implement the Children Act 1989. The amount of additional money it received from the Department of Health was £250,000 together with a message that local authorities had to find the necessary monies from within their existing budgets. It is thus no surprise that many authorities have struggled to implement the Children Act and that the Government's own Social Service Inspectorate (1993) reported that local authorities were struggling to find the resources to provide effective preventive and family support services as envisaged under Part III of the Children Act.

This points to the need to ensure better co-ordination of services and greater priority to be given to children and young people at both national and local government levels. Hitherto Government has resisted such calls prefering to believe that the present system can be made to work and that there is no need for either a Minster for Children or a Children's Rights Commissioner, both of whom might ensure that the rights and needs of children are more effectively recognised and met across government.

From this it can be seen that there are a number of reasons why politicians and policy makers are unwilling to be seen or face barriers in implementing policies which promote children's rights. Recognising these obstacles is not to excuse their inertia – there is no excuse. Politicians should have a responsibility to meet the needs of the whole community and a failure to do so is a sad indictment on our political process.

Changing practice to reflect children's rights and needs

Professional practice has improved in recent years and today there is a greater understanding of children's rights. This book contains a number of examples of good practice. It should, however, be recognised that there is still considerable room for improvement in developing a children's rights perspective to practice and that high standards are still an exception rather than a rule. Practitioners, like policy makers, have made a commitment to the principles of children's rights and if asked most will probably say that they reflect this in their work. The children and young people with whom they work will not necessarily agree, as research quoted in this book will confirm. So, again it would seem that there is a gap between the perceptions of the service providers and the experience of children and young people themselves. Why should this be so? A number of reasons can be put forward.

Practitioners – social workers, police, teachers, doctors, nurses and whoever else is working with children and young people – are not practising in isolation. They are as much influenced by the prevailing attitudes, ideology, and system of values as the policy makers, politicians and, indeed, the rest of society. While practitioners in the caring professions may be well placed to develop an alternative approach or framework, the reality of practice is that current work is so demanding and challenging and that workers face such difficulty in marshalling sufficient resources to meet the apparent needs of their 'clients' that practice is almost totally taken up with survival. Having faced a series of cutbacks in welfare provision over the last two decades, professionals now have an almost siege-like mentality. Many may want to improve practice but they do not have the energy or resources to do so.

In social work this is particularly apparent. Today social work is dominated by crisis intervention and particularly child protection. As a result procedures are almost slavishly followed and there is little room for standing back and questioning whether these are right, appropriate, or respect the rights of children and young people. The scope for preventive work and counselling is almost non-existent. The broad role envisaged for social workers has thus been considerably narrowed and it would be a brave social worker who would risk his or her reputation and career by not following a procedure and instead taking a different approach which might involve, for example, asking the child what he or she would like to happen and then attempting to take that course of action. To stand back and question the assumptions which have taken professional practice to where it is today requires the luxury of time for reflection which few practitioners have. A frequent and understandable response in child protection is one of burn out and professionals leaving the profession.

Another reason for the difficulty which some practitioners face in developing a rights perspective to their work with children is that many trained a number of years ago before the issue of children's rights achieved the significance that it has today. Many professionals will have been fortunate if they received a good training in child development but few will have been lucky enough to have been taught about children's rights. In reality the training which large numbers will have received will have been positively 'anti-children's rights' in its outlook, albeit from a paternalistic approach, and instead put forward a view that the safety and welfare of children is best promoted by adults making decisions for them. That will certainly have been the approach taken by child protection social work.

Old habits and practices die hard and while professionals may express a willingness to take up new approaches for many this can be difficult. It is not easy to change the way that one has practised over many years. To do so can involve a questioning of one's own system of beliefs and ideals and this can be both challenging and threatening. The immediate response of many professionals to the question of 'Do you really listen to children and respect their wishes and rights?' is to agree. It is only when questioning the practice which is necessary for this to happen that an element of doubt enters. When it is realised that a children's rights approach requires modifying work methods – and that this may involve increased time with the child or young person, different ways of communication, and child-friendly environments – then it is recognised that existing practice may not be as respectful of children as was first thought.

As has already been suggested, communicating with children is not necessarily easy, particularly when they have been traumatised by abuse. Many professionals will not have learnt how to listen and talk to children when they first undertook their basic training and opportunities to learn these skills now do not always exist. If professionals find communication hard with able-bodied children, they find it even more difficult with children who have disabilities and whose first language is not English. These children face a double denial of their rights.

Another reason why some professionals find it difficult to adopt a right's perspective is because to do so may undermine the relationship which the professional has established with the child's or young persons' parent or carer. This is apparent with teachers who are unwilling to take action to protect a child who they suspect may have been abused through fear that it will destroy the relationship which has been built up with the child's parent. There are worries about the repercussions of acting on suspicions which may turn out to be wrong, Doctors face similar dilemmas in relation to patient confidentiality and this may lead them not to take action to protect a child patient.

Social workers, as has been discussed in many child abuse inquiry reports (see Department of Health, 1991a), may fail to take action to protect a child because they have built a relationship with the child's parents and fail to recognise that the parenting provided is not of a sufficiently high standard and that the child is at risk. In this way the social workers collude with the parents against the child.

In some areas of work the presence of specialist posts has helped to develop good practice. This has been through the specialist either undertaking particular pieces of work with clients him or herself or through the specialist taking a lead role in developing strategies which non-specialists can follow. In the area of children's rights this development has happened with some local authorities appointing 'children's rights officers'. In some areas these posts have worked well but in other areas there have been problems as the officers have found it difficult to develop their work in quite sizeable, bureaucratic, non-child friendly structures. Many of these posts, moreover, have tended to concentrate in the narrower area of residential care rather than focussing on the rights of children in general. The rights of children who are accommodated by the local authority are, of course, very important and certainly children in such care face a number of abuses, but if a children's rights perspective is to be developed it needs to permeate all aspects of children's lives and it is expecting a great deal of a small number of children's rights officers, often working in relative isolation, to effect substantial change, or even to influence the practice of the large numbers of staff in a number of different professions who are in the employment of the local authority.

Researching children's rights

Research can make a significant contribution to the development of
both policy and practice. This book contains a number of examples
of research and evaluation relating to children's rights. The Department of Health has made a significant commitment to evaluating the
impact of the Children Act as can be seen from the annual Children
Act Reports published by the Department of Health and the Welsh
Office. Some seventeen Department of Health funded research projects are described in *Children Act Report 1993* (Department of
Health, 1994b). These initiatives, of course, are to be welcomed but
it should be noted that some relate more directly to children's rights
than others. Also, as has already been emphasised, the Government's record – and also that of the research community – cannot
stand on activity in relation to child-care law and provision alone.
Children's rights should pervade all aspects of children's lives.

With this in mind, it could be argued that there is still not a substantial body of research into children's rights. A number of reasons
may account for this.

Research does not and should not take place in a vacuum but
instead develops within the wider social and political context. It has
been argued that this context, while in principle supportive of the
concept of children's rights, in reality is hostile and many groups
will question the need to promote the rights of children. The Children's Rights Development Unit has forcefully argued that the UN
Convention of the Rights of the Child is not being implemented in
the United Kingdom. In this climate, it is, therefore, not surprising
that research organisations and individual researchers may face
difficulties in carrying out work in this area. Priority may not be
given to funding such research because children's rights are not seen
as important. It should be noted that there are some notable exceptions to this and that the work of such trusts as the Calouste Gulbenkian Foundation should be recognised. A shortage of funds for
research into children's rights will thus be a major obstacle.

Research also needs to relate to policy and practice and if, as we
have suggested, advances in children's rights are not being made in
those areas, that is likely to make the research task more difficult.
Research may inquire as to why action is not being taken to apply a
right's perspective but if those issues have not been thought through
by the subjects of the research there are likely to be difficulties.
Researchers may need to overcome unwillingness from the subjects
to take part.

Researchers face a number of methodological challenges. First,
taking up the earlier theme of communication, if work is undertaken
with children and young people, researchers will need to be skilled

in communicating with people of these ages. Children and young people may not be used to being asked their opinions and views. Techniques used for research with adults will be inappropriate for young children. The types of questions which are asked will need to be carefully worded so that they are understood. Care may need to be taken to avoid the sorts of leading questions which are used with children in everyday conversation.

It will also be necessary to secure parental consent for children to take part in the research and resistance from parents may be encountered. That particularly may be the case with research in the area of child abuse. In interviewing children, it may be necessary for the parents to be present in the room and this may affect the validity of the results as the children feel obliged to express opinions which their parents are likely to find acceptable. Researchers may also face ethical questions regarding what they can ask children and young people and the depth of probing without the research process itself becoming abusive.

Researchers may thus encounter difficulties in recruiting children and young people with whom they might work and who are representative of the population. Samples may be recruited from 'captive audiences' – children who are in care or in touch with social service organisations, for example. Research with these children and young people is, of course, very important but it should be understood that they are not representative of *all* children. Their perceptions and attitudes will be different from children who have not had contact with the care system.

Another methodological issue which needs to be considered is that if research is being conducted into a particular project or team the children and young people involved may tell the researchers what they anticipate the professionals working with them would want to be said rather than expressing their true feelings. In such situations it will be necessary to provide the respondents with reassurances that what they say will be treated in confidence and that any views expressed will not be attributed. Even having done that the problems may still remain.

Thus, for all these reasons, research into children's rights may be difficult. For researchers who surmount these problems and are then able to successfully carry out their research, there may then be the further frustration of either not seeing their work published or, even more disappointingly, not seeing their results acted upon. Children and young people are interviewed, the research is completed, and then nothing changes. While the researchers may be used to this, the children and young people involved may feel let down and be left feeling cynical about the sincerity of adults who say they want to consult with children and young people.

The example of physical chastisement

Ideally, there should be a seamless link between policy, research, and practice with each component informing the others, thereby leading to improved provision to children and young people. Unfortunately, as has been argued here, this relationship does not always exist in the context of children's rights and, indeed, policy, research, and practice may be in conflict. This can be illustrated with the case of physical punishment, currently a key issue in child protection and a good example of a children's rights issue.

Physical punishment includes any act which involves physical force intended to cause pain or distress. It will thus include hitting or beating a child or baby by hand or with an implement such as a stick or slipper. It also includes rough handling such as shaking or throwing a child, scratching, pinching, and pulling hair. The punishment is not only physically damaging but also has adverse psychological or medical effects. These may be more long lasting than the physical consequences.

Physical punishment is widespread in the United Kingdom. John and Elizabeth Newsom (1989) conducted research which found that in 1985 some two-thirds of mothers admitted to smacking their baby before the age of 12 months. They also found that 22 per cent of children had been hit with an implement by the age of 7 and another 53 per cent of 7-year-olds had been threatened with an implement. There have been a number of court cases in the 1990s which have involved parents using implements to chastise their children. EPOCH (End Physical Punishment of Children Campaign) quotes a number of such cases. For example, in October 1992 the Brighton Crown Court heard a case in which a mother had beaten her 11-year-old daughter with a garden cane and electric flex. The mother was cleared of the charges of assault and cruelty. In March 1993 North Avon magistrates acquitted a father who had admitted belting his 5- and 8-year-old sons. In this case a clinical medical officer testified that she had only twice seen such serious injuries in ten years.

Few professionals working with children would deny that physical punishment has a damaging effect. By definition, it is intended to inflict pain and distress and this is harmful. It is debated whether such behaviour constitutes 'child abuse', particularly since the law allows parents to use 'moderate and reasonable' chastisement. However, the government's guidance *Working Together* (Department of Health, 1991b), defines physical punishment as 'actual or likely physical injury to a child, or a failure to prevent physical injury or suffering to a child'.

Child protection practice and experience, as the NSPCC has

repeatedly asserted, indicates a clear link between physical punishment and child abuse. Practitioners report cases of physical assaults on children which started as punishment and which went too far. NSPCC register research (1975) found that in half of the explanations offered by parents for the abuse which led to their children being registered, the parents admitted to hitting their child – often this was said to be chastisement for alleged misbehaviour. More recently in the mid 1990s, studies by Denman and Thorpe show that in around 80 per cent of cases of *substantiated* physical assault, excessive physical punishment was the case. Disbrow, Doerr and Caulfield (1977) indicate that physical punishment is the preferred method of control used by abusive parents.

There are a number of reasons why physical punishment is unacceptable. As already indicated, it can escalate into even more damaging forms of abuse. Such punishment, moreover, does not work. Children do not respond to such behaviour and as one degree of chastisement fails the parent or carer has to resort to increased violence which will also fail. It is far better to avoid creating conflictual situations and to use forms of discipline which are effective. Violence against children sets a bad example and teaches children and young people that it is acceptable to use violence. In this way violence and its acceptability may be passed down the generations. Adults are now protected from all forms of violence and this protection should be extended to children. Parents, moreover, often report that they feel bad after they have 'administered' physical chastisement – rather than being made to feel guilty, parents should be supported in their task.

Opposition to all forms of physical and mental violence is stated quite clearly in the United Nations Convention on the Rights of the Child (United Nations, 1990). Article 19 specifies:

> States parties shall take all appropriate legislative, administrative, social and educational measures to protect the child from all forms of physical or mental violence, injury or abuse, neglect or negligent treatment, maltreatment or exploitation, including sexual abuse, while in the care of parent(s), legal guardian(s) or any other person who has the care of the child.

> Such protective measures should, as appropriate, include effective procedures for the establishment of social programmes to provide the necessary support for the child and those who have the care of the child, as well as for other forms of prevention and for the identification, reporting, referral, investigation, treatment and follow-up of instances of child maltreatment described heretofore, and, as appropriate, for judicial involvement.

The UN Committee on the Rights of the Child, which is considering the reports which governments are making to the UN on how the Convention is being implemented, has also now made it quite clear that it considers physical punishment an abuse of children's rights. Article 3 of the Convention states that in all actions concerning children 'the best interests of the child must be the primary consideration'. In this the Convention and the Children Act 1989, which covers England and Wales, would appear to be at one.

But appearances can be deceptive. Despite there being a strong view that physical punishment is abusive and that it is a violation of children's rights, the UK Government appears to condone the use of physical punishment on children. Moreover, the Government has taken this approach even though it has ratified the UN Convention. This flies in the face of both widespread professional opinion which is opposed to the use of physical punishment and also the findings of researchers who, as has been shown, point to the damaging effects of such physical violence. Government spokespeople would hail the attitude taken by the state as a 'triumph for commonsense' and a victory over 'political correctness' which is seen as so pernicious in undermining good, sensible values.

So much for the Government making 'the best interests of the child' the primary consideration in its policy on physical punishment. Instead of the Government taking a principled position, it is allowing itself to be lead by popularist opinion. The Government may feel it made a commitment to children's rights and the paramountcy principle through both its adoption of the UN Convention and through its enactment and implementation of the Children Act, but two events took place in 1992–93 which lead to a reaction against childen's rights and to a hardening of attitudes in favour of physical punishment.

The first event was the tragic death of toddler James Bulger who was killed by two children aged 10 after they had taken him away from the shopping precinct in Merseyside where his mother was shopping. James' abduction by the two children was recorded on the video recording equipment used to surveill the shopping centre, Millions of television viewers watched the poignant blurred image of James being taken away to his brutal death. In the reporting of the court case which followed the press took a highly emotive attitude and the two abductors were labelled evil monsters. Public opinon, understandably, was in sympathy with James Bulger and his family and condemned the perpetrators of the attack, without even knowing the circumstances of the boys' backgrounds. Almost literally overnight Government policy reacted and the view was put across that the commitment to children's rights had gone too far and that there was now a need for the pendulum to swing in the opposite direction. This lead to policies of harsh, punitive treatment for children and a reaction against what was seen as the 'wishy washy liberalism' of children's rights. In this climate the physical punishment of children is seen as a quite responsible approach to 'bad behaviour'.

The other event which has led to strengthening of support for physical punishment is the case of the childminder who appealed against LB Sutton's decision that as a criterion for registration, childminders should agree not to smack or physically chastise children in their care. The childminder, Anne Davies, appealed to the Magistrates and then to the High Court against this policy arguing that smacking was a necessary method of controlling children's behaviour in some circumstances.

LB Sutton, in common with the large majority of other local authorities, interpreted the Department of Health's guidance, made under the Children Act, as stating that childminders should not physically chastise children in their care. Many child-care organisations – including the National Childminding Association, the NSPCC, the National Children's Bureau, the National Foster Care Association and many others – shared that same view, all believing that physical punishment had no place in publically regulated care. Anne Davies was not prepared to make an undertaking that she would not smack a child in her care and her appeal against the decision of LB Sutton to deregister was upheld. The Department of Health, riding on a wave of anti-political correctness, supported this view, culminating in the Secretary of State for Health, Mrs Virginia Bottomley telling the 1994 Conservative Party Conference that she supported the use of smacking.

This cast great doubt on the status of the Government's own guidance which, in the light of this case would seem to mean that local authorities were at liberty to interpret the guidance as they saw fit. The Government argues that it should be left to a private arrangement between the parent and the childminder on whether the childminder should smack the parent's child while in her care. This has the implication for childminders of children from more than one family having to exercise two or more ways of disciplining a child, thereby making the childminding task that much more difficult. It also may lead to parents, childminders, and local authorities trying to determine what 'type' and 'degree' of physical punishment is acceptable. The majority of childminders are totally opposed to the use of physical punishment and the National Childminding Association has launched a national 'We're Backing No Smacking Campaign'. Other child-care specialists have also come out against the use of physical punishment by childminders.

Thus, it can be seen from this case that there is a total mismatch between policy and practise and research. The Government is disregarding the research which points to the detrimental effects of physical punishment and it is ignoring the strong views of the professionals who are required to operate the policy. It must be questioned whether the Government is making no effort to implement the second part of Article 19 which stipulates that Government should take various measures, including public education, to prevent the abuse of children. There is, at present, very little public education on alternatives to physical punishment, something which is much needed in the United Kingdom.

The case of physical punishment vividly highlights the contradictions which can exist between Government policies and principles which are publically and – in this case, through ratifying the UN Convention on the Rights of the Child – internationally espoused, the views and opinions of Government which are followed, the findings of the research community, and the knowledge and experience of the majority of the professional community. Physical punishment is an issue for child protection and these contradictions need to be reconciled.

A number of local authorities, the Association of Directors of Social Services, and local authority associations, as the Children's Rights Development Unit has shown, have adopted the UN Convention. Consideration needs to be given to how this adoption affects policy and practice on the ground. In the context of physical punishment this could mean those authorities which have adopted the Convention ensuring that the issue is discussed within the area child protection committee and that practice guidelines for professionals on responding to physical punishment are compiled and implemented. These would need to be backed with training and support to professionals on the promotion of positive discipline and on how to work with parents and carers in this area. Thus, for example, those local authorities who believe that childminders should not smack children in their care, should ensure that training is provided to this important group of carers. Public education should also be provided to the whole community, particularly to parents. Those numerous organisations which have adopted the Convention or opposed physical punishment – for example, the Health Visitors Association, the National Childminding Association, the British Paediatric Association, the British Association for Social Workers, the NSPCC, the National Foster Care Association and many others – might take action with their members and constituents to influence their attitudes, behaviour, and practice. Many of these organisations are taking some such actions. Consideration should also be given to changes in the law and pressure brought to bear on members of parliament. In these ways the right of children to protection from this form of physical and mental violence might be promoted and become a reality.

If physical punishment graphically illustrates the conflicts between policy, research and practice, it is not, of course, the only example. Recently, the emphasis in Goverment policy on secure training units for 'young offenders' has been much criticised by practitioners who believe that locking up children is not an effective way of meeting their needs and is a violation of their rights. Leading children's law specialist, Alan Levy QC, in an article for the Tom Sargant Memorial Review (Levy, 1994), has strongly criticised the Home Secretary for locking up James Bulger's young killers for at least fifteen years and for introducing gaols for 12 to 14-year olds. The Home Secretary increased the sentence recommended by the judge for these two boys by at least five years. Levy argues that the Home Secretary has 'seized every opportunity to exploit his hardline views about the police, prisons, and punishment in a bid to bolster his party politically'. He contends that sentencing should be a judicial process and not a political exercise. Levy is critical of UK governments for not having implemented legislation passed by the government in 1969 which would have raised the age of criminal responsibility to 14 thereby allowing children under that age to be dealt with by the child care system. In other countries the age of criminal responsibility is higher than it is in the United Kingdom. There are countless other examples of the mismatch between policy, practice, and research regarding the rights and needs of children.

Ways forward – the need for a policy lead

A climate needs to be created in which society as a whole views children and young people much more favourably. In the now famous words of Elisabeth Butler Sloss they need to be seen 'as people and not as objects of concern'. If they are viewed and treated as people they should enjoy the whole range of rights as other people. That is not the case in the mid 1990s. A fundamental change is needed. This will be achieved if there is a political will but that will is unlikely to emerge unless strong influences are exerted on politicians and policymakers.

That pressure will need to come from adults – the electorate, from children and young people themselves who will need to demonstrate that they are no more and no less responsible than adult members of the population, and professionals or practitioners who work with children and who can recognise the benefits for society as a whole of recognising the rights of children.

In response to this pressure there are a number of measures

which Government should introduce in order to ensure that the rights of children are safeguarded on a permanent basis. These include the establishment of a *Minister for Children*. At present there is no Minister for Children who takes responsibility for policy across *all* Government departments. A junior minister in the Department of Health, along with a range of other non-related areas, has a responsibility for children. That role, however, is exercised almost exclusively in child welfare terms and other areas of children's lives are not considered. As a result there is no strategic consideration of the needs of children. Government itself shows a marked reluctance to establish mechanisms for inter-departmental collaboration. It would be far preferable to establish a Minister for Children post, with a place in the Cabinet and a sizeable budget, whose sole purpose is to promote children's rights and who has the clout to see that their needs across all aspects of their lives are met. Just as local authorities have the task of compiling *children's services plans*, at the national level a Minister for Children might have a duty of developing a *National Plan for Children and Young People*.

Perhaps less ambitious than the creation of a Minister for Children, would be the appointment of a *Commissioner or Ombudsperson for Children*, similar to the office which exists in some other countries. Rosembaum and Newell (1991) have described the role of this post in detail. The Commissioner for Children would hear complaints from children and young people about violations of their rights, take an overview of the rights of children and young people and report to parliament, facilitate advocacy for children, and also act as an advocate. The Commissioner's remit would cover all areas of children's lives and would act as a centre for children's rights initiatives. He or she would promote good practice in working with and actively involving children. The Commissioner would not be instead of a Minister for Children, but rather the two posts would complement each other.

The legislative process invariably pays scant attention to the needs of children and young people unless the subject of the law under consideration specifically relates to their needs. One way of ensuring that these needs are not ignored would be to introduce *child impact statements* on all new pieces of legislation. Under such provisions, in making any new law Parliament and Government would be required to scrutinise the Bill and consider what are the implications for children and young people and to address the financial implictions. In this way all law could become much more child oriented and less discriminatory against children.

These three measures would go some way to ensuring that national policy adopts a greater children's rights perspective. Such measures could also be reflected at local government level where, as has already been reported, a number of local authorities have adopted the Convention. Consideration must be given to translating rhetoric into action. At this tier of Government, the children's rights officers, which already exist in some authorities, could exert a strong influence on policy and practice. These posts need to broaden their remit so that they address the needs of all children and young people and not just those who are in care. In some cases, these officers have built a rapport with local young people who have been able to influence local policy and practices. This would seem to be a good model which could be developed and extended. It needs, however, to be recognised that if these posts are to reach their full potential there are resource implications which need to be met. Simply creating children's rights posts will not be sufficient if there are insufficient resources to implement plans for meeting the needs which are identified. Unfortunately, this would seem to be the experience of some authorities.

It is also at the local level where attention must be directed towards meeting the training and support needs of professionals who are working with children and young people. Such work can be difficult and challenging and for many workers a new experience. In exactly the same way that recent years have seen effective pressure exerted for the introduction of training and support around race and equality issues, so too there needs to be a similar lobby around children's issues.

1995 is a watershed for children's rights in the United Kingdom. At the start of the year the UK Government appeared before the United Nations' Committee on the Rights of the Child to account for how the Convention was being implemented. As has already been noted, the UK government's written report to the United Nations was seen by many as being rather bland and complacent. The Government's representatives may have been expecting a straightforward and easy discussion when they were interviewed by the United Nations' Committee, in which case they were disappointed for while the Committee noted some positive aspects of the government's actions on implementation – particularly around the Children Act, strategies against bullying, and the reduction in the incidence of Sudden Infant Death Syndrome – it also highlighted many more areas of concern.

Those concerns covered sixteen separate issues affecting many areas of the lives of children and young people. The UN Committee was concerned that the Government had failed to establish effective co-ordinating mechanisms for the implementation of the Convention and that independent mechanisms for monitoring the Convention are not in place. The Committee proposed that such mechanisms should be set up and went on to suggest that 'ways and means be established to facilitate regular and closer co-operation between the Government and the non-governmental community'. The UN Committee was critical of the Government's lack of observance of the Convention's general principles and noted that the 'best interests of the child' principle seems not to be reflected in health, education, and social security legislation.

The UN Committee also reported that it was disturbed by the reports that it had received about physical and sexual abuse in the United Kingdom. The Committee said that it was 'deeply worried about the information brought to its attention regarding judicial interpretations of the present law permitting the reasonable chastisement in cases of physical abuse within the family context. Thus, the Committee is concerned that legislative and other measures relating to the physical integrity of children do not appear compatible with the provisions and principles of the Convention'. In very strong terms the Committee recommended that the physical punishment of children in families should be prohibited and that public educational campaigns should be launched to emphasise the child's right to physical integrity. The Committee felt that such measures would help create a climate of opinion which could help change public attitudes so that physical punishment would no longer be accepted.

Thus, it can be seen that the United Nations' Committee was not impressed by the UK Government's record and there was a view that an advanced democracy, such as the UK, should be taking a lead in promoting the rights of children. The reactions of the government and the press to the comments made by the UN Committee were interesting in that they felt that the Committee was being unfair in its response. The front page of the *Daily Mail*, on 28 January 1995, protested 'How dare the UN lecture us – fury as team from Brazil, Peru and other Third World countries accuse Britain of ill treating its children.' Ministers were reported as being outraged by the Committee's comments. Clearly the government has received a severe jolt which has also served to highlight the discrepancy between policy, research, and professional practice. The government will be required to consider the comments made by the Committee and should then take appropriate action. It remains to be seen what those actions might be.

1995 is also a watershed because it is the year in which the three year project which was set up by the Children's Rights Development Unit comes to an end. It will be another five years before the UK Government is required to report on its activities to the UN in 1999. In that period vigilance will be needed to ensure that complacency does not set in and further progress impeded. At this time there needs to be a close and positive relationship between policy, practice, and research so that the rights of children can become a reality. A circular relationship between children and young people, professionals, researchers, and policymakers needs to be forged with each party informing the attitudes, actions, and policies of the others. Once this dynamic process is started there is enormous potential for meeting the needs of children and young people in a spirit of partnership. Each party has a part to play and the scope for creative thinking and solutions is more narrow if one of the partners either chooses not to be involved or is excluded by the others. In the years since the ratification of the Convention there has been a considerable amount of activity around children's rights. Despite the shortcomings which have been identified in this chapter, progress has been made on a number of fronts and it is important that this momentum continues.

References

Children's Rights Development Unit (1994) *UK Agenda for Children.* London: Children's Rights Development Unit.
Creighton, S. J. and Outram, P. J. (1977) *Child Victims of Physical Abuse: a report on the findings of the NSPCC Special Units' Registers.* London: National Society for the Prevention of Cruelty to Children.
Department of Health (1991a) *A Study of Inquiry Reports.* London: HMSO.
Department of Health (1991b) *Working Together Under the Children Act 1989.* London: HMSO.
Department of Health (1994a) *The UK's First Report to the U.N. Committee on the Rights of the Child.* London: HMSO.
Department of Health (1994b) *Children Act Report 1993.* London: HMSO.
Disbrow, M., Doerr, H. and Caulfield, C. (1977) *Measuring the Components of Parents' Potential for Child Abuse and Neglect,* in *Child Abuse and Neglect,* vol 1, Nos. 2–4, 1977, pp. 279–296.
Levy, A. (1994) *Children and Criminal Justice,* in *Justice,* November, 1994.
Newsom, J. and Newsom, E. (1989) *The Extent of Physical Punishment in the UK.* London: APPROACH.
Rosembaum, M. and Newell, P. (1991) *Taking Children Seriously: a Proposal for a Children's Rights Commissioner.* London: Calouste Gulbenkian Foundation.
Social Services Inspectorate, Department of Health (1993) *Raising the Standard: the Second Annual Report of the Chief Inspector, Social Services Inspectorate 1992/93.* London: HMSO.
Thorpe, D. (1994) *Evaluating Child Protection.* Buckingham: Open University Press.
United Nations (1990) *Convention on the Rights of the Child.* New York: United Nations.

Note

The author wishes to acknowledge the contribution of EPOCH and CRDU materials to the development of this chapter.

Index